Lessons from Library Power

Lessons from Library Power Enriching Teaching and Learning

Final Report of the Evaluation of the National Library Power Initiative

➢ An Initiative of the DeWitt Wallace–Reader's Digest Fund

Douglas L. Zweizig and *Dianne McAfee Hopkins*

with

Norman Lott Webb and *Gary Wehlage*

1999
Libraries Unlimited, Inc.
and Its Division
Teacher Ideas Press
Englewood, Colorado

Libraries Unlimited, Inc.
(and Its Division
Teacher Ideas Press)
P.O. Box 6633
Englewood, CO 80155-6633
1-800-237-6124
www.lu.com

Library of Congress Cataloging-in-Publication Data

Zweizig, Douglas.
    Lessons from library power : enriching teaching and learning : final report of the evaluation of the national library power initiative : an initiative of the DeWitt Wallace-Reader's Digest Fund / Douglas L. Zweizig and Dianne McAfee Hopkins ; with Norman Lott Webb and Gary Wehlage.
        p. cm.
    Includes bibliographical references and index.
    ISBN 1-56308-833-9
    1. Library Power (Program) 2. School libraries--United States. 3. Libraries--United States--Gifts, legacies. 4. School libraries--United States--Finance. I. Hopkins, Dianne McAfee. II. Webb, Norman. III. Wehlage, Gary. IV. Title.

Z675.S3 Z94 1999
027.8'0973--dc21   99-052025

CONTENTS

List of Tables and Figures. xi

1—INTRODUCTION 1

Background 1
Evaluation Context. 6
Evaluation Approaches 7
    Introduction 7
    Surveys 8
    Case Studies 12
Organization of This Book. 16
References 17

2—COLLECTIONS 19

Introduction. 19
Improving the Collection 20
Matching the Collection to the Curriculum Through
    Collaborative Collection Development 23
Support for Improved Library Collections and Instruction. 27
Contributions of the Library Collection 30
The Future 31
Summary 33
References 34

3—ACCESS TO AND USE OF LIBRARY RESOURCES 35

Allowing Use of the Library at Times Best Suited to
    Instructional Purposes 36
Providing Appropriate Library Facilities to Support Enhanced Use. 41
Use of the Library Media Center 45
Conclusion 51
References 52

4—COLLABORATION 53

Increased Collaboration in Library Power Schools 55
Stronger Connections Between Libraries and Instruction
    Through Collaboration 60
Nature of Collaboration 61
Difficulty of Advancing Collaborative Practices 66
Levels of Collaboration As Depicted in Case Studies and
    Collaboration Logs 72
Conclusion 77
References 77

5—CURRICULUM 79

Curriculum Forms 82
Library Power Goals Related to Curriculum 83
Library Power and Curriculum in Context 85
Enhanced Awareness of the Existing Curriculum 86
New Packaging of Existing Curriculum Materials and Addition
    of New Materials 91
New Instructional Goals and Objectives 92
Improved School Capacity for Curriculum Development 97
Relationship Between Library Power and Curriculum 98
Conclusion 98
References 99

6—INSTRUCTION 101

Instruction and Intellectual Quality 103
Instruction: Improved or Changed? 105
Different Expectations 110
Analysis and Commentary 114
Constructing Knowledge Through Disciplined Inquiry 118
Improving Instruction in Decentralized Schools 122
Professional Community: The Base of Improved Instruction 124
Conclusion 129
References 131

7—LIBRARY POWER MEETS SCHOOL REFORM 133

Introduction 133
Definitions 134
Other Reform Efforts in Schools 135
Focus of the Study. 136
Reform in Three Schools 137
Library Use and Collaboration 140
The Issue of Intellectual Quality 145
  King School 147
  Hooks School 151
  Boone School 154
  Conclusions 155
Building Professional Community 155
Conclusion 160
References 164

8—PROFESSIONAL DEVELOPMENT 165

Introduction 165
Professional Development. 168
Professional Development As an Important Implementation Strategy 170
Professional Development Across the Library Power Sites 172
  Funding 172
  Professional Development Opportunities. 174
  Professional Development Content 179
Stages of Professional Development in Library Power Case Study Sites 180
  Needs Assessments 181
  Communicating the Library Power Concepts Through
    District-Wide Emphases 182
  Model School Identification and the Emergence of Leaders
    Within the District and School 182
  School-Based Professional Development 185
  Expanded Professional Development 186
  Institutionalization 187
Value of Professional Development 188
  For Librarians 188
  For Staff 188
  For Advancement of Goals 189

8—PROFESSIONAL DEVELOPMENT (continued)

Challenges 191
    Need for a Common Vision 191
    Change Takes Time 191
    Needs Exist on Many Levels 192
    Sustaining Beyond the Grant 192
Library Power Professional Development Reviewed Through Framework. 193
    Effective Professional Development Experiences Are
        Driven by a Well-Defined Image of Effective Classroom
        Learning and Teaching. 193
    Effective Professional Development Experiences Provide
        Opportunities to Build Knowledges and Skills. 193
    Effective Professional Development Experiences Model Strategies 194
    Effective Professional Development Experiences Build a
        Learning Community. 194
    Effective Professional Development Experiences Support
        Educators in Leadership Roles 195
    Effective Professional Development Experiences Provide
        Links to Other Education Parts 195
    Effective Professional Development Experiences Continuously
        Assess Themselves and Make Improvements 196
Conclusion 196
References 196

9—INSTITUTIONALIZATION 199

Introduction 199
Adoption of Practice: Roots of Institutionalization 201
Supports for and Impediments to Institutionalization. 211
    External Support 213
    Policy. 214
    Leadership. 216
    Staff Development 217
    Funding 218
Conclusion 221

10—FRAMING THE LIBRARY POWER EVALUATION

Current and Future Implications 223
A New Paradigm for Research 223
    The Unnatural Divide 225
    Evolving Practice and Perspectives 226
Understanding Integrated Practice 227
    How Well Do Library Resources Support the Needs of Instruction? 227
    How Are Library Resources Used? 229
    How Do Library Program Resources Influence the Design
        of Instructional Units? 231
    How Does Integrated Practice Contribute to the Quality
        of Teaching and Learning? 233
    How Does Integrated Practice Affect Student Achievement? 235
Implications for Educational Technology 237
The Audience for Research on the Incorporation of School Library
    and Information Resources in Teaching and Learning 238
Conclusion 238
Notes 239
References 239

Appendix A: Evaluation Personnel, Researchers, Documentors,
    and Coordinators Involved in the National
    Evaluation of Library Power 241

Appendix B: Library Media Specialist Questionnaire—1997 247

Appendix C: Principal Questionnaire—1997 259

Appendix D: Sample Design for the Teacher Survey 263

Appendix E: Teacher Questionnaire—1997 267

Appendix F: Collaborative Unit Planning Sheet 271

Appendix G: Fourteen Standards for Authentic Tasks, Instruction,
    and Student Performance 273

Index 277

List of Tables and Figures

Table 1-1   Response Rates for Library Power Evaluation Surveys 10

Table 1-2   Library Power Case Study Sites by Funding Round 13

Table 2-1   Percent of Librarians Rating Collection Currentness and
Quantity as "Excellent" or "Adequate" 21

Table 2-2   Perceptions of Teachers' Influence on Library Material Selections 24

Table 2-3   Teacher Involvement in the Collection 24

Table 2-4   An Elementary School Proposed Collection and Budget Emphasis 26

Table 2-5   Principals' Perceptions of Teacher/Librarian Collaborative
Collection Development 27

Table 2-6   Adequacy of Library Collection for Teachers and Students Since
Library Power 28

Table 2-7   Teachers' Use of Collection in Instruction 28

Table 2-8   Perceptions of Typical Involvement in Resource Gathering
and Identification for Instructional Units 29

Table 2-9   Continuation of New Library Materials and Collection Collaboration 32

Table 3-1   Scheduling in the Library Media Center in Library Power Schools 38

Table 3-2   Seating Capacity of the Library Media Centers in Library Power Schools 41

Table 3-3   Types of Spaces Available in the Library Media Centers 42

Table 3-4   Facilities Related to Scheduling of Access 44

Table 3-5   Mean Number of Students Visiting the LMC in a Typical Week 45

Table 3-6   Weekly Use of the LMC in Library Power Schools 46

Table 3-7   Groups Visiting the LMC by Quartile of Library Use Measures 47

Table 3-8   Groups Visiting the LMC by Quartile of Library Use Measures 48

Table 3-9   Teacher Report of Changes in Student Use of the Library Since
Library Power Began in the School 49

Table 3-10   Continuation of Flexible Access and On-Demand Use 50

Figure 3-1   Scheduling in the library media center in
Library Power schools 38

Figure 3-2   Spaces available in the library media centers
before and after Library Power 42

Table 4-1   Percent of Principals Reporting Collaboration Adopted
by the Full Faculty 56

Table 4-2　Percent of Principals Reporting New Collaboration Among Some Staff After School Joined Library Power 57

Table 4-3　Percent of Principals Attributing Library Power As Responsible for Collaboration Among at Least Some Staff. 58

Table 4-4　Percent of Teachers Who Reported Collaborating with Librarians in Planning and Designing Instruction, by Frequency of Collaboration. 59

Table 4-5　Percent of Teachers Who Worked with Librarians for Total Group and Percent of This Group by Level of Collaboration with Librarians in Planning, Designing, and Delivering Instruction 63

Table 4-6　Percent of Principals in 1997 Rating Levels of Collaborative Planning and Design of Instruction Between Teachers and Librarians by Year School Joined Library Power 69

Table 4-7　Percent of Principals in 1997 Rating Level of Collaborative Planning for Collection Development Between Teachers and Librarians by Year School Joined Library Power 70

Table 4-8　Percent of Principals in 1997 Rating Level of Collaborative Planning Among Teachers by Year School Joined Library Power 71

Table 4-9　Percent of Principals Attributing Library Power As Responsible for Collaboration Among at Least Some Staff by Prior Existence of Collaboration at the School 71

Table 5-1　Change in the Adequacy of the Collection over the Duration of Library Power 87

Table 5-2　Degree to Which the Library Collection Supported Needs of Teachers and Students, As Reported by Teachers Who Indicated a Positive Change in the Adequacy of the Collection over the Duration of Library Power 87

Table 5-3　Change in Teachers' Use of the Library Collection to Support Their Instruction over the Duration of Library Power. 88

Table 5-4　Teachers Who Reported They Had a Role in Their School Library's Collection 88

Table 5-5　Principals' Attribution for the Adoption of a Practice 92

Table 5-6　Frequency of Teachers Collaborating with a Librarian for the Planning and Designing of Instruction 93

Table 5-7　Topics Identified in Collaboratively Planned Activities in 1996 95

Table 6-1　Mean Scores on Professional Community Items for Librarians, Principals, and Teachers in Teacher-Sampled Schools 127

Table 6-2　Mean School Sums on Professional Community Items for Teachers in Teacher-Sampled Schools, Sorted by Mean 128

Table 8-1　Professional Development Expenditures by Round 173

Figure 8-1   Library Power average allocation for
              professional development 173

Table 9-1   Principals' Attribution of Library Power Practices 202

Table 9-2   Collaboration Between Librarians and Teachers 204

Table 9-3   Collaboration Between Librarians and Teachers 205

Table 9-4   How Teachers Report Students Visit the Library 206

Table 9-5   Teachers' Report of Collection Support 206

Table 9-6   Percent of Librarians' Ratings of Collection Areas As
              "Adequate" or "Excellent". 207

Table 9-7   Percent of Round 3 Librarians' Ratings of Collection
              Areas As "Adequate" or "Excellent" 208

Table 9-8   Teacher Ratings of Change of Collections Since Library Power Began 209

Table 9-9   Continuation of Library Power Practices. 210

1

INTRODUCTION

Douglas L. Zweizig
Dianne McAfee Hopkins

Background

Library Power began in 1988 when the DeWitt Wallace–Reader's Digest Fund provided funds to New York City public schools to improve school libraries. The Fund's interest in school libraries was in keeping with its mission, which is to foster fundamental improvement in the quality of educational and career development opportunities for all school-age youth, and to increase access to these improved services for young people in low-income communities. Shortly after its initial investment in developing New York's elementary school libraries, the Fund decided to expand its investment, making it possible within a 10-year period for 19 communities in the United States to improve their library programs.

Using *Information Power*, the 1988 guidelines from the American Association of School Librarians and the Association for Educational Communications and Technology, as a foundation, six goals were developed for the Library Power initiative:

1. Create a national vision and new expectations for public elementary and middle school library programs and encourage new and innovative uses of the library's physical and human resources.

2. Create exemplary models of library media programs that are integral to the educational process.

3. Strengthen the role of the librarian as a teacher, information specialist, and learning facilitator who assists teachers and students in becoming effective users of ideas and information.

4. Encourage collaboration among teachers, administrators, and librarians that results in significant improvement in the teaching and learning process.

5. Demonstrate the significant contributions that library programs can make to school reform and restructuring efforts.

6. Encourage the creation of partnerships among leaders in school districts, public libraries, community agencies, business communities, academic institutions, and parent groups to improve and support school library programs.

By 1998, the Fund had spent almost $45 million to improve teaching and learning through school libraries. This investment represents the largest private funding for school libraries since the Knapp Project funding of the 1960s. Much of the money went to 19 communities, which received three-year grants of $1.2 million each over the course of three years. These grants were awarded at three periods—Round 1, Round 2, and Round 3—between 1991 and 1994. The grants were awarded to communities through local education funds that were nonprofit, tax exempt, community-based organizations working to improve the quality of public education through community support. The grant process itself, involving a guided planning grant period before the formal three-year project period, contributed to the effectiveness of Library Power programs by instructing the communities on how to become involved in the planning and focus their attention on specific elements when making their case for project funding.

Communities receiving Library Power grants were:

- Atlanta, Georgia, through APPLE Corps, Inc., in collaboration with Atlanta Public School District;

- Baton Rouge, Louisiana, through the Volunteers in Public Schools in collaboration with East Baton Rouge Parish School System;

- Berea, Kentucky, through the Forward in the Fifth ("Fifth" stands for the Fifth Congressional District of Kentucky), in collaboration with area school districts, including Jessamine County School District, Pineville Independent School District, Somerset Independent School District, and Williamsburg Independent School District;

- Cambridge, Massachusetts, through the Cambridge Partnership for Public Education, in collaboration with the Cambridge School Department;

- Chattanooga, Tennessee, through the Public Education Foundation, in collaboration with Chattanooga Public Schools System;

- Cleveland, Ohio, through the Cleveland Education Fund, in collaboration with Cleveland Public Schools;

- Denver, Colorado, through the Public Education Business Coalition, in collaboration with Cherry Creek Schools, Boulder Valley Schools, Denver Public Schools, and Littleton Public Schools;

- Lincoln, Nebraska, through the Lincoln Public Schools Foundation, in collaboration with Lincoln Public Schools;

- Lynn, Massachusetts, through the Lynn Business Education Foundation, Inc., in collaboration with Lynn Public Schools;

- McKeesport, Pennsylvania, through the Mon Valley Education Consortium, in collaboration with Brownsville Area School District, Chaleroi Area District, Clairton City School District, Woodland Hills School District, and Yough School District;

- Miami, Florida, through the Dade Public Education Fund, in collaboration with Dade County Public Schools;

- Nashville, Tennessee, through the Metropolitan Nashville Public Education Foundation, in collaboration with Metropolitan Nashville Public Schools;

- New Haven, Connecticut, through the New Haven Public Education Fund, Inc., in collaboration with New Haven School District;

- New York, New York, through the Fund for New York City Education, in collaboration with New York City Public School System;

- Paterson, New Jersey, through the Paterson Education Fund, in collaboration with Paterson Public Schools;

- Philadelphia, Pennsylvania, through the Philadelphia Education Fund, in collaboration with Philadelphia Public Schools;

- Providence, Rhode Island, through the Public Education Fund, in collaboration with Providence Public Schools;

- Raleigh, North Carolina, through the Wake Education Partnership, in collaboration with Wake County Public Schools; and

- Tucson, Arizona, through the Educational Enrichment Foundation, in collaboration with Tucson Unified School District.

Most, but not all, communities represented urban environments. The level of library service provided at the time Library Power grant funds were received ranged from communities with no library media specialists and no school libraries to established school libraries, full-time librarians, and district-level library media supervisors. All communities had needs for improving their school libraries' role in promoting student learning. Most Library Power communities were single district, but three of the Library Power sites—Berea, Denver, and Mon Valley—were multi-district sites.

Using the Library Power grant funds, participating communities obtained support for library development through Library Power directors hired for the three-year grant period to provide leadership in library development, in cooperation with district-level leadership. Districts received funding for professional development programs specially designed for librarians, teachers, and principals. These programs focused on the instructional roles of the librarian and encouraged school educators to collaborate in the selection and use of library materials for instruction. Funding was also available for library facility improvements to enable libraries to accommodate multiple uses and be more inviting to users. Finally, the grant included matching funds for district expenditures to build and strengthen existing library collections for use in instruction.

Participating schools agreed to provide a full-time librarian, funds for collection development, and open access to the library throughout the school day. They also agreed to promote the use of school libraries through collaborative planning opportunities for teachers and librarians throughout the school year.

The DeWitt Wallace–Reader's Digest Fund selected the American Association of School Librarians (AASL) and the Public Education Network (PEN) as partners in the Library Power initiative. The American Association of School Librarians, a division of the American Library Association, works to improve library media programs, standards, and services in elementary and secondary schools. In the Library Power initiative, AASL coordinated Library Power on the national level and provided technical and administrative assistance to Library Power sites. The Public Education Network is an organization of local education funds. PEN helped to coordinate the Library Power initiative with the American Library Association. Its technical assistance focus was particularly valuable for local education fund agencies that received the Library Power grants.

The School of Library and Information Studies, University of Wisconsin–Madison, was selected in 1994 to evaluate the Library Power initiative, with an emphasis on Library Power at the school level. This evaluation was characterized by:

- research questions that focus on the national initiative, rather than on individual Library Power sites;

- involvement of a balance of researchers from education and library and information studies to provide joint perspectives on the contribution of the library media center to the instructional program;

- use of multiple data sources (surveys, case studies, local documentation, logs of collaboration in instruction, collection maps) from a variety of viewpoints to speak to key evaluation questions; and

- repeated measures of programs to document progress over time.

The evaluation was co-directed by Dianne McAfee Hopkins and Douglas Zweizig of the School of Library and Information Studies, University of Wisconsin–Madison, and was conducted in partnership with researchers in the School of Education, University of Wisconsin–Madison: Norman Webb of the Wisconsin Center for Education Research; and Gary Wehlage of the Department of Curriculum and Instruction, School of Education. In addition, the evaluation benefited from the consultation of Debra Wilcox Johnson, Johnson & Johnson Consulting; Carol Kuhlthau, School of Communication, Information, and Library Studies, Rutgers University; and David Loertscher, School of Library and Information Science, San Jose State University. Adam Stoll was the evaluation officer at the DeWitt Wallace–Reader's Digest Fund who monitored the evaluation. (See Appendix A for a listing of persons contributing to the evaluation of Library Power.)

Evaluation Context

The evaluation of the Library Power program took place in an organic and dynamic context. That is, while there was an overall shape to the Library Power initiative, project designs at the community level were adjusted to take into account community capacities and agendas and, even though each Library Power site had been funded on the basis of a well-organized year of planning, changes in schedules and plans could be made in response to changes in conditions. This context required a flexible, incremental, and multifold approach to the evaluation.

Initial Library Power activities began in New York City schools in 1987. Subsequent localities for Library Power projects were funded in waves or three-year projects, referred to as "rounds," with the first round of seven sites beginning their projects in 1991 and 1992. Five second-round sites began their programs in the fall of 1993. The third, and final, round of seven sites began programs in the fall of 1994, concurrent with the beginning of the evaluation. Within each of the 19 communities, practices differed with regard to the proportion of the district's schools that participated in Library Power and how schools were selected to participate. Some districts used a proposal process to select those schools that seemed best prepared to take advantage of the Library Power program. Other districts used a strategy of beginning with the most capable schools in the first of their three years and including every school in the district by the end of the three-year project. A third approach was to treat Library Power schools as demonstration projects and have them serve as models and mentors for schools that never formally became Library Power schools. Thus, a coherent initiative accommodated local conditions and was shaped by the sites and schools to meet local purposes.

The evaluation was designed to produce uniform information about each of the sites and schools as well as to learn from the local adaptations and variations that were taking place. Uniform, comparative information came from a series of surveys of the key players in each Library Power school: the library media specialist, the principal, and the teachers. Richer and more localized perspectives on the Library Power experience came from records of collection evaluation and collaborative planning that were collected from the schools. In addition, extensive case studies made direct observations of Library Power practices in the schools and at the site level. Conclusions about the performance of various aspects of the Library Power initiative were made by examining the evidence from these multiple sources.

Evaluation Approaches

Introduction

The longitudinal evaluation of Library Power began in the fall of 1994—coinciding with the third and final round of grants made as part of this initiative—and lasted through 1998. The evaluation captures the experience of schools entering Library Power under all three rounds of grant-making and reports data on a total of 456 schools. This evaluation makes extensive use of survey and case study methodologies, drawing on 1) data from annual surveys of librarians in participating schools; 2) post-program surveys from principals in participating schools and from a representative sample of teachers from across the initiative; 3) observational and interview data from longitudinal case studies done in 28 school buildings, 1995–1997;

and 4) data from activity logs that document the collaborative activities of teachers and librarians.

To examine changes resulting from the implementation of Library Power in participating schools, researchers:

- conducted time series analyses, examining changes from 1995 to 1997, including analyses examining changes in relation to time spent in the program;

- compared practices in Library Power schools with national norms, using data from the National Center for Education Statistics' School and Staffing Survey (see Chaney, 1998); and

- triangulated findings by drawing on multiple data sources on the same phenomena.

The Library Power evaluation presents data collected from more than 1,000 teachers, 400 principals, and 400 library media specialists, making it one of the largest applied research studies to examine the role school library media programs can play in supporting teaching and learning activities in schools.

SURVEYS

Library Media Specialist (LMS) Survey

An early evaluative component of the Library Power Evaluation Project was a building-level survey sent to the library media specialists in all rounds of Library Power schools in April 1995. To allow for a direct comparison of findings with contemporaneous national data for school libraries, the survey used some of the questions from the Schools and Staffing Survey (SASS) conducted by the National Center for Education Statistics. In school year 1993–94, SASS collected data from a random sample of all library media programs in the country. The Library Power evaluation team first selected SASS questions and then created others that would provide baseline data and address the major objectives of the Library Power evaluation study. The LMS Survey was repeated annually to capture information on collections, scheduling, library use, collaboration with teachers, and assessment of the Library Power experience. In 1996 and 1997, two forms of the survey were used, one for those who had responded previously and one for those responding for the first time. (Appendix B contains a copy of the LMS Survey used for those responding for the first time.)

Principal Survey

In 1996, a survey of principals in Library Power schools was added to obtain this important perspective on the place of Library Power in the instructional program of the school. To obtain the observations of principals with experience of Library Power, those in their second or later year in the project were included. The survey included a number of questions in common with the LMS Survey to allow comparisons of perspectives. This survey was repeated in 1997. (See Appendix C for a copy of the 1997 Principal Survey.)

Teacher Survey

Also in 1996, a survey was developed to obtain the perspectives of teachers in Library Power schools. (See Appendix E for a copy of the 1997 Teacher Survey.) Because of the large number of teachers involved, a sample design was employed that surveyed all of the teachers in a sample of Library Power schools selected to represent the whole in terms of grades covered, size of school, and funding round in Library Power. Again, to obtain informed observations, teachers in schools in their second or later years formed the population for the study. (See Appendix D for a description of the method used to determine the teachers to be sampled.)

Instrument Development

Although the National Center for Education Statistics' SASS provided a basic set of well-tested questions, items that related to Library Power (the degree of implementation, the acceptance of practices, the attribution of change to Library Power) had to be developed and pre-tested for this evaluation. Initial surveys of principals and teachers in 1996 provided a test of new instruments and allowed refined survey questions to be used in the post-program surveys in 1997. For items that were not changed, the repeated surveys gave some assessment of reliability in responses. In addition, interim reports were prepared for the sites as a type of validation for the survey forms.

Survey Response Rates

Obtaining responses in the spring of the school year from more than 500 schools at different stages of their Library Power grants required special attention to follow-up. Due to the support of local education funds and the cooperation of district and school staff, particularly high response rates were achieved for all three surveys in 1997 (see Table 1-1 for response rates from all three years), allowing the data to be viewed as credible representations of the national experience with Library Power.

Repeated surveys provide a time series for the entire set of Library Power schools, but the population of schools for each survey includes schools in quite different stages of their involvement with Library Power. For example, at the time of the 1995 LMS Survey, some of the respondents from Round 1 sites were in their third and final year of the Library Power project; respondents from Round 3 sites were completing their first year. In 1997, Round 3 schools were in their final year, and Round 1 sites had ended their formal Library Power funding two years before. To clarify movement in the program, some analyses have looked at a matched set of Round 3 schools in 1995 and 1997; in this case, the great majority of the schools were ending their first school year in the program in 1995 and completing their three-year project in 1997. Some other analyses looked at Library Power measures in terms of the school's time in the program, to gain a sense of change over time. The repeated surveys in 1996 and 1997 of principals and a sample of teachers cannot provide strong evidence in terms of change over time but do provide a kind of test-retest reliability for relatively new instruments.

TABLE 1-1
Response Rates for Library Power Evaluation Surveys

Survey	1995 Response Rate	1996 Response Rate	1997 Response Rate
Library Media Specialist Survey	82.6	74.6	82.4
Principal Survey	n/a	66.9	76.7
Teacher Survey	n/a	65.5	78.4

In addition to the three surveys, two documentation forms were used by librarians to record critical aspects of their Library Power programs: collection maps (graphical representation of the topical strengths) and collaboration logs.

Collection Maps

In the school year 1995–96, David Loertscher provided training to the Round 2 and 3 sites individually in the development of collection maps for their schools' collections. Arrangements were made with each site for the timing of sending copies of collection maps done for 1995–96 to the evaluation office. The spring 1997 LMS Survey asked that the current version of the school's collection map be returned with the survey. Collection maps were used by case study researchers to understand how the collection was being built in the school and by writers of evaluation chapters focusing on collection issues.

Collaboration Logs

Most Library Power programs encouraged teachers and library media specialists to collaboratively plan units of instruction. To monitor the kind and quality of this collaboration, the evaluation team sought information about the extent to which this sort of collaboration was occurring, the instructional areas in which it was occurring, and its significance by asking library media specialists to keep logs of collaboratively planned units of instruction during the 1995–96 and 1996–97 school years. (See Appendix F for a copy of the Collaboration Log form developed by David Loertscher.)

Librarians were given instruction in what would be considered collaboration and asked to log units done with:

a. individual teachers;

b. grade-level teams;

c. interdisciplinary teams;

d. special teachers such as counselors, art teachers, and reading specialists; or

e. the entire faculty (all-school projects).

In spring 1996 and 1997, librarians were asked to include photocopies of the five most successful units with the LMS Survey, along with a summary chart of all the units in the notebook modeled on the "Collaborative Unit Summary Chart" included with the survey. Collaboration logs were used by case study researchers to identify key collaborations taking place in the school and by writers of evaluation chapters focusing on collaboration and instruction issues.

CASE STUDIES

INTRODUCTION

The case study was another method used to study the Library Power initiative. This method was selected to obtain a more in-depth, internal look at the workings of Library Power than could be obtained through self-reporting mechanisms such as surveys. Case studies represent the preferred strategy when "how" or "why" questions are being posed; when the investigator has little control over events; or when the focus is on a contemporary phenomenon within some real-life context (Yin, 1994, p. 1). The Library Power case studies focused on all aspects of Library Power and sought to answer various questions, including: How has Library Power changed the nature of learning in the school? What activities occur in a library on a typical day? How are services of the library affecting what occurs in the classrooms? How does collaboration between librarians and teachers occur? What are students and teachers doing in the library? What are the levels of activity in the library? What is a typical day like for the Library Power librarian? In what ways is the collection used?

SITE SELECTION

Case studies were conducted at both the site and the school level. Two Library Power communities were selected from Round 1 sites when case studies began in spring 1995. Three communities were selected from Round 2 sites, and three communities were selected from Round 3 sites. These case studies began in fall 1995. Case studies continued until the end of the 1996–97 school year.

Communities were selected to represent the range of library programs and services available at the time the Library Power grants began. Thus Paterson, New Jersey, a Round 1 community without full-time librarians and libraries in its elementary and middle schools, was selected for case study, as was Round 1 community Baton Rouge, Louisiana, which had full-time librarians and a district-level library supervisor. Communities were selected to reflect the variety that Library Power encompassed as well. Although the majority were urban communities, rural communities were also represented. For example, New Haven, Connecticut, an urban community, was selected from the Round 3 sites, and the Berea, Kentucky area (especially the communities associated with the Forward in the Fifth local education fund), a largely rural area, was also selected from Round 3. Table 1-2 shows the sites chosen for case study, by funding round.

TABLE 1-2
Library Power Case Study Sites by Funding Round

Round 1	Round 2	Round 3
Baton Rouge, LA (Site + 3 schools)	Chattanooga, TN (Site + 4 schools)	Atlanta, GA (Site + 3 schools)
Paterson, NJ (Site + 3 schools)	Denver, CO area (Site + 4 schools)*	Berea, KY area (Site + 4 schools)*
	Lincoln, NE (Site + 3 schools)	New Haven, CT (Site + 3 schools)

*Multi-district sites

In selecting case study sites, the University of Wisconsin–Madison research team sought the recommendations of the program associate at the DeWitt Wallace–Reader's Digest Fund. In addition, recommendations were sought from the two technical assistance providers, AASL and PEN. Both AASL and PEN had begun working with Library Power sites in 1992, and both had made several visits to the sites. It was believed that this background information, as well as a familiarity with the proposals and planning grants submitted by the sites, gave these individuals unique information that would be helpful in site selection.

In addition to the considerations named in the previous paragraph, criteria for case study selection were to reflect the variety of approaches being used in Library Power sites and to focus on settings from which it was felt the most could be learned. Thus, sites focusing on interdisciplinary unit development were included, as were sites in which Library Power operated within existing school reforms. In addition, although the majority of case studies were conducted in elementary schools, several were also conducted in middle schools or K–8 schools. Diversity of approach was an important secondary criterion.

A total of 34 case studies were conducted, 8 of which were site-level case studies in each of the communities selected. The first studies were conducted in spring of the 1994–95 school year in the selected Round 1 schools. Then, beginning in fall 1995, case studies began in the six Round 2 and Round 3 case study sites. In addition to general case study approaches, two sets of thematic case studies were conducted in the areas of school reform and information-seeking behaviors. Led by Professor Gary Wehlage, school reform case studies were conducted in selected schools in three districts. These case studies specifically looked at the Library Power initiative in schools emphasizing strong linkages between Library Power and school reform initiatives that were underway. The second thematic focus was led by Professor Carol Kuhlthau. Three case study research studies were conducted in selected schools in three districts. The focus of these case studies was on the use of the school library for student information seeking.

Selection of Case Study Researchers and Reports

Because the Library Power initiative was interdisciplinary, it was important that the case study researchers represent the range of educational emphases that were a part of the initiative. The evaluation team sought and secured case study researchers representing not only library media programs, but also educational administration, reading and language arts, school reform, and elementary education. The majority of the researchers were university professors from schools of library and information studies or schools of education. Individuals were invited to participate based on their research preparation, particularly in qualitative research methodology; educational background in the areas being sought; knowledge of the role of school libraries in instruction; and letters of recommendation. Teams of case study researchers representing broad backgrounds were selected for each of the sites. (See Appendix A for a list of all case study researchers.)

An initial group of case study researchers was selected for the two Round 1 case studies in fall 1994. They were trained as a group in November 1994 regarding the purpose of the case studies and primary questions to address. Observations began in January 1995. Following an interim Round 1 researchers' group meeting conducted by the University of Wisconsin–Madison evaluation team, these researchers returned to their sites in spring 1995. Thus, there were two one-week observations during the second semester, 1994–95. A written draft report of the visits for each case study was submitted to the evaluation team for review.

Additional case study researchers for the Rounds 2 and 3 sites were selected in summer 1995. Case study researchers, especially those already engaged in case study research, were given the opportunity to assume up to two case study responsibilities. The researchers for Rounds 2 and 3 were trained as a group in a manner similar to the training for the Round 1 researchers. This time, selected Round 1 researchers provided first-hand accounts of their experiences. Rounds 2 and 3 case study researchers began work in fall 1995. A mid-course meeting was held in winter 1996, led by the evaluation team, and case study researchers returned for a second one-week school-year visit in spring 1996. Written draft reports of the visits were submitted to the evaluation team for review. Based on that review, questions for the next year's study were prepared and discussed in a series of telephone conference calls in summer 1996 with case study researchers grouped by site. Case study researchers also received summaries of survey results, pertinent to their site or school, for study. Most individuals returned for a final one-week, on-site visit during the 1996–97 school year. Final written reports were submitted to the evaluation team in May 1997.

Documentors

For all Round 2 and 3 sites selected for case studies, documentors were used beginning in spring 1995 to create records of Library Power as it developed at the site and school levels. Documentors were individuals from the local communities who had special knowledge of the district(s) involved. They were recommended by local education fund and district leadership. Documentors came with a variety of backgrounds and included recently retired teachers, principals, librarians, central office district-level staff, and substitute teachers. Following training in December 1994, documentors began their work in the second semester of 1995.

Documentors received written guidelines about what materials to collect, what observations to make, and how these should be reported. In addition to general instructions for data to be collected, documentors received specific areas for observations at specific times, governed by what was being learned about Library Power. They submitted monthly reports, which were forwarded to case study researchers, listing documents obtained, general observations, and specific observations as directed in monthly instructions. Documentors attended professional development meetings, provided initial observations on the use of the library, collected relevant school newsletters and local newspaper articles, and interviewed librarians and teachers as requested.

Documentors preceded the on-site work of case study researchers in Rounds 2 and 3 case studies. They provided important background information that served to introduce case study researchers to their sites or schools before the first visit. Most case study researchers met with the documentors for their sites or schools when they were conducting the case study.

Documentors were used in Rounds 2 and 3 in spring 1995 and during the 1995–96 school year. Because the background information had been provided, beginning in the 1996–97 school year, only site-level documentors for multi-district sites continued to be used. These remaining documentors completed their work at the end of the 1996–97 school year. (A list of documentors and their sites is included in Appendix A.)

Regional Coordinators

An additional source of observations of progress at Library Power sites was provided by five regional coordinators who were employed to communicate with the sites about the evaluation. They visited each assigned site once a year, maintained telephone and e-mail contact, and informed evaluation staff of any concerns with the evaluation. The regional coordinators were university educators with affiliations in education and librarianship. (See Appendix A for a list of the coordinators.)

Organization of This Book

The chapters in this book are organized around key questions of the evaluation. Chapters 2 through 4 address the implementation of the key components of Library Power: 1) improved collections, 2) flexible access to an improved library facility, and 3) a collaborative approach to using library resources in instruction. Chapters 5 through 7 cover some of the consequences of Library Power programs in the schools: 1) how the Library Power program interacted with the curriculum planning (Chapter 5) and instructional operation of the school (Chapter 6) and 2) how Library Power operated in conjunction with various school reform initiatives also present in many schools. Chapter 8 discusses how professional development was used as a strategy to communicate the intentions of the program, transmit needed skills, and foster the formation of teams in schools, with a focus on the use of library materials in instruction. Chapter 9 examines the degree to which key Library Power practices can be seen to have been incorporated into school practice and the likelihood of their continuing after the end of formal grant funding. Finally, Chapter 10 presents reflections on the evaluation process from the perspective of an evaluation officer at the DeWitt Wallace–Reader's Digest Fund.

References

Chaney, B. (1998). *School library media centers: 1993–94.* NCES 98–282. Project Officer, Jeffrey Williams. Washington, D.C.: U.S. Department of Education, National Center for Education Statistics.

Yin, R. K. (1994). *Case study research: Design and methods* (2d ed.). Thousand Oaks, CA: Sage Publications, Inc.

Dianne McAfee Hopkins

CHAPTER 2

COLLECTIONS

Introduction

One of the first ways in which libraries support a program of instruction is through the collection. A library collection needs to match the curriculum, be current in its information and its appearance, and have materials in sufficient quantity to support varied use by classes, small groups, or individual students engaged in research and inquiry.

A major challenge faced by school librarians today in achieving full curriculum involvement is outdated library collections. Another challenge has been connecting the library collection to classroom instruction. The Library Power initiative addressed both outdated collections as well as the selection and use of library materials in instruction. Collection development was recognized as a critical foundation for teaching and learning collaborations between librarians and teachers.

Improving the Collection

In applications for Library Power grants, Library Power communities articulated needs for improving the library resources that were available to students and teachers. Problems with dated collections were often cited because dated, inaccurate materials would be unlikely to be useful in today's teaching and learning efforts. In the early to mid-1990s, when grant applications were submitted, many schools reported collections with books averaging copyright dates from the 1960s and the 1970s. Therefore, an important question to answer is, "Are collections improving in Library Power schools?"

The answer to the question is yes. Collections have improved substantially. In annual surveys, librarians were asked to rate 14 parts of their collections. The questions were modeled on those used by the National Center for Education Statistics for the survey of school librarians nationally (Chaney, 1998). The Center's Schools and Staffing Survey (SASS) is an integrated set of surveys periodically conducted to assess the state of U.S. education. The most recent national data on school library collections is from a SASS survey reporting on the 1993–94 school year. In a survey, conducted by the Library Power evaluation, of library media specialists in all Library Power schools in 1995, the general finding was that collections were rated "less than adequate" (less than two on a three-point scale) in both currentness and quantity. When compared to the SASS survey results focusing on the 1993–94 school year for elementary schools, the estimate of the state of the Library Power collections is similar. Thus, the SASS data provide a national context for the beginning years of Library Power data collection and a benchmark against which to measure change. By 1997, the overall collection ratings in the evaluation's survey of library media specialists in all Library Power schools, had uniformly improved. Many collection areas were now rated "better than adequate." These areas are picture books, fiction, biography, reference sources, science and technology, social sciences, and literature. Among the top-rated collection areas were those most likely to be used in reading improvement or reading motivation efforts, such as picture books and fiction. Table 2-1 shows these improvements from a subset of school librarians who completed the survey instrument in both 1995 and 1997. It shows the percentage of librarians estimating their collections to be "excellent" or "adequate" in the areas shown.

TABLE 2-1
Percent of Librarians Rating Collection Currentness and Quantity as "Excellent" or "Adequate" (SASS 1993–94; Matched LMS Surveys, 1995 and 1997)

	Currentness			Quantity		
Collection Area	SASS %	LMS 1995 %	LMS 1997 %	SASS %	LMS 1995 %	LMS 1997 %
Reference	65	83	95	65	86	93
Science/Technology	54	81	95	55	61	90
Mathematics	40	51	77	38	38	63
Geography	52	61	86	53	57	80
History	63	70	85	60	62	81
Biography	66	88	91	68	88	92
Social Sciences	59	73	93	58	71	88
Fiction	79	75	95	77	82	91
Picture Books	72	88	96	70	82	91
Literature	64	75	91	64	72	83
Fine Arts	48	62	81	46	53	74
Foreign Language	25	42	70	22	26	58
Careers	36	48	61	36	37	53
Health	47	65	85	44	52	77
Total Responding	*	221	221	*	221	221

*Data from the 1993–94 Schools and Staffing Survey are estimates for the 56,272 elementary schools in the United States having school library media centers.

There are two particularly important points about changes in the collections:

1. Table 2-1 shows that ratings for all 14 areas within the collection improved in both currentness and quantity from 1995 to 1997.

2. In a separate analysis of mean ratings, the currentness of collections in the areas of reference, science/technology, geography, history, social sciences, and health is rated significantly higher in schools that have been in the Library Power program longer (p<.05).

These positive changes in the currentness and quantity of materials relate, in part, to the availability of additional money for the purchase of library materials. Library Power funds for collection development were offered as matching funds, so that most participating Library Power schools received at least twice their normal funding for library resources. During these years, many schools also allocated higher budget amounts for collections from local funds. In this way, they received higher funding from Library Power through matching. In addition, most Library Power sites also offered mini-grants, a source of special funding already popular in some local education funds (LEFs) even before Library Power. Mini-grants provided special grants that usually ranged between $500 and $1,000. Mini-grants encouraged teachers to work with the librarian to develop instructional proposals with important collection components.

An item from the federal SASS study was repeated in the Library Power LMS Surveys: "Rate the adequacy of the entire collection to meet the needs of multicultural education." Improvements can be noted in librarian responses here, as well. In 1995, 72% of Library Power librarians rated the entire collection as "adequate" or "excellent" in meeting the school's needs in multicultural education. This improved to 86% in 1997. In 1995, slightly more than one in five, or 22.2%, rated the multicultural education collection as "excellent." In 1997, slightly more than one in four, or 26.9%, rated the collection as "excellent."

Library Power librarians rated their collections higher, in both the 1995 and 1997 surveys, in meeting the needs of multicultural education than did librarians completing the SASS survey in 1993–94. At that time, only 56.2% of the national sample of librarians rated the entire collection as "adequate" or "excellent" in meeting the needs of multicultural education in their schools. It is possible that Library Power librarians stressed multicultural materials because they represented, for the most part, urban environments with multicultural school populations. SASS respondents, on the other hand, represented urban, as well as rural and suburban school communities. Rural and suburban schools may not have stressed the value of multicultural materials as much as their urban counterparts.

Thus, all Library Power library collections improved. In addition to general collection areas, the multicultural component was strengthened during the Library Power years.

Matching the Collection to the Curriculum Through Collaborative Collection Development

Increased funds for the purchase of library materials was one reason the collections improved. Another important reason was the collaborative manner in which materials were selected. In the past, many librarians traditionally sought to involve teachers in the selection of materials with limited success. The result was that even when current library materials were available and appropriate for instruction, they were less likely to be used by either teachers or students in conjunction with teaching and learning. Too often there was a lack of connection between the collection development process and instruction. Library Power sought to connect teachers and librarians through library materials. By doing so, new collection development practices were promoted. These practices led to more relevant collections that were more likely to be used in instruction.

In Library Power schools, teachers became actively involved in selection of library materials. In the 1997 surveys, both teachers and principals reported this involvement in their schools in response to a question that asked: "At this school, how much influence do teachers have on selecting materials to be added to the library." Eighty-one percent of teachers felt they had influence in selection, and 97% of principals felt that teachers had influence in selection. Table 2-2 shows these data.

Not only did teachers feel they had influence in the selection of materials, but most teachers actively participated in selection and many participated in assessing the quality of the collection. Table 2-3 reports teachers' responses in the 1997 survey to the questions, "Do you play any role in helping to select materials for your school library's collection?" and "Do you play any role in helping to assess the quality of your school library's collection?"

TABLE 2-2
Perceptions of Teachers' Influence on Library Material Selections
(Teacher and Principal Surveys, 1997)

	Teachers	Principals
A Little		
1	8.1%	.7%
2	10.7%	2.2%
3	28.1%	15.3%
4	32.5%	42.3%
5	20.5%	39.4%
A Great Deal		
Number Responding	1,166	411

TABLE 2-3
Teacher Involvement in the Collection
(Teacher Survey, 1997)

	Selection	Assessing the Quality
Yes	68.9%	45.7%
No	31.1%	54.3%
Number Responding	1,163	1,153

The involvement of teachers in collection development was promoted in several ways. Principals encouraged teachers and librarians to collaborate on instructional areas including selection and use of materials. Principals also provided planning time both during and after the school day for librarians and teachers. Site-level leadership made improving the collection a major thrust of the Library Power initiative, in keeping with Library Power goals, and offered professional development opportunities to support collection development. Professional development topics focused on collection building and the library's role in teaching and learning. They also introduced the concept of collection mapping.

Developed by library educator David Loertscher (1996), collection mapping is the systematic development of a school library collection based on the actual curriculum that is being taught and involving the school's librarian, teachers, and principal in the collection development process. By engaging in a collection mapping process, library material purchases are based on areas of focus within the curriculum. Library materials with direct ties to the curriculum can be used readily by teachers and students alike. Collection maps outlining plans to connect future library purchases with the school's curricular emphases were created by many librarians following consultation with teachers. Table 2-4 is an example of a proposed collection plan for a Library Power school.

The collection development collaboration between teachers and librarians was widely adopted, according to principals who believed that the practice of collaboration on the collection had been adopted by most of the faculty. Table 2-5 shows the principals' responses to the 1997 survey.

Most principals, 71%, indicated that the practice of collaborative collection development did not exist before Library Power. More than half of the principals, 52.5%, attributed the changes in collection development solely to Library Power, while an additional 38% felt that the changes were based on a mix of school reform initiatives that included Library Power.

TABLE 2-4
An Elementary School Proposed Collection and Budget Emphasis

Emphasis Area	Number of Titles	Focus	Proposed Additions	Library Power Funds 1996-97*	Other Funds 1996-97*
Fiction	1,635	Build	160	$400	$2,000
Picture Books	987	Build	175	$1,000	$1,625
Core Collection	1,306	Maintain	60		$900
Poetry	213	Maintain	25		$375
Folklore	352	Maintain	22		$330
Biography	460	Build	35		$525
United States	220	Build	80	$1,000	$200
Canada	20	Build	40		$300
Latin America	30	Build	35	$525	
Home State	16	Build	100	$1,500	
Native Americans	13	Build	50		$750
Life Science	557	Build	200	$3,000	$600
Earth Science	96	Build	100	$900	$600
Health/Anatomy	84	Build	5		$75
Math Concepts	12	Build	50	$550	$200
Arts	280	Maintain	20		$300
Reference	85	Build	15	$225	
Emergent Readers	42	Build	60	$900	
Periodicals	35	Build	11		$1,120
Accelerated Readers	400	Build	6		$100
Total	6,843		1,249	$10,000	$10,000

*Dollar amounts are 1996 U.S. dollars.

TABLE 2-5
Principals' Perceptions of Teacher/Librarian Collaborative Collection Development
(Principal Survey, 1997)

Not Adopted At All	
1	.3%
2	12.0%
3	44.5%
4	43.2%
Adopted by Full Faculty	
Number Responding	391

Support for Improved Library Collections and Instruction

As envisioned, improved library collections tailored to match the curriculum and collaborative teacher involvement in the selection of library materials resulted in greater use of the collection for instruction. Eighty-five percent of teachers found the collection to be better for themselves and students than before Library Power. Almost 60% of teachers said they used the collection more in instruction than they did prior to the Library Power program. Among the many examples is that of a teacher of gifted and talented students who said, "Having more materials in the collection has made it easier to do independent projects with my students. Before Library Power, I would have to go to the public library and the junior college library to find materials for my students to use. I don't have to do that anymore." Tables 2-6 and 2-7 show the data from the 1997 Teacher Survey.

TABLE 2-6
Adequacy of Library Collection for Teachers and Students Since Library Power
(Teacher Survey, 1997)

	Supports Needs of	
	Teachers	**Students**
Much Worse	.4%	.7%
Somewhat Worse	1.3%	1.4%
About the Same	13.4%	10.4%
Somewhat Better	34.0%	30.8%
Much Better	50.9%	56.7%
Number Responding	1,143	1,145

TABLE 2-7
Teachers' Use of Collection in Instruction
(Teacher Survey, 1997)

Much Less Than Before	
1	5.2%
2	5.4%
3	29.5%
4	31.3%
5	28.6%
Much More Than Before	
	1,103
Number Responding	

When librarians work with teachers on instructional units, that work often centers around the identification and use of materials. More than half of all teacher respondents, 59%, indicated that librarians usually participated in the planning and implementing of instructional units by identifying and gathering materials and resources. Librarians indicated that they were almost always involved in instructional units, with 99% citing their involvement in resource identification and gathering. Principals offered yet another positive perspective. Principals saw both librarians and teachers as being involved in working on instructional units through material identification and gathering. The principals indicated in the 1997 survey that more than 94% of teachers and librarians were involved in instructional unit planning in this way. By all accounts, librarians became more directly involved in unit planning, particularly through the use of the library collection, through Library Power. Table 2-8 contains combined data from the 1997 surveys.

TABLE 2-8
Perceptions of Typical Involvement in Resource Gathering and Identification for Instructional Units (Teacher, LMS, and Principal Surveys, 1997)

	Respondents		
Who's Involved?	**Teachers**	**Librarians**	**Principals**
Classroom Teacher	89.2%	53.9	94.4
Other Teachers	45.8%	14.9	54.7
Librarian	58.6%	98.7	97.3
Other Specialists	15.8%	16.4	44.3
Number Responding	1,162	475	413

Contributions of the Library Collection

Library Power made many contributions to the schools in addition to improvement of collections, such as renovated facilities, flexible access, collaboration, reading promotion, school reform support, and professional development. However, in response to an open-ended question in the 1997 Library Power evaluation survey completed by teachers in which they were asked to cite the most important contributions of Library Power to their teaching, unprompted, 64% of teachers (794 out of 1,239) named the collection as the most important contribution of Library Power to their teaching. Principals, similarly, found the renewed collection to be of value, with 35% (140 out of 395) responding that materials were among the most important contributions of Library Power to teaching.

The overall success of flexible access to the library has also been attributed in part to collection development. More than 60% of teachers indicated that since Library Power began, students used the library more and had more positive attitudes toward the library. In explaining the positive changes in students, teachers often connected new materials to the frequency with which students used the library. Among reasons often cited by teachers at all grade levels for why students used the library frequently were to get new, exciting books; use the large variety of materials; and use up-to-date materials. In addition, a review of teacher comments gathered through case study interviews showed less reliance on encyclopedias and better instructional material support for students.

The availability of new materials encouraged a link between the collection and other aspects of Library Power, including collaboration, instruction, and classroom use. Principals indicated that because the library had so many resources, team planning and teaching occurred more easily between teachers and the librarian. The comment that follows was typical of those given by principals in interviews, "Everyone became aware and wide awake to the importance of resources, research value, student interests and teaming of staff efforts. Our library media specialist became a true library media specialist in every sense of the word. The realization that together we can do a better job for our students became a beacon." Some principals expressed the belief that teaching and instruction had improved significantly, noting that teaching and collaboration had generally brought forth a wealth of creative ideas and the use of teaching materials and tools that made learning exciting and fun for students.

Case studies also showed that librarians viewed the collection as essential to collaboration between themselves and teachers. They saw direct connections between curriculum improvements and improved library collections. A change as basic as the opportunity to order library materials according to need throughout the year (rather than being limited to predetermined periods) was sufficient to provide new opportunities for teacher support and freedom in the creation of curriculum.

In particular, the collection proved to be necessary to support curriculum where resource-based teaching was in place. In one Library Power school, the teachers had stopped using textbooks even before Library Power, but were unable to depend on the library to meet their material needs. Instead, one second-grade teacher indicated, "Before Library Power, we had to go to three different public libraries to get the books we needed to teach our units." After Library Power, collections improved and relevant materials were available for specific topics. In another community where a strong emphasis on thematic units for instruction was evident, an up-to-date collection was also important. Several schools in Library Power communities also developed collections of duplicate titles to aid in instruction. The library collection was also critical to many school reading initiatives.

Some school reforms were strengthened with good library collections. An example of this is Literacy League, a Public Education Business Coalition initiative found in several Denver, Colorado, area school districts. It emphasized improving students' reading and writing through literature, and involved extensive training of school faculties. In schools where Literacy League was coupled with Library Power and where the librarian participated fully in training, collection selections and use were also an important part of this initiative.

Thus, new, up-to-date materials in the library collection supported the frequent use of the library, formed the foundation upon which collaborations were based, and offered a variety of materials useful to instruction. The improved, focused collection was one of Library Power's most important contributions.

THE FUTURE

Collection development practices involving teachers and librarians were well received throughout the Library Power school communities. Evidence suggests that new collection development practices will continue. Two relevant collection development questions about practices that will and should continue in the future were asked of librarians, teachers, and principals in 1997. The first related to the addition of large quantities of new library materials. The second related to continuation of collaboration between librarians and teachers in developing the collection.

The majority of respondents felt that the better resourced collection and the more inclusive collection development process had become valued in schools to the point where they would be sustained beyond the grant period. In terms of new materials, the majority of respondents believed that the infusion of large quantities of new materials would continue. Teachers were more optimistic than librarians that large quantities of library materials would continue to be purchased, with 80% estimating continuation. There was almost unanimous agreement among librarians, teachers, and principals that the purchase of large quantities of new materials *should* continue. Table 2-9 presents the data from these surveys.

TABLE 2-9
Continuation of New Library Materials and Collection Collaboration
(Teacher, LMS, and Principal Surveys, 1997)

	Respondents		
	Librarians % Yes	Principals % Yes	Teachers % Yes
Addition of large quantities of new library materials			
Will continue	51.9%	98.3%	79.9%
Total responding	422	360	793
Should continue	96.7%	99.2%	96.2%
Total responding	460	361	1,038
Collaboration between teachers and librarians on developing the library's collection			
Will continue	94.9%	98.3%	88.4%
Total responding	452	360	813
Should continue	99.1%	99.2%	96.0%
Total responding	452	361	1,026

As shown in Table 2-9, there was substantial agreement among librarians, teachers, and principals about collaboration between teachers and librarians in collection development. Almost 95% of librarians felt that teacher/librarian collection collaboration would continue, and more than 88% of teachers and 98% of principals agreed. There was almost unanimous agreement across all respondent groups (96% or greater) that collection collaboration *should* continue.

Summary

The strengthening of library collections through the Library Power initiative had many benefits. Collections of up-to-date materials became available for student and teacher use. Thanks to strong professional development programs and the support of principals, teachers actively engaged in selecting library materials. The process of upgrading library collections shifted the attention from the librarian as the sole selector of library resources to that of a partnership between the librarian and classroom teachers in the schools. Teachers used the collections more in instruction and found that the collections met their needs. Their involvement in the selection of library materials helped to assure that the collections responded to the curriculum. The curriculum connection between librarians and teachers encouraged in national library media guidelines became a reality for many schools during the Library Power years.

The collection also promoted instructional participation of the librarian. The collection was the primary basis for collaborations occurring between librarians and teachers. Students appreciated the upgraded collections as well. They were eager to use the library and had more positive attitudes. Major findings about the collection follow:

- New collection development practices led to improved collections and expanded use of collections in instruction.

- Strong connections were established between library collections and instruction.

- Changes in collection development practices are well regarded by librarians, teachers, and principals. There is a desire to sustain the new practices.

- Both teachers and principals cite the materials obtained through Library Power as major contributions of the initiative to the teaching done in the school.

- Changes in collection development represent an improvement that goes well beyond strengthening the collection. It is clearly the primary basis for collaboration efforts between most librarians and teachers.

References

Loertscher, D. V. (1996). *Collection mapping in the LMC: Building access in a world of technology.* Castle Rock, CO: Hi Willow Research and Publishing.

Chaney, B. (1998). *School library media centers: 1993–94.* NCES 98–282. Project Officer, Jeffrey Williams. Washington, D.C.: U.S. Department of Education, National Center for Education Statistics.

ACCESS TO AND USE OF LIBRARY RESOURCES

Douglas L. Zweizig

Use of school library resources takes many forms and occurs in a variety of places. Resources are used by students to provide individually-chosen reading, answer questions on assignments, pursue individual topics of interest, and support assigned papers, as well as by teachers to prepare lessons. Use of library resources occurs in classrooms and workrooms as well as in the school's library. The surveys and case studies of the Library Power evaluation have attempted to capture some of this complexity by asking librarians to make counts of usage, by asking teachers to describe their students' use of the library, and by having case study researchers observe students and staff in libraries and classrooms.

Other chapters in this book, particularly those on collections and collaboration, describe the promotion of the use of library resources through improvements in library collections and joint planning of instruction by librarians and teachers. This chapter reports how access to libraries in Library Power schools was provided, the changes in facilities and equipment that were made, the amounts and kinds of usage that occurred, how practices and facilities were related to usage, and how teacher involvement in Library Power activities related to use of the library by students.

Allowing Use of the Library at Times Best Suited to Instructional Purposes

One of the premises of Library Power is that library facilities and resources can best support instruction if they are available at the time most suited to the lesson or when spontaneous interests arise. Therefore, one of the requirements for a school to participate in Library Power was to make a commitment to using a flexible schedule. This meant that individual, group, or class access to the library would not be limited to rigidly scheduled times of the day or week but would be possible, when needed, for a range of instructional activities. Flexible scheduling also implies that the library would support multiple activities taking place in the library at the same time, such as small groups, classes, and individual students working in the library simultaneously.

A basic question for Library Power schools is whether students and teachers are getting sufficient access to the facilities and the materials to support instructional efforts. Library Power schools were asked to move to a flexible schedule if they were on a traditional schedule of, for example, once-a-week library visits. Such a change in the program can cause a major disruption in a school's working philosophy, and the transition is not always easy; in fact, the flexible schedule might be extremely controversial and could become a major political problem for the administrator and the library media specialist. Further, an important question is whether the practice of flexible scheduling continues when the requirement from the initiative is no longer present.

The National Center for Education Statistics' Schools and Staffing Survey (SASS) found that library media centers in elementary schools in the 1993–94 school year were regularly scheduled in 57% of the schools, were mixed in 27%, and were fully flexibly scheduled in 17%

(Chaney, 1998).This national pattern is in strong contrast to scheduling as surveyed in the Library Power schools in 1997 (see Figure 3-1).

In a series of annual surveys, librarians in Library Power schools were asked which of the following described how access to their library was scheduled:

◆ All classes are regularly scheduled into the library media center (LMC).

◆ Some classes are regularly scheduled, other classes flexibly.

◆ The LMC is completely flexibly scheduled (classes, small groups, and individuals are scheduled for varying time periods appropriate to need).

As illustrated in Figure 3-1, in the spring of 1997, 94.8% of the Library Power libraries reported having full or partial flexible access to the library. However, this set of libraries included schools that were nearing the end of their Library Power program in 1997 as well as schools that had ended their formal funding two years previously. Although Figure 3-1 shows the amount of flexible access achieved as of 1997, it does not give a sense of how this changed for schools over the course of their three-year program. A clearer pattern is seen if a matched set of Round 3 libraries, which began their Library Program in school year 1994–95, is compared (see Table 3-1). Here we find that 85.9% of the Round 3 libraries reported having full or partial flexible access to the library in the spring of 1995 (the end of their first school year in the program) and 98.3% reported such access in 1997. In fact, 91.9% of these libraries were reported as fully flexibly scheduled in 1997. From survey data and case study observations, it appears that schools moved quickly to implement flexible access to the library in response to the Library Power requirement.

An additional question to consider is whether the practice of providing flexible access to the library persists after the end of the grant period. Overall (n = 480) in 1997, librarians in 95% of Library Power schools reported at least partial flexible access for their school libraries. Sites funded in Round 1 ended their Library Power funding in 1995. In 1997, two years beyond the grant period, libraries in 84% of those schools were wholly or partially flexibly scheduled. In Rounds 2 and 3 schools, 97% of the libraries were scheduled flexibly, in-whole or partially.

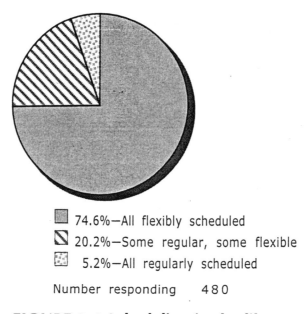

74.6%—All flexibly scheduled
20.2%—Some regular, some flexible
5.2%—All regularly scheduled

Number responding   480

FIGURE 3-1 Scheduling in the library media center in Library Power schools. (LMS Survey, 1997)

TABLE 3-1
Scheduling in the Library Media Center in Library Power Schools (Matched Round 3 LMS Surveys, 1995 and 1997)

Schedule	1995	1997
All regularly scheduled	14.1%	1.6%
Some regular, some flexible	25.0%	6.4%
All flexibly scheduled	60.9%	91.9%
Number Responding	64	62

*1995 and 1997 could not represent a clear pre- and post-test because schools were already completing their first year in the program in 1995 and were completing their third year in 1997.

Behind the strong survey findings there are various complexities to consider: school staff beliefs about and reactions to flexible scheduling, administrative support, and policies on student use. Case studies indicate that because school staff held differing beliefs about flexible scheduling, it was implemented in a variety of patterns and with varying effects on use of the library. Some teachers, for example, believed that kindergarten and first-grade students should not go to the library unaccompanied by a teacher; others believed that the students' developmental needs were served best by regular, predictable schedules, and in those schools regularly scheduled times were maintained for those classes. In other schools, teachers were reluctant to send students spontaneously because the librarian might be too busy to supervise or help them or because they did not believe in the students' ability to work independently. Some schools scheduled classes on a flexible basis, but maintained a regularly scheduled checkout time for the whole school. This was seen as a "step toward total flexibility."

Librarians, teachers, and principals have made adaptations to help flexible scheduling work for their schools. In one school, for example, half-classes visit the library for half a period, allowing for better attention for students in the library and giving the teacher a smaller group to work with in the classroom. Then the half-classes switch places, so the other half gets to visit the library. In many libraries, librarians keep a schedule on which teachers can sign up for blocks of time; in one library, teachers can sign up for a study table in the library for a group from their class to use. In some schools, going to the library as an individual was a reward for good behavior or for finishing lessons in the classroom; in others, students were dropped off at the library to prevent them from disrupting the class. Because methods for tracking which individual students gained access to the library were rarely evident, it must be assumed that some students gained access more easily than others, but the patterns of such use are not known.

The report of one case study researcher illustrates how librarians at one school struggled with the concept of a full flexible schedule and produced a thoughtful compromise that met the purposes of on-demand access:

> Neither the librarians nor teachers felt the continuation of weekly checkout periods represented a significant compromise in flexible scheduling. Retaining a brief weekly checkout period was seen as a service provided to students above and beyond the library's increased involvement in instruction vis-à-vis flexible scheduling. Most

students would have used the library at least once a week in any event, the librarians reasoned, so weekly checkout periods helped streamline library traffic associated with non-instructional student needs. Furthermore, weekly checkout periods did not compromise the philosophy of flexible scheduling as it applied to individual students because students were still permitted to come to the library any time they wanted. But the main reason librarians did not see problems with the weekly checkout is that they did not feel it detracted from what they themselves could do, or actually did do, with students. As [a librarian] noted, the main idea behind flexible scheduling was to make the interaction between students and librarians more purposeful, and School 1's hybridized scheduling approach did not hamper them in that objective.

An analysis of the relationship between scheduling of access and staffing of the library found a significant ($p<.05$) relationship between scheduling patterns and the number of support staff in the library. Overall, Library Power libraries had an average of less than one-third full-time equivalent (.31) support staff. However, libraries that had regularly scheduled access had an average of .076 full-time equivalent support staff, compared with an average of .341 for libraries with fully flexible access. The presence of support staff has been noted as necessary for a library to be responsive to multiple and spontaneous demands for services.

Perhaps the most painful aspect of moving from a regular to a flexible schedule is that many teachers lost a planning period. Under the regular schedule, the class would often be left at the library while the teacher would be free to plan lessons or perform other individual tasks. Many of these teachers had to gain experience with the flexible schedule before they could develop a sense of the benefits it could bring to their teaching. In a number of case studies, the principal was credited with the movement to a flexible schedule by strongly supporting the practice and creatively finding alternative times for both the teachers and the librarians to plan instruction. By 1997, case study researchers were reporting that many initially reluctant teachers had come to value flexible access to the library. However, responses to the Teacher Survey in 1997 indicated that there was a segment (11%) of the teachers who did not believe that flexible scheduling should continue, probably because some teachers had difficulty making use of the library in their instruction.

Providing Appropriate Library Facilities to Support Enhanced Use

Renovations were made in all of the libraries to make them more suitable to support instruction, allow multiple uses, and signal to the school and community that major change was occurring. Funds from the initiative were provided to pay for materials needed to renovate the libraries; each school district was required to provide the labor. In many cases, the labor was obtained through volunteers in the communities.

The easiest change to measure in facilities was the addition of more seats in nearly half the participating libraries, reflecting a more than 10% increase in seating capacity since Library Power began in the schools (see Table 3-2).

TABLE 3-2
Seating Capacity of the Library Media Centers
in Library Power Schools
(LMS Survey, 1997)

	Range	Mean	Median
National Library Power Schools			
Seating capacity before Library Power	0-320	51	40
Seating capacity after modification	3-400	57	50
Total Responding	422		

More important were changes designed to make libraries more attractive and more accommodating to different kinds of uses, especially those that relate to flexible scheduling. The evaluation inquired into the kinds of spaces available in the library and whether the type of space had undergone renovation with Library Power grant funds.

Figure 3-2 shows the change in schools' library media center spaces before and after the three-year Library Power program. Table 3-3 lists the total types of spaces found in 1997, with an indication of the number and percentage of libraries that had added or renovated those spaces during Library Power participation.

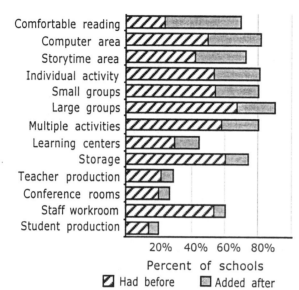

FIGURE 3-2 Spaces available in the library media centers before and after Library Power. (LMS Survey, 1997)

TABLE 3-3
Types of Spaces Available in the Library Media Centers (LMS Survey, 1997)

Type of Space	Number Having in 1997	Percent Having	Number Adding During LP	Percent Adding
Comfortable quiet reading areas	308	69.1%	204	45.7%
Computer access area or laboratory	364	81.6%	145	32.5%
Storytime area	322	72.2%	134	30.0%
Individual read/view/listen	361	80.9%	123	27.6%
Small group (< 5) reading/viewing areas	357	80.0%	115	25.8%
Large group (5+) reading/viewing areas	400	89.7%	101	22.6%
Space enough for multiple activities	358	80.3%	100	22.4%
Areas for learning centers	198	44.4%	64	14.3%
Storage (equipment, etc.)	330	74.0%	63	14.1%
Production areas for classroom teachers	128	28.7%	33	7.4%
Conference rooms	120	26.9%	31	7.0%
Workroom for LMC staff	267	59.9%	30	6.7%
Production areas for students	88	19.7%	27	6.0%
Total Responding	446			

Nearly half of the Library Power schools added more space for comfortable reading. A third of the libraries added spaces where students could work on computers and where teachers and librarians could read aloud to groups of students. One-fourth of schools added space where individual students could read, view, or listen to library materials. Schools also provided areas where students could work in small groups or large groups and spaces to allow different simultaneous activities. In relatively few schools facilities were added to allow students or teachers to use library resources to produce materials (such as handouts, overhead transparencies, and bulletin board displays) that would support instruction. Overall, more than three-quarters of Library Power libraries now can support large and small groups, reading aloud, computer use, and multiple simultaneous activities.

In addition to supporting the alterations made to the library spaces, Library Power funds were used to furnish the libraries with more attractive and comfortable furniture, such as lower bookshelves to open up or define spaces, warm carpeting, rocking chairs, reading nooks, and other features to make the library media center more inviting to students.

In many schools, there was a clear interaction between the facilities renovations and the degree to which they were implementing flexible scheduling. Table 3-4 indicates the relationships found to be significant (p<.05) between kinds of spaces added or owned in 1997 and the kind of access provided. There is a clear pattern of libraries providing more flexible access being more likely to have added such spaces and to have such spaces in 1997. For example, no libraries that were regularly scheduled added space for individual reading, viewing, or listening. Almost 80% of libraries having such spaces were fully flexibly scheduled. Most striking is the capability to support multiple activities in the library at the same time. Almost 80% of the libraries with such capacity were fully flexible scheduled; less than 60% of those not having such capability were fully flexible scheduled.

In addition, in a separate analysis, there was a relationship between seating capacity in the library and the form of scheduling. Libraries that allowed only regularly scheduled access reported an average of 43 seats; libraries with a mix of access scheduling reported an average of 50 seats; and libraries providing fully flexible access reported an average of 61 seats.

These data cannot support a causal conclusion either that facilities determine scheduling or that scheduling affects facilities. It is clear, however, that those aspects of facilities and scheduling reported in Table 3-4 occurred in ways unlikely to be due to chance.

TABLE 3-4
Facilities Related to Scheduling of Access Significant at p<.05 (LMS Survey, 1997)

	All Regularly Scheduled 5.2%	Some Regular, Some Flexible 20.2%	All Flexibly Scheduled 74.6%		n
Individual read/view/listen—					
% adding during LP	0.0%	24.0%	76.0%	100.0%	441
% not adding	7.2%	18.7%	74.1%	100.0%	
Individual read/view/listen—					
% owning at end of LP	2.8%	19.0%	78.1%	100.0%	441
% not owning	15.5%	25.0%	59.5%	100.0%	
Comfortable quiet reading areas—					
% adding during LP	2.0%	21.8%	76.2%	100.0%	441
% not adding	7.9%	18.8%	73.2%	100.0%	
Comfortable quiet reading areas—					
% owning at end of LP	3.3%	20.0%	76.7%	100.0%	441
% not owning	9.6%	20.6%	69.9%	100.0%	
Storytime area—					
% owning at end of LP	5.0%	24.2%	70.7%	100.0%	441
% not owning	5.7%	9.8%	84.5%	100.0%	
Production areas for classroom teachers—					
% owning at end of LP	3.2%	12.7%	84.1%	100.0%	441
% not owning	6.0%	23.2%	70.8%	100.0%	
Production areas for students—					
% owning at end of LP	3.4%	11.5%	85.1%	100.0%	441
% not owning	5.7%	22.3%	72.0%	100.0%	
Space enough for multiple activities—					
% owning at end of LP	31.3%	17.6%	79.3%	100.0%	441
% not owning	13.6%	30.7%	55.7%	100.0%	

Use of the Library Media Center

Because the purpose of improving facilities and scheduling is the use of the library for the support of instruction, the evaluation has used several measures of the uses made of the library: visits by individuals, small groups, and classes; circulation of materials; and teachers' reports of student use. The most common measure of library use is the number of visits by users. Librarians were asked to record on each day of a typical week the number of large groups, small groups, and classes that visited the library. The numbers of students contained in each of these groups was added to the number of individual student visits to obtain the number of visits in a typical week. Table 3-5 reports the mean response for that measure over three years and the number of visits per week per student in the school. For comparison purposes, the 1993–94 SASS figure for the mean number of visits per week is given for elementary schools nationally.

TABLE 3-5
Mean Number of Students Visiting the LMC
in a Typical Week*
(Matched LMS Surveys, 1995 and 1997; SASS)

	Library Power		SASS
National Library Power Schools	**1995**	**1997**	**1993-94**
Mean # of student visits	514	856	414
Mean # of students in the school	581	572	463
Mean # of visits per student per week	0.91	1.58	0.89
Total reporting	188	210	

*The survey item used to gather data in 1995 was modified to request more detailed information in subsequent years. Some of the reported increase in library media center visits may be related to this change in the instrument.

On average, a student in a Library Power school would visit the library over one and one-half times a week. This represents an increase over the expected once a week found under rigid scheduling of library use by classes. This count includes visits by individuals, classes, and other groups; on average, about one-quarter of the weekly visitors were reported to be individual students. On these visits, libraries circulated an average of one book per student per week. (See Table 3-6.)

TABLE 3-6
Weekly Use of the LMC in Library Power Schools
(Matched LMS Surveys, 1995 and 1997)

Type of Use	1995	1997
Mean number of large groups in a week (2+ classes)	2.4	2.8
Total Responding	205	211
Mean number of classes in a week	13.3	18.1
Total Responding	208	211
Mean number of small groups in a week	12.5	21.2
Total Responding	205	210

In a week, the average Library Power school library would be visited by 4 large groups (averaging 35 students), 21 classes (averaging 24 students), and 25 small groups (averaging 6 members). These averages are larger than those obtained in 1995, when 3 large groups, 15 classes, and 14 small groups were reported. In addition, in 1997, 30% of the librarians would have helped to teach an average of 3 classes outside the library. (See Table 3-6.)

Flexible access to the library appears to affect the patterns of use of the library. Although there was no significant difference found between the number of large groups in a week for regularly scheduled access and fully flexible access (averages of 3.61 for regular versus 3.33 for flexible), there was a strong difference between those libraries with a mixed schedule (an average of 1.5 large group visits per week) and those with fully flexible access, which had twice as many large group visits in a week (3.3). The number of small group visits seemed even more strongly affected by scheduling. The number of small group visits to libraries with a regular schedule was less than 10 in a week (9.56), while the number of small group visits to fully flexibly scheduled libraries was more than twice as many (21.39).

With the move to flexible access and more direct support of the curriculum, the question of the capacity of the library to support instruction is raised. The average Library Power school had approximately 30 classroom teachers. Visits by each class of an average of once a week would come close to exhausting the resources of the library and staff, particularly considering that each of the visits under a flexible schedule is for a unique purpose. Under the regular schedule, the same lesson could be repeated for a number of classes. In addition, and often simultaneously, there are visits by small groups and individuals. Therefore, while there is an increase in use from 1995 to 1997, it is unknown at this point whether a limit of capacity is being reached.

Table 3-7 reports the distribution of use levels reported from all Library Power libraries in 1995 and 1997, showing that a number of very active libraries raise the overall average.

TABLE 3-7
*Groups Visiting the LMC by Quartile of Library Use Measures
(LMS Surveys, 1995 and 1997)*

Type of Grouping	1st Quartile 25%	2d Quartile 50%	3d Quartile 75%	90+ Percentile 90%	n
1995					
Large groups per week	0	1	3	5	271
Classes in a week	5	11	19	25	273
Small groups	5	10	17	30	271
Visits/student/week	0.57	0.88	1.05	1.45	242
1997					
Large groups per week	0	1	3	8	425
Classes in a week	10	17	23	30	425
Small groups	9	16	27	45	423
Visits/student/week	1.03	1.38	1.84	2.33	418

As indicated in Table 3-7, although each kind of visit shows substantial increases from 1995 to 1997, there are still 25% of the schools with low levels of activity: no large groups in a week, 10 class visits, and 9 small group visits. It is reasonable to conclude that in these schools in the bottom quartile many teachers have not found good ways to make use of flexible access.

Again, change in levels of use brought about by the initiative can be examined by a matched comparison of Round 3 Library Power libraries in 1995, the first year of their project, and in 1997, as they completed the three-year funding. Although the overall pattern of Table 3-8 is similar to that of Table 3-7, the upper 10% of libraries were even more heavily used in 1997 in this cohort than in all Library Power libraries, and the median number of small groups per week is more than 40% higher.

TABLE 3-8
Groups Visiting the LMC by Quartile of Library Use Measures (Matched Round 3 LMS Surveys, 1995 and 1997)

Type of Grouping	1st Quartile 25%	2d Quartile 50%	3d Quartile 75%	90+ Percentile 90%	n
1995					
Large groups per week	0	1	3	8	61
Classes in a week	7	14	21	29	60
Small groups	4	10	21	32	62
Visits/student/week	0.55	0.89	1.05	1.65	55
1997					
Large groups per week	0	1	5	13	62
Classes in a week	13	19	26	36	62
Small groups	10	23	38	50	62
Visits/student/week	1.14	1.50	1.85	3.08	62

As an additional measure to the counts kept by librarians, teachers, in a sample survey across the initiative, were asked for their observations on student use of the library. Overall, 65% of the teachers reported an increase in library use since Library Power began. Further, 60% noted an increase in use of the library on the students' own initiative, and 72% described student attitude toward using the library as more positive. (See Table 3-9.)

TABLE 3-9
Teacher Report of Changes in Student Use of the Library
Since Library Power Began in the School
(1997)

Student Frequency of Using the Library

Much less than before	5	4	3	2	1	Much more than before	n
	5.7%	5.5%	24.0%	32.5%	32.3%		1091

Student Frequency of Using the Library on Their Own Initiative

Much less often	5	4	3	2	1	Much more often	n
	7.2%	6.5%	26.4%	32.1%	27.9%		1076

Student Attitude Toward Using the Library

Much more negative	5	4	3	2	1	Much more positive	n
	3.1%	2.8%	22.4%	32.1%	39.6%		1084

The change in attitude toward using the library was described by a principal in a case study school:

> The old library was not tied to the curriculum in any way. You went to the library to check out a book. Period! Now classes of students, half classes of students, one student, two students, depending upon what is going on in the classroom … determines who needs to go. … They go in there with their problem … that they were trying to find information about … They go right to it. Librarians, parents, volunteers, or assistants, at times, are in there to help.

In the two years, you almost needed to be here to see the … change. But now students have a completely different view of the library … They enjoy going to the library … enjoy solving problems that they … can solve in the library … I have seen some of that. "We are going to the library to see what we can find out. We do not agree on this … so we are going to the library." We still have students who want to check out books, but now they check out books related to some things happening in the classroom, almost every time … not just some isolated book.

A further source of insight into the acceptance of flexible scheduling was obtained by asking librarians, principals, and a sample of teachers whether they felt key Library Power practices would and should continue beyond the formal funding period. In particular, they were asked about flexible scheduling and on-demand use of the library. (See Table 3-10).

TABLE 3-10
Continuation of Flexible Access and On-Demand Use (1997)

	Librarians % Yes	Principals % Yes	Teachers % Yes
Flexible scheduling of classes in the library (vs. regular weekly visits)			
Will continue	92.2%	96.4%	93.1%
Total responding	403	363	851
Should continue	98.2%	97.8%	85.3%
Total Responding	405	362	1006
On-demand use of the library by individual students or groups (vs. at pre-set times)			
Will continue	93.2%	96.9%	90.7%
Total responding	404	360	830
Should continue	97.0%	98.0%	90.0%
Total Responding	403	355	1008

Overall, all three groups of respondents believe that the practice of as-needed access to the library will continue and should continue. Teachers are somewhat less supportive of the practice: More think that flexible scheduling *will* continue (93%) than believe it *should* continue (85%). Schools that had completed their Library Power grant periods two years previously had somewhat lower expectations for continuation of these practices; however, the lowest percentage of agreement found from Round 1 librarians, teachers, or principals is 82%, showing a strong support for Library Power practices and an expectation that they would continue. Again, the lowest percentage is of Round 1 teachers agreeing that flexible scheduling should continue. The overall high expectation for continuity is supported by persistence of the practice in a large number of Library Power schools.

The attitudes and behaviors of the teachers appear to be strongly related to their degree of involvement with Library Power practices. Teachers were asked to rate their level of "participation in Library Power activities, such as flexible use of the library and joint planning of instruction with the librarian." Teachers who rated their participation as more active also said more often that their students visited the library "as a class," "in small groups," and "as individuals." They also reported that their students used the library more than before, used the library more often on their own initiative, and had a more positive attitude toward using the library. The teachers who had been more involved with Library Power were more convinced that the practices of "flexible scheduling of classes in the library (vs. regular weekly visits)" and of "on-demand use of the library by individual students or groups (vs. at pre-set times)"should continue. Teachers who reported increased use of the collection to support their instruction were also significantly more positive that these practices should continue. Teachers who rated their level of participation with Library Power as more active were also statistically significantly ($p<.05$) more positive that both flexible scheduling of classes in the library and on-demand use by individual students should continue.

Conclusion

It appears that the Library Power initiative has spurred major change in the way school libraries are used to support instruction. While the facilities' improvements are an immediate and visible sign of change in the school, the move to flexible scheduling was a more profound change in the operation of the school. It is clear from the survey and case study data that this change in the timing of access to the library is well under way, but there is also ample evidence that it is often not smooth; is interpreted in various ways by different librarians, teachers, and principals; and it raises significant concerns about the evenness of access within the school and the classroom. However, while the adjustment to a flexible schedule is often difficult, there is also reason to believe schools that persist will find ways of working through the complexities, and instruction will be better served by their doing so.

As the practices of Library Power continue to be employed in these schools, a number of issues will require attention:

◆ How to move to quality and equitable support for all of the classrooms in the building.

◆ How to provide full flexibility that supports regular visits as well as spontaneous uses.

◆ How to allow general checkout visits as well as more targeted uses.

◆ How to design appropriate visiting practices for different grade levels.

◆ How to determine the amount of use that is desirable for each class.

◆ How to allocate the limited staff resources of the library to provide the fullest support of the curriculum.

References

Chaney, B. (1998). *School library media centers: 1993–94.* NCES 98–282. Project Officer, Jeffrey Williams. Washington, D.C.: U.S. Department of Education, National Center for Education Statistics.

4 *COLLABORATION*

Norman Lott Webb

Collaboration is one of the main tenets of Library Power and is one of the six goals for the program:

To encourage collaboration among teachers, administrators and librarians that results in significant improvement in teaching and the learning process (collaboration within schools).

As indicated by this goal, advancing collaboration was a major change strategy for Library Power that would lead to a stronger connection between what occurs in classrooms and what occurs in the library. That is, increased collaboration among library media specialists, teachers, and others in schools is essential for library media specialists and libraries to become more central to the instructional missions of schools. In theory, increased collaboration among librarians and teachers will produce more effective planning for instruction and more effective use of library resources. By discussing plans and expectations with teachers, the librarian will be better able to order materials and develop a collection that is aligned with and supportive of the curriculum. Teachers will have more flexibility in planning instructional activities by using the librarian as another teacher and expanding instructional activities into the library. Joint monitoring of instruction by teachers and librarians will result in meeting the needs of students more effectively.

Library Power contributed to increasing collaboration in general in schools and, in particular, between library media specialists and teachers. The requirements for being a Library Power school, and the program's strong emphasis on linking the library with instruction, encouraged schools to develop a climate of collaboration. In working more closely together, library media specialists coordinated their activities with teachers, both in improving the libraries' capacity as a resource for instruction and in incorporating information resources into teaching and learning. A significant number of library media specialists and teachers went further and actively planned and designed lessons together. Further, Library Power not only advanced collaboration among teachers and library media specialists, it also encouraged collaboration between teachers.

Many different levels of collaboration were observed in Library Power schools. What is evident from the study is how complex advancing collaboration in schools can be. A few of the schools claimed to have engaged all of the faculty in this process with the library media specialists, but in most of the schools only about half of the teachers actually collaborated with the librarian. Increasing the proportion of teachers who collaborated with the library media specialist over time was very difficult and proceeded slowly. A number of library media specialists reported that they had to seek out individual teachers for them both to learn how to engage in productive collaboration and to find the time to interact with each other. The difficulty that some schools had in fostering collaboration among their faculty contrasts with the progress made in other schools.

This chapter discusses the advances made in furthering collaboration in Library Power schools. The results of Library Power are expressed within the context of other studies of collaboration in schools. The information reported is organized in four categories:

1. Library Power increased collaboration in schools.

2. Collaboration strengthened the connection between libraries and instruction.

3. Identifying the nature of the collaboration.

4. Advancing collaborative practices in schools is difficult.

Increased Collaboration in Library Power Schools

Developing collaboration and strong collegiality are emerging as important conditions for teaching. The roots of Library Power reach into the early stages of the school reform movement begun in the 1980s, which was fueled by the need to reduce the isolation of teachers and others in a school (Nelson, 1994, p. 19). Teaching was narrowly perceived as an adult in a classroom engaging students in activities. The teacher rarely left the classroom and rarely had the opportunity to communicate with other teachers, much less the librarian. Students were dropped off at the library once a week. Teachers perceived this break in their schedule as an opportunity for their own planning or grading rather than for instruction. Students used this time less for learning and more for checking out books. As reform took hold in the latter part of the 1980s and the early 1990s, it included rethinking what it means to be a teacher or a librarian and what instruction is. Teaching as predominantly telling and showing—the lecture-demonstration model—was being replaced by teachers supporting students' active learning (Simon, 1997, p. 60). Teaching in schools became a process of understanding how individual students make sense of important ideas, how they develop concepts and skills, and what activities will most likely advance student learning. Redefining instruction to more actively engage students in authentic learning by having them understand the connections among ideas and applications can be facilitated by teachers and librarians collaborating with each other. Accepting this new view of instruction requires time for those working with students to learn and advance collegiality to better manage student learning.

This chapter draws on data from longitudinal case studies, collaboration logs, and surveys from teachers, principals, and librarians. Principal and teacher surveys were conducted in 1996 and 1997. Because all of the sites had begun their projects before 1995, these data represent schools well into their Library Power process or after the project had been completed. It would not be expected to find important movement from 1996 to 1997, but consistency between the years provides a test-retest of reliability of measurement and the increases that did occur suggest movement in desired directions. Overall, library media specialists, principals, and teachers agreed that Library Power contributed to increasing collaboration between librarians and teachers and, though to a lesser degree, between teachers and teachers. Some collaboration between teachers and librarians was reported in nearly all of the Library Power schools, based on an analysis of questionnaire data and confirmed by the case studies. Ninety-nine percent of the principals (n=456) of the Library Power schools reported that the librarians had worked with at least some teachers to plan and design instruction and develop the collection. In 1997, 36% of the principals reported that their schools had fully adopted collaborative planning and design of instruction between the librarian and teachers. An even higher percentage of the principals (43%) reported that their schools had fully adopted collaboration between the librarian and teachers in developing the library's collection (see Table 4-1).

TABLE 4-1
Percent of Principals Reporting Collaboration
Adopted by the Full Faculty
(Principal Survey, 1996 and 1997)

Year	Number Responding n	Teachers with Librarians Instructional Units %	Teachers with Librarians Collection Development %	Teachers with Teachers Instruction Planning %
1996	350	34	45	34
1997	433	36	43	37

A high percentage of principals indicated that since their schools had joined Library Power at least some teachers had begun to collaborate for the first time. In 1997, 80% of the principals reported that at least some teachers at their school had begun to collaborate in planning and designing instruction with the librarian. (See Table 4-2.) A lower percentage (72% in 1997) reported that some teachers had begun to collaborate with the librarian in planning for collection development. A slightly lower percentage, but still nearly two-thirds of the principals, reported that at least some teachers had begun to collaborate with other teachers in planning instruction. The ordering of these percents reflects, in part, what was in existence before Library Power and the focus of Library Power. In many schools, teachers already had been collaborating with each other. What Library Power contributed was to include the librarian in this process.

TABLE 4-2
Percent of Principals Reporting New Collaboration
Among Some Staff After School Joined Library Power
(Principal Survey, 1996 and 1997)

Year	Number Responding n	Teachers with Librarians Instructional Units %	Teachers with Librarians Collection Development %	Teachers with Teachers Instruction Planning %
1996	350	81	69	63
1997	433	80	72	62

Nearly all of the principals attributed the increase in collaboration at their schools, at least in part, to Library Power. Over half of the principals attributed the increase in collaboration among librarians and teachers mostly to Library Power. (See Table 4-3.) Almost 40% attributed the increase in collaboration to both Library Power and other school reforms. Overall, 90% of principals attributed the increase in collaboration between teachers and librarians to Library Power working alone or as part of a mix with other school reforms. As one principal wrote, "Library Power goals and practices encouraged, and even mandated, the collaborative process."

Library Power was not as frequently cited in furthering the adoption of collaborative planning just among teachers. However, one-fourth of the principals did credit Library Power with increasing this type of interaction. Over half, 55%, attributed improved collaboration among teachers to a mix between Library Power and other school reforms. The similarity in percentages in both 1997 and 1996 provides some indication of reliability in the percentages reported.

TABLE 4-3
Percent of Principals Attributing Library Power As Responsible for Collaboration Among at Least Some Staff (Principal Survey, 1996 and 1997)

Year	Number Responding n	Teachers with Librarians Instructional Units		Teachers with Librarians Collection Development		Teachers with Teachers Instruction Planning	
		Mostly LP %	LP+ Reform %	Mostly LP %	LP+ Reform %	Mostly LP %	LP+ Reform %
1996	337*	56	37	51	43	28	50
1997	416	59	35	52	39	26	55

*The number of principals can vary depending on the number who responded to a specific item.

Librarians supported the findings from principals that Library Power had increased collaboration in schools. A greater proportion of the teachers in schools had regularly collaborated with the librarians after the school had joined Library Power than before. Prior to their school's joining Library Power, librarians reported that they had regularly collaborated in planning or providing instruction with 22% of the teachers in their schools. After the schools had joined Library Power, the total percentage of teachers that librarians reported they had regularly collaborated with was over half of those on the faculty (56%) in 1997. However, there was a large variation among Library Power schools. Of all the schools and librarians who completed a questionnaire, 75% of the librarians collaborated with more than 40% of the teachers; the upper 25% of librarians collaborated with 85% or more of the teachers in their schools.

Data from teachers confirmed the responses from the principals and librarians. In 1997, when asked to respond on a four-point scale—"Not at all" (1) to "Very often" (4)—how often they collaborated with the librarian for planning and designing instruction, 17% of the teachers reported "Very often" and 34% reported "Some" (3) (see Table 4-4). The total who reported at least some collaboration (51%) is very similar to the percentage of teachers the librarians reported they had collaborated with (56%). Data from both the librarians and teachers indicate that, on the average, a little more than half of the teachers in Library Power schools in 1997 were regularly collaborating with librarians. Only 18% of the teachers reported they were not at all collaborating with the librarians.

TABLE 4-4

Percent of Teachers Who Reported Collaborating with Librarians in Planning and Designing Instruction, by Frequency of Collaboration (Teacher Survey, 1996 and 1997)

		Frequency of Collaboration				
Year	Number Responding n	Very Often %	3 (Some) %	2 (Little) %	Not at All %	Total %
1996*	969	21	34	31	14	100
1997*	1,152	17	34	31	18	100

* In 1996, 54% (n=526) of the teachers said Library Power had increased their participation in collaboration. In 1997, 46% (n = 529) of the teachers said the same.

Using an open-ended question format, teachers were asked to identify the two most important contributions of Library Power. The response identified by the highest proportion of teachers (more than 70%) was the resources they had been given. The second most frequently cited contribution was collaboration. Further, 5% of the teachers gave collaboration as their first choice.

Various unknown factors inhibited full implementation of collaboration in Library Power schools. Schools varied in the proportion of teachers at the school who collaborated with the librarian and with other teachers. Only one-third of the principals reported that the full faculty adopted collaboration on instruction. One principal acknowledged that in her school only a small number of teachers were involved in collaboration: "Limited collaboration with about four members of the staff, which is an improvement over none that existed before." The teachers' responses supported those of the principals in indicating that not all teachers participated in collaboration.

In summary, Library Power increased collaboration to at least some extent within schools. More than 90% of the principals attributed to Library Power at least some increase in collaboration in their schools. Library Power was more effective in fostering new forms of collaboration between teachers and the librarian than only among teachers, in part because interactions among teachers had existed prior to Library Power. About one-third of the principals reported that collaboration on instruction had been fully adopted by the faculty in their schools. This, along with a majority of the teachers in Library Power schools collaborating with librarians, establishes a strong relationship between the initiative and the interaction among faculty. (See Table 4-4.)

Stronger Connections Between Libraries and Instruction Through Collaboration

Collaboration among colleagues in schools is compatible with research on how teachers change. Professional learning (Loucks-Horsley et. al., 1998) is recognized as an important component of the teaching profession that requires more than short, after-school workshops once per quarter. Such experiences do not provide the ongoing, interactive, cumulative learning and the experimentation necessary to develop new conceptions and patterns of work (Fullan, 1991, p. 85; Webb, Heck, and Tate, 1997; Stocks & Schofeld, 1997). More effective approaches facilitate interaction among peers that can be sustained over time and provide input at the critical times when the need is the greatest. Among other strategies for professional learning are coaching and mentoring (working one-on-one with an equally or more experienced teacher); professional networks (linking with teachers and others to explore and discuss topics of interest, pursue common goals, and share information); and partnerships with those in business, industry, and universities (working collaboratively to improve teacher content knowledge, instructional materials, access to facilities, and access to new information) (Loucks-Horsley et. al., 1998, pp. 43–44). There are many ways in which teachers and library media specialists can collaborate to improve both their own professional skills and instruction of students.

Nature of Collaboration

What constitutes collaboration is a matter of interpretation. This section discusses what collaborative activities Library Power teachers and librarians engaged in as reported by principals, librarians, and teachers. In general, more librarians reported participating in planning for instruction by identifying goals and activities than before their schools joined Library Power. However, librarians' major responsibilities remained identifying and gathering resources in support of instruction, teaching information skills, and helping students create products. Teachers retained sole responsibilities for evaluating students and grading.

Collaboration can be analyzed by both its form and its substance. There are degrees of collaboration ranging from only tangential activities to significant cooperation among people who all have equal stakes in the endeavor. Five levels depict a range and a variation in the nature of collaborative activities. These levels are not distinct and do not form a strict hierarchy. In any one school, faculty could be engaged at times in all different levels of collaboration, each fulfilling different purposes and different means for meeting students' needs. The five levels are:

1. Aware: Teachers and the librarian are aware of each others' activities.

2. Parallel: Teachers and the librarian engage in parallel activities, teachers in the classroom and the librarian in the library.

3. Coordinated: Teachers and the librarian coordinate a division of labor and responsibilities for instructional activities in one location such as the library.

4. Interactive: Teachers and the librarian cooperate with each other and assume equal responsibility for planning and delivering instruction.

5. Shared: Teachers and the librarian share full responsibility for their own learning and the learning of students. A professional learning community has been created.

The focus of teachers collaborating with librarians can vary greatly from planning and designing instruction, to evaluating the degree the library's collection is aligned with the curriculum, to providing instruction to students. All of these foci, and others, were documented in Library Power schools. To understand how collaboration is functioning within schools, both the focus and form of collaboration must be considered.

Nearly all of the principals, more than 95%, reported that both teachers and the librarian participated in identifying and gathering materials, teaching information skills, and helping students create reports. Principals reported that the teachers and librarians delivered instruction and designed unit activities. In two-thirds of the schools, principals reported that teachers and librarians created goals and objectives. According to principals, librarians in about one-third of the schools were involved in designing student evaluations or evaluating performance.

Teachers worked with librarians in a variety of ways (see Table 4-5). Of the approximately 1,185 teachers who responded to the 1997 Teacher Survey, the highest percentage of teachers reported that the librarian worked with them to teach information seeking/research skills (63%). Slightly lower percentage reported that they worked with the librarian to identify/gather materials (59%) and help students create products (52%). One interesting finding is that even though teachers reported they had worked with the librarian on these specific activities, a small percentage of teachers did not perceive that activity as collaboration. From 1% to 6% of teachers who said they had worked with the librarian on seven of the different activities (see Table 4-5) responded "Not at All" when they were asked if they collaborated with the librarian in planning and designing instruction. This suggests that at least some teachers who worked with a librarian did not consider this to be engaging in collaborative planning with the librarian.

Table 4-5 identifies the subset of teachers who reported working with the librarian when carrying out each of eight different tasks. For those teachers working with the librarian on a given task, the frequency of collaboration in planning and designing instruction with the librarian is reported to show how intensively the teacher and librarian were working together.

For those instructional activities librarians have traditionally done—identify/gather materials (D), teach information seeking/research skills (F), and help students create products (G)—the percentage of teachers who very often collaborated with the librarian in planning and designing instruction was markedly lower than for activities more traditionally identified with the teacher—creating/writing unit's goals and objectives (A), designing unit activities (B), and so forth (see Table 4-5). Fewer teachers worked with librarians on these activities more traditionally done by teachers. When they did work with the librarian on these activities, they were more likely to be collaborating frequently with the librarian in planning and designing instruction. For example, a low percentage of teachers (7%) worked with a librarian to evaluate student performance. However, 53% of this group collaborated very often with a librarian in planning and designing instruction (see item H in Table 4-5). That is, working with librarians on instructional activities was positively related to collaborating with the librarian in planning and designing instruction.

TABLE 4-5
Percent of Teachers Who Worked with Librarians for Total Group and Percent of This Group by Level of Collaboration with Librarians in Planning, Designing, and Delivering Instruction (Teacher Survey, 1997)

				Of Teachers Who Worked with Librarian:			
		Teachers Who Work with the Librarian		Frequency of Collaboration			
	Total Number Responding			Very Often	3 (Some)	2 (Little)	Not at All
Instructional Activities	n	n	%	%	%	%	%
A. Create/write unit's goals/objectives	1,140	300	26	40	44	15	1
B. Design unit activities	1,143	359	31	36	45	17	2
D. Identify/gather materials	1,135	672	59	25	43	26	5
E. Deliver instruction	1,129	300	27	39	40	19	2
F. Teach information seeking/research skills	1,120	708	63	24	41	29	6
G. Help students create products	1,115	576	52	26	42	26	6
H. Evaluate student performance	1,140	85	7	53	36	6	5
I. Calculate and provide course grades	1,131	23	2	70	26	4	0

Principals validated that teachers and librarians had engaged more in planning for instruction. Of nearly 370 principals who responded to an open-ended question as to what extent and in what ways Library Power had affected the collaborative process, 43% gave some response that indicated teachers and librarians had increased their joint planning on instructional units. Comments from some of the principals illustrate this point:

> Now the librarian is intricately involved in planning instruction and carrying it out.

> Prior to Library Power, the librarian was not a participant in the creation of instructional units. This has evolved to a nice collaboration between all parties.

> Library Power had a positive impact in that it encouraged teamwork and collaborative planning which was non-existent on some grade levels.

> Library Power has increased the dialog in our school about curriculum and the types of assignments students should be given. All may not agree on substance of assignments, etc. but teachers are now collaborating.

> Before Library Power, collaboration was almost non-existent. As we get more training we are changing from individually developed units to those collaboratively planned. We have made progress in this direction with still some ways to go.

Some of the principals described how Library Power had led to an increase in collaborative planning between teachers and librarians. One reason given was that Library Power provided the professional development needed by staff to learn about collaboration. Additional comments from principals illustrate the importance of professional development:

> Staff received directions and orientation to the collaborative planning process as a result of our involvement in the Library Power Program.

Through training and resources provided by Library Power, staff was trained in collaborative planning and provided time to do it.

Each of the years that [our school] has participated in Library Power, there have been significant inservice activities focused on interdisciplinary planning for staff.

A second reason principals gave for increased interaction between teachers and librarians was that Library Power afforded more time for collaboration and planning. The following comments from four principals show how this happened:

As a setting with built-in flex time for children to come to library alone or in small groups, more support for individualized work. More planning opportunities with librarian were available.

Through Library Power teachers were given training in the collaborative process and provided the time to participate in the process.

Time has been provided for planning between teachers and librarian.

Library Power provided funds for substitutes to give teachers release time to collaborate.

Some principals held teachers and librarians accountable for collaborating with each other, another contributing factor to increasing their collaboration. As one principal reported:

Because of Library Power our LMS has worked with every teacher in the collaborative process. Each teacher must document for me at least three projects he/she has planned with the LMS.

In summary, teachers and librarians engaged in a variety of collaborative activities. The highest percentage of librarians reported that they worked with teachers in activities more traditionally identified with librarians: teaching information seeking/research skills, identifying and gathering materials and resources, and helping students create products. However, there was strong evidence, both from the principals and teachers, that librarians were becoming more active in the instructional mission of the schools through increasing their participation in planning for instruction by writing goals and objectives, designing units, and delivering instruction. At the same time, a high percentage of librarians remained removed from evaluating or grading students.

Difficulty of Advancing Collaborative Practices

Instituting collaboration among teachers and librarians in a school is difficult. How this can be done will vary from school to school. Each school has its own culture, with established patterns of work, set time schedules, and defined responsibilities and roles. Changing the work patterns within a school will require changing beliefs about what is important, control over time, and territorial boundaries. Even if a school adopts an innovation, rarely is it fully assimilated into the school as intended by its developer (Popkewitz, Tabachnick, & Wehlage, 1982; Romberg & Pitman, 1990). Developing collaboration among staff in a school is an attempt to change the school culture. The skills of collaboration can be learned through study groups, coaching and mentoring, networks, and case discussions. These activities can equip school staff with tools and techniques to build and maintain supportive, professional communities in their schools (Loucks-Horsley, et. al., 1998, p. 199). More difficult is changing the beliefs of teachers and librarians that collaboration is good for them and their students and for them to assume ownership of this new practice.

Collaboration among colleagues, as with most education improvement approaches, is not without problems if attempted blindly and superficially. Poorly conceived collaboration, or contrived collaboration, can be as much a negative force as a positive one (Fullan & Hargreaves, 1991). Productive collaboration is a skill that has to be learned. Teachers and librarians need to learn how to communicate with each other and how joint planning can benefit the work of each. They need to learn how to solve problems, offer productive criticisms, understand the expectations and needs of the other person, and establish a common language. School staff members may have individual goals and styles that inhibit working with others. Incentives for promotion or recognition may encourage individuals on a staff to strike out on their own (Raths, 1993, p. 264). Some may not have the confidence or comfort level to open up their classroom practices and reveal their perceived inadequacies to fellow teachers and librarians. Collaboration requires time (Loucks-Horsley, et al., 1998, pp. 197, 224–228). Teachers' and librarians' professional time during a week is already full, not only with teaching responsibilities but also with supervision duties, parent conferences, record keeping, and lesson preparations. Not only must staff members learn the needed skills to collaborate with their colleagues, they must be given the necessary support to create a climate where collaboration is valued. School principals and district administrators have to give teachers the time needed for effective collaboration.

Collaboration as a change strategy depends heavily on individuals, their commitment, and their willingness to participate (Webb & Romberg, 1994, p. 207). Left to individuals, collaboration leads to incremental change affecting isolated groups or individuals rather than to school- or system-wide change. Strong administrative efforts and staff ownership are needed for collaboration among staff to reach its full potential to improve instructional effectiveness within a school. In the absence of these features, other than products that may be produced through collaboration, such as boxed lessons, the collaboration is unlikely to have ripple effects. One challenge faced by this evaluation of how collaboration has been incorporated into Library Power schools, and to what ends, is to ascertain how pervasive collaboration has been and how the program has served to increase the proportion of those who participate.

Certain changes require a learning curve or time to implement. This was not the case for collaboration and Library Power. Very little change was observed in schools with full adoption of Library Power based on the number of years the school had participated in Library Power. The natural expectation would be that collaborative practices would be expanded to a greater proportion of faculty in schools that had participated in Library Power over a longer period of time. This did not happen. Regardless of the year that the school had started in Library Power, there was essentially no variation in the percentage of principals who reported full faculty adoption of collaborative planning among teachers and librarians on instructional units (see Table 4-6). The variance was only 9%. Principals at schools that had participated in Library Power the fewest number of years (one to two), reported full faculty adoption in nearly the same percentage (36%). This was only slightly less than the 39% reported by principals of schools in Library Power for three years and more than the 30% reported by principals of schools in Library Power for four years.

There was an increase in collaboration related to the length of time a school had participated in Library Power in the "Some" collaboration category. It appears that about one-third of the schools achieved full adoption of collaborative practice independent of time spent in the initiative, perhaps as a result of administrative direction or school-wide policy. Other schools increased, at least to some degree, the concentration of faculty engaging in collaboration the longer they were in Library Power, but still not to a sufficient degree to increase the percentage fully adopting collaboration.

Schools joining Library Power in 1996–97, the year the survey was completed, had a significantly higher percentage of principals who reported that collaboration had already existed at their schools before joining Library Power than principals whose schools had joined Library Power in one of the three previous years. (See right-hand column in Table 4-6.) More than one-third of the schools in the 1996–97 cohort (35%) reported that collaboration had already existed. This is 16% to 23% higher than the percentage of principals who reported prior collaboration in the schools joining Library Power between 1993 and 1995. The data are insufficient to decipher exactly why this was the case. One explanation could be that schools late in joining Library Power were slow in participating because they were already employing collaboration and other features of the program, or there could simply be an anomaly in this cohort of schools. Schools and districts did vary in conditions by the round in which they joined Library Power. Several Round 1 sites, for example, did not have libraries or library programs prior to joining Library Power. What is clear is that there was a large increase from the 19% of schools that had already adopted collaboration among their faculty prior to joining Library Power to the 87% that had adopted these practices, to at least some degree, after joining Library Power (see Table 4-6).

For each of the five cohort groups of schools, a higher percentage of principals reported full faculty adoption of teachers and librarians collaborating on collection development than on planning and designing instructional units (see Tables 4-1, 4-6, and 4-7). For each of the five years, from 3% to 10% of the schools had more teachers and librarians collaborating on collection development than on instructional planning and design. As is shown in Table 4-7, there was no discernible pattern by year in the rate of faculty adoption of collaboration between teachers and librarians on collection development. The only observed variation by year was on the percentage of principals who indicated "Little" (2) collaboration on collection development. Those schools that had joined Library Power in 1992–93 (the first cohort of schools) had a higher percentage at this level than schools that joined Library Power in 1994–95 (21% compared to 7%). The first cohort of schools, those schools that had been in Library Power the longest, appears to be somewhat lower in collaboration on collection development than those joining in later years.

TABLE 4-6
Percent of Principals in 1997 Rating Levels of Collaborative
Planning and Design of Instruction Between Teachers and
Librarians by Year School Joined Library Power
(Principal Survey, 1997)

		Degree of Adoption of Collaboration Among Faculty				Existed Before LP
Initial Year in Library Power (Years in Library Power)	Number Responding	Fully Adopted	3 (Some)	2 (Little)	Not at All	
	n	%	%	%	%	%
1992–93 (4 years)	33	30	54	15	0	20
1993–94 (3 years)	67	39	55	6	0	12
1994–95 (2 years)	112	36	55	9	0	19
1995–96 (1 year)	83	37	43	18	1	16
1996–97 (<1 year)	44	36	45	18	0	35*
Total	339	36	51	12	0.3	19

* Statistically significant difference from three previous years (1993–94, 1994–95, 1995–96).

   Some difference was also detected between schools in the first cohort group and the other cohort groups in the low adoption rate among teachers who collaborated on planning with other teachers (see Table 4-8). A higher percentage of schools in the third cohort group (1994–95) reported at least some collaboration among teachers than did those in the first cohort group (1992–93), 93% compared to 78%. There was an increase in percentage of principals who reported that collaboration among teachers had existed prior to the school's joining Library Power, from 28% in 1992–93 to 47% in 1996–97. This, accompanied by a higher percentage of principals in the 1996–97 survey attributing collaboration among teachers to school reform (27% compared to from 8% to 20% for the other years), suggest that Library Power was a less important factor for establishing collaboration among teachers than other reasons, such as school reforms.

TABLE 4-7
Percent of Principals in 1997 Rating Level of Collaborative Planning for Collection Development Between Teachers and Librarians by Year School Joined Library Power (Principal Survey, 1997)

Initial Year in Library Power (Years in Library Power)	Number Responding	Degree of Adoption of Collaboration Among Faculty				Existed Before LP
		Fully Adopted	3 (Some)	2 (Little)	Not at All	
	n	%	%	%	%	%
1992–93 (4 years)	33	33	45	21	0	26
1993–94 (3 years)	67	45	45	10	0	31
1994–95 (2 years)	112	46	46	7	1	21
1995–96 (1 year)	81	40	46	15	0	21
1996–97 (<1 year)	44	41	43	16	0	31
Total	337	42	45	12	0.3	28

With respect to the different forms of collaboration, Library Power contributed more to librarians and teachers collaborating on instructional units and on developing the library collection than it did to collaboration between teachers on instructional planning (see Table 4-9). Ninety percent of principals at schools where collaboration on librarian-teacher instructional planning or collection development had not existed before Library Power attributed this form of collaboration mostly to Library Power. This is nine times the percentage of principals attributing this form of collaboration to Library Power at schools where these forms of collaboration had existed before. The difference in the percentage of principals attributing collaboration mostly to Library Power at schools where the practice did not exist prior to Library Power and where it did exist was somewhat smaller for the third form of collaboration: 84% and 16% for teacher-teacher collaborative planning.

TABLE 4-8
Percent of Principals in 1997 Rating Level of Collaborative
Planning Among Teachers by Year School Joined Library Power
(Principal Survey, 1997)

Initial Year in Library Power (Years in Library Power)	Number Responding n	Fully Adopted %	3 (Some) %	2 (Little) %	Not at All %	Existed Before LP %
1992–93 (4 years)	33	36	42	21	0	28
1993–94 (3 years)	68	38	46	16	0	26
1994–95 (2 years)	113	38	55	6	1	41
1995–96 (1 year)	80	35	48	16	0	38
1996–97 (<1 year)	45	36	56	9	0	47
Total	339	37	50	12	0.3	37

Degree of Adoption of Collaboration Among Teachers

TABLE 4-9
Percent of Principals Attributing Library Power As Responsible
for Collaboration Among at Least Some Staff by Prior Existence
of Collaboration at the School
(Principal Survey, 1997)

Existed Prior to LP?	Teachers with Librarians Instructional Units Mostly LP %	n	Teachers with Librarians Collection Development Mostly LP %	n	Teachers with Teachers Instruction Planning Mostly LP %	n
No	91	202	90	177	84	79
Yes	9	20	10	19	16	15

In summary, only a few differences were detected in the rate of collaboration in schools attributable to the year the school joined Library Power, particularly in the rate of full adoption by faculty. This implies that even though schools became more experienced in Library Power, they did not necessarily increase the percentage of teachers who collaborated with the librarian and did not eventually reach all of the faculty in the school. Factors other than time in the program were more important. Those shifts in collaborating practices that were reported were from little collaboration to some collaboration. Library Power was credited more for teachers collaborating with librarians on collection development than for teachers collaborating with librarians in instructional planning, or for collaboration between teachers. What is clear is that a high percentage of schools (more than 60%) that joined Library Power had incorporated collaboration among faculty where this practice had not existed prior to the school joining Library Power.

Levels of Collaboration As Depicted in Case Studies and Collaboration Logs

Quantitative data collected by questionnaires established the extent to which people in schools reported the existence of collaboration; the percentages of schools, teachers, and librarians engaging in collaboration; and in general terms some activities that teachers and librarians worked on together in collaborating. The collaborative logs and case studies provide more information about what happened in collaborative activities.

Librarians and teachers in Library Power schools were asked to document five cases of collaboration during the 1995–96 school year and during the 1996–97 school year by completing a collaboration log on the activity. Both the librarian and those teachers involved in the activity were instructed to report the goals and purposes for the activity, the content area, the grade level(s), the time spent in planning, the distribution of work doing the instructional activity, and an evaluation of how they felt the activity worked. For the 1995–96 school year, 307 schools submitted collaborative logs covering nearly 1,500 collaborative activities. The percentage of activities when examined by grade level ranged from 20% in grade 3 to 9% for both kindergarten and grade 8. The highest frequency of activities was in the social studies content area (37%), followed by science (29%), language arts (24%), and reading (12%).

Thirty-one schools (10%) were randomly selected from the 307 schools whose librarians had submitted collaborative logs. One collaboration log was randomly selected from each of these schools for analysis. From the information provided, an inference was made about the level of collaboration: aware (level 1), parallel (level 2), supportive (level 3), interactive (level 4), and shared (level 5). Forty percent of the 31 activities coded were judged to be level 2. At this level the librarian and teachers planned an instructional activity together, but the actual instructional activity was done with the librarian in the library and the teacher in the classroom. One example of an activity judged as a level 2 (parallel activity) was described as follows:

> Library media specialist will assist eighth grade students as they select fairy tales in their student elements. Eighth grade teacher will teach elements of fairy tale and direct the writing of an original fairy tale.

Another 43% of the activities were judged to be below level 2. Two examples follow:

> [Teachers] discussed the library's holdings and decided which ones would be helpful. Scheduled research periods to ensure that each child came to the library.

> Met with teacher to plan curriculum objectives and to organize culminating activity. Teacher worked with students on research skills and techniques for giving effective oral presentation. Librarian worked with students to access relevant information. Culminating activity was a women's history festival where students gave oral reports.

None of the activities was rated at level 5 (librarian and teachers sharing fully the responsibility for their own learning and the learning by students) or level 4 (interactive). Less than 20% of the reported activities demonstrated that the teachers and librarian had coordinated a division of labor and responsibilities (level 3). One example of a level 3 was a grades 1–2 science activity on polar regions:

Teacher and library media specialist will instruct students in the use of maps and atlas as they locate the polar regions. Teacher and library media specialist will prepare Book Bags containing fiction and nonfiction books and a puppet for students to use for research and enjoyment at home.

Teacher and librarian media specialist will read and discuss fiction and nonfiction books, show videos, guide the use of CD-ROMs, and assist students in finding answers to questions. The library media specialist will teach students to gather, organize, and record information.

The collaborative logs provide only some indication of the form of collaborative practices within the Library Power schools. The range of activities reported indicates that teachers and library media specialists were working together to provide instruction for their students. The dominant form of this work appeared to be cooperative planning, with a division of labor in performing the activities (level 2). There were some examples of more coordinated, interactive, or shared instructional activities indicating a more sophisticated level of collaboration. These examples occurred in about one out of every five activities.

Understanding the full range of collaboration in Library Power schools and the full depth to which library media specialists and teachers engaged in collaborative practices goes beyond the study conducted. Even with the large amount of information collected, sometimes the data from different evaluation instruments on the same school were not confirming. These instances of disagreement indicate a need for more refined data collection to fully understand what took place.

For example, consider these data from one case study school. Whereas the principal's and teachers' responses to the surveys would imply a high level of collaboration between teachers and the librarian, the case study researcher reported that collaboration when done was usually the librarian working with individual teachers where each engaged in coordinated activities. On a questionnaire, the principal wrote that there was a great deal of collaboration between the librarian and classroom teachers. The librarian who indicated collaborating with 88% of the teachers in the 1996–97 school year confirmed this. The collaborative logs indicated that the librarian and teachers had worked to produce integrated units and units in science. Units were identified for a range of grade levels and teachers.

Two grade 5 integrated units were "How to Spend a Million Dollars" (a mathematics and social science unit) and "Earth at Risk" (a science and social studies unit). One grades 1–2 science unit was "Night Animals." Two grades 2–3 science units were "Frogs and Toads" and "Ocean Animals." It was difficult to determine exactly how teachers and the librarian collaborated on these units, but the responsibilities appeared to have involved the librarian more than the teacher. On four of the units, the teachers' roles included "background knowledge" (Frogs and Toads); "prior knowledge and partner in research" (Earth at Risk); "prior knowledge and coach on written report" (Ocean Animals); and "background knowledge, team with research, and help shape product" (How to Spend a Million Dollars). The librarian's role was more extensive and included doing the "resource tour, small groups beginning to end, and Venn diagrams" (Frogs and Toads); "mini lessons, resource tour, and partner in research" (Earth at Risk); "resource tour, browsing, mini lessons, index, coach in note taking, product making and presentation" (Ocean Animals); and "resources (tours), research, internet ML, resource ML" (How to Spend a Million Dollars). On the fifth activity, "Night Animals," the teacher's role was stated as "send small group," whereas the librarian's role was listed as "research with small groups, KWLW/illustrates wall story, present in Bubble (a tall inflated plastic tent)." All of these activities appeared to be mainly conducted in the library media center.

The case study on this school indicated that the "principal's leadership clearly influenced teachers to collaborate with the librarian." Not all of the teachers had participated in collaborating with the librarian. A few were identified as "resisters." Even though the librarian moved into a new role as an instructional leader, only about one-third of the teachers had accepted her in this role. There was some evidence of change in the level of collaboration over two years. The study attributes the curriculum resource teacher at a school in 1995 as reporting, "most teachers viewed the librarian as a 'resource for instruction'—to help teachers and students find and use library materials—but not as a curriculum leader who could formulate unit objectives, plan content, select teaching materials, design assessments, etc." In 1997, the same resource teacher wrote more positively about the librarian's role in collaboration: "The curriculum resource teacher described her as a 'strong leader' and praised her for 'becoming more flexible and changing her approach' to teaching the research process by creating new materials and using new methods to reach students and teachers."

Units identified as resulting from collaboration between teachers and the librarian usually began with a conference between the teacher and the librarian. It appears that most of these conferences involved one teacher meeting with the librarian rather than the librarian meeting with a group of teachers. Individual meetings can over-extend the time of the librarian. One grades 2–3 teacher met with the librarian to discuss strategies for a unit. A grades 4–5 teacher met with the librarian to plan students' science fair projects. Another grades 2–3 teacher had a conference with the librarian to plan the unit on ocean animals. As a result the librarian was identified as doing the research part. Nearly all of these units, as reported in the case study and in the collaborative log, incorporated some research where students were required to find information on a topic. Many of the units required the students to produce a product and sometimes to make a presentation to others. Collaboration did not appear to involve team teaching, but rather coordinated activities between the teacher and librarian. The librarian's role, it appears, was primarily assisting students in locating research materials and in doing research, with some coordination with classroom instruction.

The case study researcher confirmed that at least one unit, "Night Animals," was done in the library with some time each day of the week spent there. This unit involved the grades 1–2 students in higher order thinking because they manipulated the information they collected and made generalizations or gave explanations about their animals. The librarian reported that she spent about three hours a week collaborating with teachers. One product attributed to the librarian's collaboration with teachers was using the "sentence strip" method to help students with the research process. Using this method, students could manipulate their color-coded written facts and place them in categories.

The evidence from multiple sources from this school supports the conclusion that Library Power contributed to the advancement of some form of collaboration. More teachers collaborated with the librarian as Library Power continued. The principal provided leadership and accountability for teachers to engage in collaboration. What was presented in logs and the case study as collaboration was the teaching of curriculum units, some of which were integrated units. A major role of the librarian was assisting students in doing research. Teachers and the librarian did not appear to engage in team teaching as much as they did in coordinated activities. When instructional activities were described in the case study, generally either the teacher *or* librarian was described working with the students, rather than both working together. Many of the activities did take place in the library.

This one example illustrates the complexity in revealing the full story of collaboration within schools. What is apparent was the engagement between the librarian and teachers to provide students with instructional activities. To begin differentiating among different levels of collaboration would require a more in-depth analysis.

Conclusion

An important outcome of Library Power has been the increase in collaborative activities within schools. The data support the conclusion that Library Power has contributed to library media specialists and teachers working more closely together to plan and design instructional units, develop the library collection, and deliver instruction.

The collaboration logs indicate that the dominant forms of collaboration were parallel activities (level 2) or coordinated activities (level 3). From evidence presented in the collaboration logs, few of the collaborative activities reached an interactive (4) or shared (5) level. Some of those that did are discussed in Chapter 6. For most of the reported activities in the logs, the librarian had the responsibility to provide resources for the activity, whereas the teacher was responsible for giving students the background knowledge they would need to engage in the activity, such as working on a weather unit or studying the life cycle of butterflies.

Increasing collaboration within schools is an important element of the current school reforms. Collaboration is a means for expanding the resources within a school and for existing resources to be used more efficiently and effectively. Library Power has helped schools to move in that direction.

References

Fullan, M. G., & Steigelbauer, S. (1991). *The new meaning of educational change.* New York: Teachers College Press.

Hargreaves, A. (1989). *Curriculum and assessment reform.* Milton Keynes, United Kingdom: Open University Press.

Little, J. W. (1990). The "mentor" phenomenon and the social organization of teaching. In C. Cazden (Ed.), *Review of Research in Education* (Vol. 16, pp. 297–351). Washington: American Education Research Association.

Loucks-Horsley, S., Hewson, P. W., Love, N., & Stiles, K. E. (1998) *Designing professional development for teachers of science and mathematics.* Thousand Oaks, CA: Corwin Press, Inc.

Nelson, B. S. (1994). Mathematics and community. In N. L. Webb, & T. A. Romberg (Eds.), *Reforming mathematics education in America's Cities: The urban mathematics collaborative project* (pp. 8–23). New York: Teachers College Press.

Popekewitz, Thomas S., Tabachnik, B., & Wehlage, Gary (1982). *The myth of educational reform: A study of school responses to a program of change.* Madison, WI: University of Wisconsin Press.

Raths, J. (1993). Organization and support systems associated with science and mathematics education. In R. Stake, J. Raths, M. St. John, D. Trumbull, M. Foster, S. Sullivan, & D. Jenness (Eds.), *Teacher preparation archives: Case studies of NSF-funded middle school science and mathematics teacher preparation projects.* Urbana, IL: Center for Instructional Research and Curriculum Evaluation, University of Illinois.

Romberg, T. A., & Pitman, A. J. (1990). Curricular materials and pedagogical reform: Teachers' use of time in teaching mathematics. In M. Ben-Peretz, & R. Bromme (Eds.), *The nature of time in schools* (pp. 189–226). New York: Teachers College Press.

Simon, M. A. (1997). Developing new models of mathematics teaching: An imperative for research on mathematics teacher development. In E. Fennema & B. S. Nelson (Eds.), *Teachers in transition* (pp. 55–86). Mahwah, NJ: Lawrence Erlbaum Associates.

Stocks, J. & Schofeld, J. (1997). Educational reform and professional development. In E. Fennema & B. S. Nelson (Eds.), *Teachers in transition* (pp. 283–308). Mahwah, NJ: Lawrence Erlbaum Associates.

Webb, N. L., Heck, D. J., & Tate, W. F. (1997). The Urban Mathematics Collaborative Project: A study of teacher, community, and reform. In S. A. Raizen & E. D. Britton (Eds.), *Bold ventures: Vol. 3. Case studies of U.S. innovations in mathematics education* (pp. 245–360). Dordrecht, The Netherlands: Kluwer Academic.

Webb, N. L., & Romberg, T. A. (Eds.). (1994). *Reforming mathematics education in America's cities: The urban mathematics collaborative project.* New York: Teachers College Press.

5 CURRICULUM

Norman Lott Webb

Few terms as critical to schooling as curriculum are given so many different meanings. Learning and instruction, both essential to schooling, pale in comparison to the variety of imposed interpretations of this all-encompassing word. Curriculum can mean the scope and sequence of topics covered in a course; the goals and objectives that guide learning; the materials used with students; the classroom activities students do; what students learn; or all of these or something entirely different. Pinpointing this elusive construct is even more difficult when trying to establish a relationship between it and an effort toward school reform.

The National Library Power Initiative sought to improve the teaching and learning process in schools by using the school library media program as a catalyst for school reform. The Library Power program sought to have the school library media program become more central to instruction in schools. Library Power was not a curriculum program, and it did not directly seek to have an impact on curricula. Initially the evaluation of Library Power devoted little attention to seeking information on curricula in schools. The importance of the relationship between Library Power and curriculum grew increasingly clear only as the program matured and a greater understanding emerged from its evaluation. The evaluation gathered more information on curriculum in the last round of case studies conducted during the 1997–98 school year than it did in surveys and case studies conducted prior to that time. Thus, for understanding how Library Power had an impact on curricula, the greatest sources of information are the case studies, with some general information distilled from the quantitative survey information.

Three of the National Library Power Program's goals have curriculum implications:

1. To create model library programs that are an integral part of the education process.

2. To demonstrate the significant contributions that library programs can make to school reform and restructuring efforts.

3. To encourage collaboration among teachers, administrators, and librarians that results in significant improvement in the teaching and learning process.

Because curriculum is so embedded in schooling, it is impossible to even consider affecting the education process, reforming and restructuring schools, or improving teaching and learning without touching curriculum— the goals and outcomes for students' learning—in some way.

This chapter discusses the interaction of Library Power with school curricula and how Library Power contributed to curriculum changes. Two primary data sources from the National Evaluation of Library Power provide the bulk of evidence. Library Power's relation to curriculum issues was revealed through the rich, descriptive information included in the case studies. Case study researchers gathered and interpreted information on curriculum and its connections with Library Power directly and through investigating collaboration and collection development. All 27 of the case studies from each of eight selected sites were searched for examples of how Library Power interacted with the curriculum. The examples that were found and are reported here demonstrate that at least in one or more schools Library Power had some influence on curriculum.

A second source of data was the responses of teachers, library media specialists, and principals to surveys administered in 1995–96 and 1996–97. The percentage of responses to these surveys was sufficiently large to draw conclusions about all of the schools and districts participating in

Library Power. A set of questions on these instruments pertained to curriculum issues. Library media specialists were asked the following:

- How well did the library media center's resources support the instructional program in a range of content areas?

- What were changes to the library and information skills program?

- Did teachers generally feel responsible for carrying out the goals of the school?

- Who generally was involved in collaboratively writing a unit's goals and objectives?

- How likely was it for collaborative planning on instructional units to continue?

Teachers were asked many of the same questions. In addition they were asked the following:

- How much influence did teachers have on designing the curriculum to be taught?

- How often did they collaborate with other teachers on planning and designing instruction?

- Had Library Power increased this collaboration?

- What were the most important contributions of Library Power to their teaching?

Principals were asked many of the same questions as those listed above. In addition, they were asked if collaborative planning among teachers and librarians on instructional units was attributable to Library Power.

The analysis of the quantitative and qualitative data shows that Library Power had an impact on school and district curricula in four important ways. First, Library Power enhanced school staff's awareness of curriculum. Professional development, collaborative planning, and collection improvement all contributed to library media specialists', teachers', and principals' attending more to curriculum. Second, schools developed a greater capacity for engaging in curriculum development and change. Collection mapping and curriculum mapping instituted in schools because of Library Power increased staff's knowledge of both the existing curriculum and the relationship among topics. Added resources and requirements of the program gave schools the impetus to think more about their curriculum. The library media specialists gained a greater perspective on the curriculum across grade levels through collaborative planning with teachers from the different grades. In some schools, the library media specialist's new perspective helped reduce redundancy in the curriculum. Third, schools and districts introduced new goals and content into the curriculum because of their participation in Library Power. The new goals and content arose from raised expectations for learning, more emphasis on research skills, and increased emphasis on understanding the relationship among concepts through thematic units. Fourth, existing curriculum topics were covered in greater depth and breadth. Schools gave greater attention to promoting reading. Flexible scheduling helped provide conditions more conducive to engaging students in research and inquiry. Additional topics were included and a higher quality of units was implemented through collaborative planning among library media specialists and teachers.

Curriculum Forms

Any discussion of curriculum requires clarification of the boundaries to be imposed on its use. Most often, curriculum refers to the goals and objectives for student learning. Goals and objectives can be stated very generally, as in district or state standards for learning, or very precisely, as in expectations for what students are to learn from one lesson. Goals and objectives for students are not limited to cognitive learning; they can include attitudes, dispositions, habits of mind, and democratic ideals. Commonly stated goals, such as "Students will become lifelong learners and responsible citizens," encompass all of these. For students to become effective library users, researchers, and information processors, aspects of these important qualities are also required.

The qualities of a curriculum can be implied or construed by specific decisions and other factors (Robitaille, et al., 1993; McKnight, et al., 1987; Goodlad, et al., 1979). The functions a curriculum serves help clarify its nature. Content goals and objectives stated in frameworks, guidelines, policies, regulations, and textbooks are the *intended* curriculum. These are official statements about what students are to learn and be able to do. The materials and instruction teachers make available to students constitute the *implemented* curriculum. Teachers are important decision makers and providers of instruction to students. Even with a highly structured and mandated official curriculum, teachers decide daily what content to include or exclude and what points to emphasize or de-emphasize. These decisions are important determinants of what students learn and what they have the opportunity to learn and experience.

The *assessed* curriculum, or students' content knowledge that is measured, places additional boundaries on what students are to know and do and on what they actually learn. Rarely are students ever fully assessed on the intended curriculum or even the implemented curriculum. Nearly all assessments require sampling from a domain of knowledge. Sometimes widely used national assessments will measure only those goals and objectives common among a large number of schools and districts, increasing the likelihood that the assessments will not be fully aligned with the curriculum of any one school or district. High stakes assessments, such as those used to censure schools or to promote students to the next grade, can have a strong influence on what instruction teachers give to students and what is officially recorded as what students know. Because of these and other forces, the assessed curriculum can become the surrogate for the intended or implemented curriculum.

All three of these forms of the curriculum represent, to some degree, what is desired for students to learn. A fourth version, the *attained* curriculum, is the outcomes from schooling. The attained curriculum is the knowledge, habits, and attitudes students actually gain from schooling. These attainments will be influenced by the intended, implemented, and assessed curriculum, but will vary from student to student and could include outcomes that exceed any expectations of the other curriculum forms.

Library Power Goals Related to Curriculum

In theory, the goals and action plan of Library Power are strongly related to influencing curriculum. Curriculum is central to teaching and learning. For Library Power to make library programs more integral to the education process, contribute significantly to school reform and restructuring, and improve teaching and learning, Library Power has to have an influence on and be influenced by curriculum. The evaluation demonstrated that at both the school and district levels, changes attributed to Library Power initiatives did affect the curriculum. This chapter describes those influences in some detail and the relationship between Library Power and curriculum. It covers primarily the goals and objectives for learning—that is, the intended curriculum. Also, some discussion is devoted to the implemented curriculum. Because of the close relationship among the implemented curriculum, instruction, and learning opportunities, chapters on those areas will also provide information on curriculum.

A Library Power program within a district could affect goals and objectives for learning (the intended curriculum) in a number of ways. Introducing or increasing collaborative planning among the library media specialist and teachers at a school provides an opportunity to formulate new goals and instructional objectives and to interpret differently or impose a new sequence on existing goals and objectives. This could lead to new lessons added to the existing course of study. Teachers working with the library media specialist to strengthen the library collection by weeding outdated books and acquiring new books to build weak areas have the potential to force the instructional staff to consider more carefully their instructional goals and objectives as they consider existing and needed resources. Aligning the collection with the curriculum, or checking on the alignment, can cause the instructional staff to reflect on both. This can result in changes in what teachers expect their students to be able to learn and in what books and other materials teachers will use to support this learning. Teachers and students having greater access to the media center, through flexible scheduling or structural changes from refurbishing the physical area, can lead to teachers and others rethinking the cognitive level of instructional goals or setting goals previously thought unattainable. Greater access to the media center as a place to do research and with more trade books can lead to incorporating more authentic goals into the curriculum. Increasing the instructional resources available to students can improve the opportunity they have to apply their knowledge by doing extended projects or more in-depth explorations to answer questions.

A Library Power program can influence the implemented curriculum by helping school and district staff plan and manage instruction. Packaging and storing materials by instructional units in the media center can affect what content teachers present by making it easier for them to manage and organize the necessary materials for an instructional unit. The library media specialist becomes another hand to more effectively prepare for instruction. Introducing a Library Power Advisory Committee in a school where there has not been any school-based planning group can lead to empowering the school's instructional staff to engage in more long-range planning and greater reflection on what the school curriculum should be and how it can be better managed. Providing teachers, administrators, and library media specialists with professional development and other experiences can serve to broaden the instructional staff's perspective about the curriculum. This can result in the staff's refining their skills for defining goals and objectives and implementing instructional units. In these and other ways, Library Power, at least in theory, has the potential to influence the curriculum.

Library Power and Curriculum in Context

Library Power, as an initiative to improve the teaching and learning process in schools, joins many other programs and reform efforts. Some of the Library Power sites are in states with strong reform efforts, such as Kentucky and Louisiana. Some reforms are standards-based, whereas others are assessment-based. Some districts have adopted approaches to school reform such as Comer or Paideia. Gary Wehlage discusses some of these related issues in more detail in Chapter 7.

In addition to these other initiatives, decisions about the curriculum are influenced by how education systems are organized and structured. Some states and districts have a highly centralized system, with system-mandated tests, system-wide textbook adoptions, and rigid regulations imposed on the curriculum. Other states and districts are more locally controlled. In these systems, curriculum decisions are made locally at the district, school, or even classroom levels. School-based management may be in place at one site, whereas at another site main curriculum decisions are made by the district.

Library Power sites varied greatly in the degree to which teachers had the authority to make curriculum decisions. In 1997, one-fifth of 1,166 teachers who responded to a survey said they had a great deal of influence on designing the curriculum; about the same proportion of teachers reported they had little influence on that area. Overall, 45% of the teachers reported they had a significant influence on designing the curriculum (those who marked a 4 or 5 on a 5-point scale, where 5 represented "A great deal"). Similar proportions of the 452 principals who responded to a 1997 survey confirmed this finding. A total of 56% of these principals reported that teachers had a strong influence on the curriculum (a 4 or 5 on a 5-point scale). These figures represent an upper bound on what significant effects Library Power can have on the curriculum. Only about half of the teachers had a high influence on designing their curriculum. Thus, whatever initiatives are introduced through Library Power to develop new relationships between library media specialists and teachers, it is reasonable to expect that only about half of the schools in the Library Power program would have the potential for major effects.

Another contributing factor to variations in the potential impact of Library Power on curriculum was that library media specialists differed greatly in background and experience. Some had strong teaching backgrounds, having taught a number of years before becoming library media specialists. Some were nearing retirement whereas others were new to education. Some schools had had a library media center and a specialist for a number of years, while other schools had had a full-time library media specialist and a media center for only a short period of time. All of these factors govern to some degree what influence any Library Power initiative could have on the intended and implemented curricula at any one site. These and other contextual factors are important in drawing meaning from the evidence gathered by the evaluation about the relationship between Library Power and curriculum.

Enhanced Awareness of the Existing Curriculum

Library Power contributed to teachers' and library media specialists' awareness of the intended and implemented curriculum in their schools. Reflective practices advanced by Library Power, including collaborative planning, collection mapping, and curriculum mapping, forced school staffs to analyze the curriculum, uncover holes, reveal outdated materials, and incorporate instructional activities requiring students to engage in higher cognitive activities. In Atlanta, for example, collaborative planning forced teams at schools to take a closer look at curriculum objectives. Improvements in library collections made the collections more valuable resources to support both teachers' and students' activities. Professional development experiences sponsored by Library Power included helping teachers and library media specialists increase their expectations of what students could do.

A high percentage of the teachers in Library Power schools in 1997 reported that over the time Library Power had been implemented, the adequacy of the library collection had improved to better support teachers' (85%) and students' (87%) needs (see Table 5-1). Of those who reported an improvement, 82% reported that the collection was more than adequate for their needs and 85% reported the collection was more than adequate for their students' needs (see Table 5-2). Not only had teachers in Library Power schools observed improvement in the collection, they were also highly satisfied with what the collection provided them and their students.

TABLE 5-1
Change in the Adequacy of the Collection over
the Duration of Library Power
(Teacher Survey, 1997)

	Better		Worse		Total Number Responding
Type of Support	%	n	%	n	
Supports teachers' needs	85	904	2	18	1,066
Supports students' needs	87	933	2	22	1,067

TABLE 5-2
Degree to Which the Library Collection Supported Needs
of Teachers and Students, As Reported by Teachers Who
Indicated a Positive Change in the Adequacy of the
Collection over the Duration of Library Power
(Teacher Survey, 1997)

Type of Support	Very Well 5	4	3	2	Not Well 1	Total Number Responding
Supports teachers' needs	48	34	16	1	1	904
Supports students' needs	51	34	13	1	0.2	933

Related to increased satisfaction with the collection is the 1997 finding that a majority of the teachers (60%) in Library Power schools were using the library collection more than before Library Power to support their instruction (see Table 5-3). In addition, 69% of the teachers reported they had a role in selecting materials for the collection and 46% of the teachers reported they had a role in helping to assess the quality of the collection (see Table 5-4). These results support the conclusion that the library collections in Library Power schools became more connected and important to the implemented curriculum. These findings also suggest that teachers had more resources at their disposal to incorporate into their instruction, increasing the likelihood that students could go into more depth and breadth in topics studied.

TABLE 5-3
Change in Teachers' Use of the Library Collection to Support Their Instruction over the Duration of Library Power
(Teacher Survey, 1997)

Much More than Before				Much Less than Before	Total Number Responding
5	4	3	2	1	
29	31	30	5	5	1,103

TABLE 5-4
Teachers Who Reported They Had a Role in Their School Library's Collection
(Teacher Survey, 1997)

Teachers' Role	% Yes	Total Number Responding
In selecting materials	69	1,165
In helping to assess the quality	46	1,155

Comments from principals and data from the case studies help to clarify the nature of the changes that occurred as a result of Library Power and how these have contributed to increasing the depth and breadth of the existing curriculum. When asked what were the major contributions of Library Power, some principals' responses reveal a positive relationship with the curriculum:

Opened and extended materials available in the library. More persons to extend and expand plans for units.

The librarian has been able to work across grade levels with the collaborative process. Teachers are eager to work together and to extend the learning process. Our students are challenged more with the collaborative work of the teachers.

Because of increased resources in the library, teachers use the library with their students.

The librarian has been included in the development and carrying out of the new curriculum process. She expands and teaches research skills.

Library Power has increased the dialogue in our school about curriculum and the types of assignments students should be given.

Library Power was the impetus for teacher/media specialist collaboration. Subsequently instructional units are becoming more divergent in material, technology, projects, rubrics, etc.

Having both teacher and librarian working together has definitely improved students' thinking skills since instruction now brings together many methods of learning and teaching.

Library Power led to improvements in some schools simply through improving the connection between the library and the curriculum. A librarian in one Kentucky school had received professional development through Library Power at the same time she was weeding the school's library collection. She reported that the training was invaluable because collection mapping and developing a collection based on the curriculum were new ideas to her. Collection mapping revealed for one Atlanta school that its social studies collection was inadequate. This resulted in the librarian targeting the need to increase the library's collection in historical fiction and biography.

Collection maps resulting from Library Power were not always of high quality, but even with some variance in quality, the process of trying to align the collection with the curriculum helped to reveal weak areas. At one Chattanooga school, the curriculum maps were organized largely by topics even though the school emphasized a theme- and concept-based curriculum. The maps did not reflect integrating themes or central questions, but represented a traditional scope and sequence chart. Even with the topical structures, the curriculum maps played a central role in staff discussions of future work and generated a focus for teachers' collaborative planning with the librarian during the school year. The curriculum maps revealed a "bloated" curriculum in social studies that tried to cover too much and was fragmented and disconnected. The curriculum map gave at least one teacher at this school a better awareness of the curriculum demands with respect to the school's shifting to standards-based assessments. She observed, "Something's got to give." In this case, Library Power helped to accelerate and sharpen the school's focus on the curriculum and expectations of students. A similar situation was reported in Kentucky. A librarian at one school credited Library Power with influencing her to zero-in on specific content, rather than to supply the needs of all library users, by having her align the collection and the curriculum.

Library Power helped improve the intended curriculum's quality and the implemented curriculum's efficiency. In the 1996 survey, one principal claimed that collaborative planning resulted in more comprehensive units being taught. In other schools, through engaging the librarian in curriculum planning, repetition in the curriculum across grade levels was reduced. The library media specialist became the one person who had an overview of the curriculum at each grade level because of planning collaboratively with teams from all of the grade levels in the school. According to one principal, the librarian became the one staff member who had "the big picture" of the curriculum and who could report on what had been done in other grades. At a Chattanooga school, different from the one noted above, a librarian's overview of the curriculum was credited by one third-grade teacher for enabling the school to avoid unnecessary duplication in topics covered. The case study researcher observed that "a continuity and coherence to the curriculum across the entire school prevented duplicating activities and field trips done in other grades. Instead, the teachers and librarian worked to broaden the variety of experiences available to the students."

New Packaging of Existing Curriculum Materials and Addition of New Materials

By making materials more accessible to teachers and easier to use, Library Power had some impact on the implemented curriculum. This impact was a result of teachers' incorporating different or a greater variety of topics in their courses, rather than making significant changes in their expectations, objectives, or goals for student learning (intended curriculum). Working together, the library media specialist and teachers in some schools developed "trunk units." All materials for one instructional unit (for example, a unit on spiders) were put in one box or tub, stored in the library, and made available for teachers to check out. These trunk units were developed frequently through the collaboration of teachers with the library media specialist. A principal of one Kentucky school commented, "Library Power has been the catalyst for developing the trunk curricula." In Chattanooga, a librarian reported, "We have been able to create fabulous curriculum tubs for every area of our curriculum, from biomes in kindergarten to ancient civilizations in sixth." The extra funding provided by Library Power helped to purchase needed materials and, in some schools, to remodel the space in the media center to store the units. Trunk units appeared to be prepared most frequently in the science subject area because individual science units commonly require a large number of manipulatives. Teachers were more apt to teach a unit on a topic such as spiders or penguins because everything that was needed was easily accessible in one container.

Librarians, through collaborative planning, became more knowledgeable regarding implemented curriculum used by teachers in their classrooms. Because of this increased communication with teachers, librarians were able to "target order" books for the library. Library collections became more responsive to the implemented curriculum. In some schools, the collection was improved by enhancing the materials available for specific instructional units. A librarian reported, "I can't wait until our curriculum map is done to help me target my ordering. I have to spend the money now. I need more help." However, not all of the Library Power schools targeted specific curriculum areas to strengthen the collection. In Atlanta, the library media specialists and volunteers at one of the first schools to join the Library Power program continued to order books that children wanted rather than supplement the collection based on curriculum need.

New Instructional Goals and Objectives

New content and goals were added to schools' curricula because of Library Power. The two greatest influences on introducing new content and goals into a school's curriculum were 1) professional development experiences sponsored by or funded at least in part by the Library Power program and 2) collaborative planning among teachers and the media specialists. The introduction of new content and goals was primarily done by individual teachers rather than more formally at the school or district levels.

Library Power was responsible for increased collaboration between librarians and teachers in schools. In 1997, 87% of the principals indicated that at least part of the faculty collaborated with a librarian in planning on instructional units and in developing the library collection. A majority of the principals (52%) attributed these practices mostly to Library Power, and over 90% attributed these practices at least in part to Library Power (see Table 5-5). More than half of the teachers in 1997 (51%) reported that they had collaborated with a librarian in planning and designing instruction (Table 5-6). On the average, librarians reported they had collaborated with about half of the teachers in their schools, an increase from about 20% prior to Library Power.

TABLE 5-5
Principals' Attribution for the Adoption of a Practice
(Principal Survey, 1997)

Collaboration Between Teachers and Librarians	Mostly Library Power %	Mostly School Reforms %	A Mix %	Total Number Responding
Planning on instructional units	59	5	35	432
Developing the library's collection	52	6	39	421

TABLE 5-6
Frequency of Teachers Collaborating with a
Librarian for the Planning and Designing of Instruction
(Teacher Survey, 1997)

| Very Often | | | Not at All | |
4 %	3 %	2 %	1 %	Total Number Responding
17	34	31	18	1,152

Schools' incorporating more storytelling into the existing curriculum is one example of how Library Power influenced the curriculum. Librarians, teachers, and principals, through professional development provided by Library Power, changed their expectations about what students could learn and the intended curriculum. One librarian in a Kentucky school, after attending a Library Power in-service, decided to introduce storytelling into the curriculum. She claimed that students who were struggling to write stories were better able to write when they were able to tell their own stories. In this way, storytelling became an intermediate goal for furthering students' writing skills. A principal of a Louisiana school reported a similar scenario. This principal used Library Power funds to attend a national meeting, where she heard a presentation on storytelling. Based on this experience, she decided to incorporate a storytelling experience into a school year and invited the storyteller she heard to visit her school and work with students.

Library Power changed some teachers' expectations about what research younger students could do. At one school in Baton Rouge, the librarian worked with a beginning first-grade teacher to demonstrate how her students could do "picture" research. Initially, this teacher did not believe that her young students could respond to questions by seeking information and forming explanations. The librarian gave her a few jungle pictures and helped her formulate questions to use with her students. This positive experience for this teacher increased her expectations about first graders' abilities. This was not an isolated event and was replicated at other sites. A New Haven teacher reported on the teacher questionnaire that Library Power had raised her expectations and now she understood that first graders could do research. However, not all teachers associated with Library Power were convinced that younger students were ready for research. On the questionnaire, when asked to identify the most important contributions of Library Power, a kindergarten teacher from Nashville wrote, "I haven't found it to be a help at all—rather a problem because of lack of time to meet with the librarian. Kindergarten should not be involved in this because of the lack of library skills relevant to the curriculum."

Both teachers and librarians received training through Library Power on teaching research skills. Even if the inclusion of research skills in the curriculum was not new, the experiences teachers and media specialists had in incorporating research skills into the curriculum did result in schools placing a greater emphasis on students doing research. One principal of a Baton Rouge elementary school, whose child attended the school, credited Library Power for her son's successful completion of a very comprehensive research project. Her son was in fifth grade at her school the year that the school became a part of the Library Power program. She recalled, the night before the project was due, "So . . . he brought it out. I started to look at it. I mean just the cover and everything. Wow, a lot of things he had taken from the computer and cross-referenced it in front and all that. He said you had to show the whole thing. He had to show the note cards, so there were his note cards. He brought them out. The note cards were wonderful. 'When did you do this?' And then there was a timeline in it when he did all this with the librarian." Her son's English teacher in middle school was very impressed with his knowledge of research skills and his independence in completing work for the class. His mother and former principal attributed his success, at least in part, to Library Power.

Library Power's impact varied somewhat by content area. Teachers found Library Power's efforts to be more relevant in some content areas than others. One teacher did not think Library Power was relevant to mathematics. The view of this teacher was shared by about one-third of the 484 library media specialists who responded to the 1997 building-level survey. They reported that their library's resources poorly supported the currentness of the instructional program in mathematics. Over one-third, 37%, of the library media specialists reported that resources were poor in quantity in mathematics. Careers and foreign languages were the two other content areas identified as poor in currentness and quantity by the highest percentage of library media specialists (even slightly higher than the percentages for mathematics). These results were not uniform across the sites.

In Baton Rouge, the media center's resources were reported by the highest percentage of the library media specialists (over 90% on current-ness and over 85% on quantity) to adequately support the instructional program in reference, science/technology, and fiction. The library media specialists in 1997 rated the foreign language collection highest in currentness and quantity. The district had just received a large grant from the U.S. Department of Education to support foreign language education. The first expenditures of this grant went to libraries, due in part to the increased knowledge people had gained about the expanded uses of the library achieved through Library Power.

Librarians and teachers were asked to identify the content area of the five activities they recorded on the collaboration logs (see Chapter 4). The distribution of these topics provides one indicator of how Library Power interacted with the different content areas (see Table 5-7). Social studies (37%) and science (29%) were the two most frequently recorded content areas, followed by language arts (24%) and reading (12%). Interdisciplinary was only recorded for 9% of the activities, although 35% of the other activities involved more than one content area. The highest percent of collaborative activities were for grade 3 (20%), followed by grade 2 (19%), grade 4 (17%), grade 5 (16%), and grade 1 (13%).

TABLE 5-7
Topics Identified in Collaboratively Planned Activities in 1996 (Collaboration Logs, 1996)

Topics*	Percent of 1,482 Activities Recorded
Social Studies	37%
Science	29%
Language Arts	24%
Reading	12%
Interdisciplinary**	9%
Mathematics	5%
Literature	3%
English	2%

*A collaboration activity could have been coded as more than one topic, so the sum of the percentages will be more than 100%.

**Even though only 9% of the activities were explicitly identified as interdisciplinary, 44% of the activities were identified as either interdisciplinary or including more than one topic.

At a number of the sites, teachers and librarians received professional development on thematic or interdisciplinary units through Library Power. Teachers attributed to Library Power the incorporation of thematic units into the curriculum; however, not all of the credit can be given solely to the library initiative because thematic units are one of the characteristics of a number of current school reforms. What the Library Power programs in districts were able to accomplish was to facilitate the training of teachers and media specialists in how to prepare thematic units and implement them with students. Summer institutes and academic training sessions sponsored by the Library Power programs focused on training teachers how to write thematic units. In Baton Rouge, a centerpiece of the unit was a web showing the connections among themes for the unit, the learning objectives for seven content areas (language arts, mathematics, music, physical education, arts, social studies, and science), and information processing skills. The overall impact of Library Power on introducing thematic units is tempered to some degree. Only about 2% of the unprompted teachers identified thematic units as among the initiative's two most important contributions.

Thematic units were a concrete way that librarians and teachers could engage in collaborative planning, team instruction, and curriculum decision making. At least initially instigated by the librarians, development of these units forced the consideration of how the library space would be incorporated. This meant that attention was given to where learning centers were to be set up, how children were to move about the space along with the routine flow of students, what resources needed to be available, and how hands-on materials were to be packaged.

The incorporation of thematic units increased the likelihood that a teacher's intended curriculum would include objectives for students to understand the connections between different content areas within one theme. A Lincoln, Nebraska, teacher reported on the 1997 teacher questionnaire, "Library Power created an environment in which students' ideas were used frequently in planning instructional activities and thematic units drive more of the curriculum." On the questionnaire they completed in 1997, school principals at at least three sites credited Library Power for the development of thematic units and interdisciplinary instruction. Some noted that these units had resulted in new and better learning by students.

Library Power, with perhaps a few exceptions, tended to influence the interaction between teachers and the library media specialist to different degrees for teachers at different schools. In some cases, what teachers reported as a significant contribution of Library Power identified more the role of the library media specialist as a provider of resources, rather than being central to the instructional program. These teachers reported that they used the library media specialist to gather resources for lessons; they made no mention of collaborative planning. At at least one site Library Power did not address student outcomes. One case study researcher wrote, "Library Power had been global in addressing how we go about implementing change and sustaining change. It has not been definitive on how we measure student outcomes."

Improved School Capacity for Curriculum Development

Teachers in Library Power schools indicated that Library Power had facilitated the development of their own curriculum because of the additional resources in libraries and specific professional development experiences. In Kentucky, one of the goals for statewide school reform was for teachers to design their own curriculum. Motivated by the reform efforts and the support from Library Power, teachers in at least one of the Kentucky Library Power schools increased their engagement in curriculum development. Several conditions associated with Library Power helped this process, including a current and responsive collection, flexible scheduling, the principal arranging release time from duties to meet with others, and informative workshops on how to use the library in teaching. The case study researcher attributed these changes to the interaction between the state reform initiative and Library Power.

Other components of Library Power contributed to teachers' and library media specialists' becoming more understanding of curriculum issues. Improvements to the physical environment provided conditions that allowed staff to give more focus to the curriculum. Libraries became a physical environment and a context that served cooperative planning among teachers and gave students a place to digest information, evaluate ideas, and plan what to do next.

Library Power helped school staff see the potential for having the library become more integral to the instructional mission of schools. People took this knowledge with them if they transferred to other schools. A new principal at one Atlanta school, one without Library Power, had been a curriculum specialist at a Library Power school. She reported that her experience with Library Power had focused her attention on what was possible. She saw the librarian as a teacher rather than as a clerical person. Another Atlanta principal, through Library Power, understood how a strong librarian could influence the curriculum and refused to accept unqualified persons when hiring for the position. The opportunity to order books according to need throughout the year, rather than at the outset of a new year, gave teachers the support and freedom to do what Kentucky's Reform Act (KERA) wanted them to do: create curriculum. The librarian of one school in Kentucky reported that the "library became the textbook of the school."

Relationship Between Library Power and Curriculum

Library Power has had an impact on the intended curriculum of participating schools. This impact was not uniform, but varied from school to school and among sites. About half of the teachers (54% in 1996 and 46% in 1997) attributed to Library Power increased collaborative planning and designing of instruction with a librarian. Less than one-third of the teachers (32% in 1996 and 22% in 1997) attributed to Library Power increased collaborative planning and designing of instruction with other teachers. Collaborative planning was not the only way that Library Power could influence the curriculum, but it is a central component of its underlying principles and coincided with other reform theories. Collaboration was central to major links between Library Power and the curriculum that emerged from the data.

Conclusion

Library Power has contributed to changes in both the intended and implemented curricula in schools. It is impossible to determine the full impact of the reform initiative on curriculum from the data collected by this evaluation. However, there is enough information to infer that a number of components of Library Power, and the changes schools made when implementing Library Power, contributed to teachers' and library media specialists' rethinking learning goals for students and incorporating new activities in their instruction. Library Power increased collaboration between teachers and library media specialists in planning instructional units and in developing the library collection. More than half of the teachers in schools with Library Power engaged in these practices. Other changes advanced by Library Power, including physical changes to library space and flexible scheduling, also had an influence on both the implemented and intended curricula.

Teachers and library media specialists heightened their awareness of curriculum issues. They set more challenging learning goals and developed instructional activities requiring greater intellectual engagement by students. They introduced new topics and lessons for the first time. Schools and staff developed both institutional capacity and individual capacity to better align library collections with the curriculum and to use library media specialists more centrally in the instructional mission of the school. These and other changes affected a number of content areas, but most intensively social studies and science.

References

Fullan, M. G., & Steigelbauer, S. (1991). *The new meaning of education change.* New York: Teachers College Press.

Goodlad, J. (1979). The scope of the curriculum field. In J. Goodlad, et al. (Eds.), *Curriculum inquiry: The study of curriculum practice.* New York: McGraw-Hill.

McKnight, C., Crosswhite, F. J., Dossey, J. A., Kifer, E. A., Swafford, J. O., Travers, K. J., & Cooney, T. J. (1987). *The underachieving curriculum: Assessing U.S. school mathematics from an international perspective.* Champaign, Illinois: Stipes.

Nelson, B. S. (1994). Mathematics and community. In N. L. Webb & T. A. Romberg (Eds.), *Reforming mathematics education in America's cities: The urban mathematics collaborative project* (pp. 8–23). New York: Teachers College Press.

Popekewitz, Thomas S., Tabachnick, Robert, & Wehlage, Gary. (1982). *The myth of educational reform: A study of school responses to a program of change.* Madison, WI: University of Wisconsin Press.

Robitaille, D. F., McKnight, C., Schmidt, W. H., Britton, E., Raizen, S., & Nicol, C. (1993). *Curriculum frameworks for mathematics and science.* TIMSS Monograph, 1. Vancouver, Canada: Pacific Educational Press.

Romberg, T. A., & Pittman, A. J. (1990). Curricular materials and pedagogical reform: Teachers' use of time in teaching matematics. In M. Ben-Peretz & R. Bromme (Eds.), *The nature of time in schools* (pp. 189–226). New York: Teachers College Press, Columbia University.

Webb, N. L., & Romberg, T. A. (Eds.). (1994). *Reforming mathematics education in America's cities: The urban mathematics collaborative project.* New York: Teachers College Press, Columbia University.

6 INSTRUCTION

Gary Wehlage

This chapter describes teachers' instructional practices in Library Power schools. Examples from lessons, observations by field researchers, and testimony from teachers and administrators provide insights into the impact of Library Power on instruction. Our analysis goes beyond the question of whether Library Power promoted changes in instructional practices and explores the extent to which it helped to improve the quality of instruction. We investigate whether teachers who made use of Library Power did so in ways that produced higher-quality instruction for their students. The data tell us much about the relationship between Library Power and instruction; however, because no baseline data are available to describe instruction before the initiative, it is not possible to answer causal questions about the amount of change or the degree of improvement in instructional practices.

Making value judgments about instruction is inherently part of the task of our evaluation assignment. Certainly the DeWitt Wallace–Reader's Digest Fund intended that Library Power facilitate better instruction. While the official goals as stated by the Fund do not use the term "improved instruction" per se, they strongly imply it. The goals for the national initiative include 1) creating model library programs that are an integral part of the educational process; 2) strengthening the role of the librarian as a teacher and information specialist who assists teachers and students; and 3) encouraging collaboration among teachers, administrators, and librarians "that results in significant improvement in the teaching and learning process" (The Fund, 1997). Such language, when placed in the context of national school reform and restructuring efforts, implies changes to instructional strategies to make them more intellectually challenging and engaging for students.

Most schools envisioned better instruction because of Library Power, and many of the sites incorporated into their proposals and rationales specific language that called for improving instruction through Library Power. What such improvement would look like was articulated similarly in many proposals. For example, proposals discussed using Library Power to help children become problem solvers and critical thinkers; promoting active learning in contrast to traditional and outmoded methods of teaching that placed students in the role of passive receivers of information; taking instruction beyond the pages of the usual textbooks and basal readers and drawing on new sources of information; collaboration among teachers and librarians to produce instruction that was "resource based" and interdisciplinary; and providing open access to the library to make instruction learner-centered as opposed to teacher-centered. In general, the tone set by the proposals was one of using Library Power as a lever to help teachers change the way they delivered instruction. Clearly the purpose of such change was to produce not only different but higher-quality student outcomes. Having said all this, we also recognized that, in the very early stages of the initiative, Library Power was not conceived and presented to schools as a program to improve instruction.

An abundance of testimony and anecdotal evidence gathered by field researchers indicated that in fact instruction did change to some extent in almost all schools. Many teachers affirmed that they had redesigned at least some of their instruction in an effort to make use of Library Power resources. Collaboration in planning and carrying out some instruction occurred in every case study school. Frequently such collaboration resulted in units aimed at promoting some variation of what teachers called "resource-based" teaching. Observers described students visiting the library with the purpose of using its resources to inquire, do research, and answer questions. The following sections provide a number of examples of such practice and analyze the intellectual demands it placed on students. Our analysis addresses questions such as: What did resource-based teaching, inquiry, and research ask students to do? How intellectually challenging was such instruction?

Instruction and Intellectual Quality

The term *instruction* has a variety of meanings that overlap with notions of curriculum and student learning, two topics that are explored elsewhere in this book. Instruction is sometimes equated with teachers' verbal behavior in the classroom, but we are unable to report much about such behavior because little direct systematic observation of teaching was conducted as part of the evaluation. In this chapter, instruction is defined as the tasks teachers give to their students. Tasks are also called *assignments* or *learning activities* that direct students' efforts toward some purpose.

To the extent possible, we examined the purposes and objectives of teachers' instructional tasks, especially those that made use of library resources. Many of the instructional tasks that we describe and analyze here included some degree of collaboration between teachers and librarians. When educators talked about changes in instruction due to Library Power they often made reference to collaboration, a relatively new activity for many teachers and librarians. However, we do not focus on the collaborative relations that were part of the instructional process because this topic is covered in Chapter 4. Although instructional change can address who teaches as well as what and how students are taught, in this chapter the emphasis is on the what and how of instruction, especially the kind of academic performance asked of students.

To the extent allowed by the data, we characterize teachers' instructional tasks in terms of the intellectual quality demanded in students' academic work. The standards of intellectual quality used to describe and judge instruction are those developed by the Center on Organization and Restructuring of Schools (CORS) at the University of Wisconsin (Newmann, Secada, & Wehlage, 1995; Newmann & Wehlage, 1995). These standards are presented in more detail in Appendix G and are used in Chapter 7 to assess the impact of restructuring. Standards are important to this evaluation because some criteria are necessary to make evaluative judgments. The standards developed by CORS were chosen to evaluate the extent to which instruction in Library Power schools was likely to result in student performances that are "authentic achievements" (Newmann & Associates, 1996). Such achievements meet three requirements: students construct knowledge; students engage in disciplined inquiry; and the products of students' work have some personal, aesthetic, or utilitarian value.

CORS developed rubrics and a scoring manual to assess the intellectual quality of instruction and student performances, but in the Library Power evaluation no systematic effort was made to use these devices to score teachers' tasks. Rather, the standards serve as an orientation and backdrop against which we discuss the quality of instruction associated with Library Power. In using the standards to evaluate instruction, we are very much aware that not all instruction should be expected to score high on standards of authentic achievement. These standards emphasize relatively complex cognitive operations and clearly there are times when teachers need to direct student learning toward objectives that include acquiring simple factual knowledge and basic skills as part of a base from which to launch into higher-level work. Our assertion is that a range of instructional complexity is necessary to good teaching but that the overall goal is one of authentic achievement. The standards from CORS are used here to make some evaluative judgments about tasks that occupied a significant portion of school time, such as a week or more, had the potential to challenge students cognitively, and utilized important human and library resources. We believe that it is fair to assume that major instructional units involving Library Power resources should have as a central goal to challenge students cognitively by engaging them in authentic achievement tasks.

Data for the chapter came primarily from two sources. One was the set of 29 case studies written by on-site observers who were members of the national evaluation team. Each case provided a more detailed picture of one of the eight sites, the districts, or a particular Library Power case study school. All case studies included a section on instruction. Each case was read to understand the overall context of instruction and the use of library resources for instruction. The second data source was the set of "collaboration logs" kept by librarians as part of the national evaluation methodology. These logs usually summarized five collaboratively planned instructional units from the school year. Logs were designed to provide the school and the national evaluation with evidence of collaboration between teachers and the librarian. The log form provided for statements of goals; subject topics; resources; and corresponding tasks for the teacher, librarian, and students in a unit of study. Presumably these entries presented what the librarian and teachers saw as good examples of both their collaboration and use of library resources for instruction.

A sample of entries from these logs was selected to gain a picture of typical instructional activity in Library Power schools. Another search of the logs was made to identify a few selections that appeared to offer high-quality instruction based on the CORS standards identified above. The purpose of these examples was to illustrate higher-quality instruction and indicate the potential for instruction based on Library Power resources. Exactly what portion of all instruction could be scored high on standards of intellectual quality, we do not know, but it was probably relatively small. As stated above, scoring of examples of instruction using the technical rubrics for authentic achievement was not possible, but our discussion of these examples in light of the standards provides some general insights into issues of instructional quality when schools used Library Power resources.

To foreshadow the main finding, the quality of instruction was found to range considerably both within schools and across sites. In the following sections, we present a number of examples of instruction that spans this range from low to high quality. Our examples suggest that some teachers were able to respond to Library Power by using it to offer exciting new experiences that challenged students to think and struggle with important ideas, while other teachers seemed unsure of how Library Power could make an important difference in what and how they taught; their instruction often presented rather undemanding tasks albeit in a new setting, the library. Most instruction fell somewhere between these two ends of the quality continuum.

Although the examples of instruction sometimes refer to Library Power sites by name, and this is done to give the reader a context for the data and findings, the evaluation is not designed to make judgments about the relative success of any particular school, district, or site in implementing Library Power. Rather, through an analysis of the examples we hope to provide the Fund and the education and library professions some general insights into successes and difficulties of using Library Power to improve the intellectual quality of instruction.

Instruction: Improved or Changed?

Testimony about instructional change attributed to Library Power could be found at every site. In Lincoln, Nebraska, for example, teachers were quick to identify Library Power as an important support for improving their instruction. Here change was not so much doing something new or different, but building on and enhancing what they were already doing. Using the library to promote resource-based teaching was already a practice for a number of teachers. Reportedly instruction was already thought to be of high quality and, according to the site observer, the Lincoln system generally was not aggressively pushing an agenda of reform in teaching. One kind of support from Library Power that teachers identified was assistance from the librarian through collaboration. Just over two-thirds of the teachers in the district who responded to the national evaluation questionnaire indicated that they and the librarian collaborated in designing activities, identifying and gathering instructional materials, teaching information-seeking skills, and helping students create products and reports.

What did instruction look like when teachers and librarians collaborated? In one Lincoln school it was reported that the librarian conducted a number of lessons on research skills tailored to different grade levels. The purpose of the librarian's instruction was to help children become information users as they prepared to undertake various classroom assignments requiring research. The research skills were said to be taught by the librarian "as needed." Lessons on how to use the library were based on previous work by a cadre of teachers in the Lincoln district who had developed a Guide to Integrated Information Literacy Skills (GIILS). GIILS focused on the "Big Six" research steps and provided a number of actual lessons to illustrate use of the various skills, such as identifying relevant sources, comparing information from different sources, and using the skills to produce a written report. The collaboration log at one school showed that all but one of five collaborative units focused on teaching information-seeking skills as a main learning objective.

Reports indicated that instruction requiring student research followed a standard format: Students selected a topic, went to the library to look up some information, and then produced a written report. For example, in a ninth-grade biology class students were told to choose an animal to study. Subsequently they went to the library to look up facts for their written reports and to produce some kind of accompanying visuals. The teacher had encouraged them to study an unusual animal: A koala bear report was accompanied by a model constructed of spray-painted cotton balls; a tapir was modeled from papier-mâché. Finally, students were told to write stories about their animals that contained at least five "facts." The collection from the class was bound into a volume entitled "Animal Stories."

Such units were cited by teachers as evidence of enhancement and improvement of their instruction. They seemed to enjoy teaching these kinds of units and student engagement was apparently high. On the other hand, it was not clear that these kinds of tasks greatly challenged students' cognitive capacities.

In Atlanta, Georgia, rhetoric espousing instructional change through Library Power echoed a refrain heard in most other districts. According to the district's proposal, the library was to be the "intellectual hub" for students and teachers. Instruction should help students become "problem solvers and critical thinkers." Teachers were to help students use "instructional technology . . . to expand their learning experiences beyond the pages of the textbook and the walls of the classroom." Students were to have free access to the library as individuals and in small groups. Assessment of student learning should be used to modify instruction and to use "every teaching innovation" in promoting greater student achievement. Clearly, such rhetoric promised to use Library Power to improve teachers' instructional practices.

Testimony from teachers credited Library Power with helping them change their practices for achieving such goals. After three years of the initiative, the director of Library Power in Atlanta saw evidence that the program had moved instruction toward some of the outcomes promised:

> When you look at the products that come out of this (instruction), you . . . have a process that kids are engaged in based on the plan. As a result . . . you have a product, you will see a diorama. For example, the little covered wagons—they have learned the structure of the wagon, who the people are, where they were going. The product is the talk, paper and a project.

The director also cited reports from principals that "something different is happening. More kids are in the library. More kids are doing different kinds of things." Principals saw that teachers were offering instruction featuring activities in the library. These observations were supported by data from the case studies and collaboration logs. Exactly what students were learning as a result of such activities was not clear, however.

Atlanta's local education fund conducted its own evaluation and reported that during 1995–96 the level of sophistication for such instruction varied considerably. It was found that some teachers asked students simply to gather information without much purpose or substance. Some instruction was devoted simply to looking up answers, some called for learning to use information-processing skills, and a few tasks asked students to use information to solve problems. The report found that of the 46 collaboratively planned units they reviewed, only 6 to 11 were judged to involve students in higher levels of problem solving and critical thinking.

The next year, one middle school listed 11 units in the collaboration log that were developed by teachers and the librarian. Summary descriptions were provided for 5 of the units. One for eighth graders on the topic of the nervous system illustrated the way in which the library was used (by teachers in Atlanta and elsewhere). The objective for the unit was: "Students will know the parts of the nervous system and their importance." Students used the library to gather information from reference books and other sources about the nervous system and to "create a picture/illustration" about how the system works. The librarian provided them with the necessary materials, instructed them in the use of computers, and monitored their use of information skills such as indexing and taking notes. This kind of task involved students in an information-seeking activity in the library, but it did not appear to be substantially different from lessons that relied on textbooks in the classroom.

A somewhat more challenging task was presented by eighth-grade teachers at the same school in their unit on the Revolutionary War. The objectives called on students to evaluate the causes and effects of the war; compare and contrast the cultures and beliefs of the British, Patriots, and Indians; and evaluate the importance of various people and/or events during the American Revolution. These tasks also called for the retrieval of correct answers, but additionally they demanded some higher-level thinking when students were evaluating causes and effects of the war and comparing and contrasting cultures and beliefs.

Chattanooga, Tennessee, was a district intensely interested in reforms aimed at instructional improvement. Like many other sites, this one argued in its proposal to the Fund that the main purpose of Library Power should be the improvement of instruction. The chances of such change were increased somewhat because the Library Power initiative was leveraged by other reforms, mainly those sponsored by the Edna McConnell Clark Urban Middle School Reform Program in the middle schools and the Paideia Project in several elementary schools. The directors of the three school reform initiatives merged much of their staff development effort to support a common agenda, one that included having teachers use library resources to promote student inquiry. The depth of commitment in Chattanooga to improving instruction through Library Power was such that several schools in the district were denied funding for Library Power when they embraced Distar, a program emphasizing direct instruction of basic skills. The Distar program was seen as incompatible with the kind of instruction that Library Power hoped to engender.

In one school, Paideia had already led to changes in instructional practice before Library Power arrived on the scene. The principal indicated that teachers had for some time de-emphasized textbooks and had begun using literature and library resources for instruction. With the arrival of Library Power, teachers increased their use of library resources. For example, a first-grade teacher testified that her instruction had not changed much, but she quickly added that instruction had been "enriched and enhanced by Library Power." As an example of this enhancement, a second-grade teacher explained that she was teaching about the Navajo in class while "the kids do other tribes, gather information in the library, and share with everyone else." And a fifth-grade teacher in the same school said, "[Library Power] enhanced the way I teach. . . . We have time to more effectively address individual needs. I see the kids do more group things." Such testimony was typical of teachers interviewed in Chattanooga. Such use reflected an important aspect of Library Power success. Nevertheless, while having kids gather information more often or participate in more group activities may indicate a degree of change, it is not necessarily a sign of improved instruction.

A number of teachers in the district testified about the impact of Library Power in other ways. A second-grade teacher remarked that her students knew what research was and how to do it. In a unit on Native Americans, she gave her students a worksheet that asked for basic information about tribes such as where they lived, the kinds of clothing they wore, and the types of homes each tribe lived in. A "bonus question" (that is, optional for students) asked: "What effect did where your tribe lived have on how they lived?" From the perspective of promoting authentic achievement, this kind of question should be an integral part of an instructional task because it presents students with more of an intellectual challenge than simple factual searches. Certainly students' understanding of research ought to include notions of interpretation as well as factual accumulation.

A fourth-grade teacher believed that by the time students came to her they were proficient in many of the requisite library skills. She said that they could be relied upon to go to the library alone or in small groups to do research. While they might have copied material verbatim in the past, she claimed that they now paraphrased what they read. Another fourth-grade teacher indicated that because of Library Power her students had been "weaned from the encyclopedia. They go to the computer or to books first. They are more independent in that they are less teacher directed. You can give them a basic outline of what to do, and they do it."

A third-grade teacher had students doing research on "pirates." Using resources from the library included looking up answers in the dictionary, an atlas, and an online service. Students had to supply correct answers to questions such as "What is a pirate?" (For historians, this question has proven vexing rather than simple.) Other activities that were part of the assignment included drawing a treasure map, a pirate ship, or a pirate flag. These activities appeared to engage students, but the intellectual quality was judged to be shallow.

The kind of instruction described above illustrates how teachers, students, and librarians frequently used the library, not only in Lincoln, Atlanta, and Chattanooga, but at a number of other sites. Library Power was credited with helping to further trends in instructional practice that were underway in a school or district. The evidence suggests that teachers used the library to enhance resource-based teaching and help students practice information-seeking skills. But the evidence, reflected in the examples cited above, does not support an argument for seeing such change as an improvement in the intellectual quality of the tasks teachers assigned students. What had not yet occurred was to use Library Power to offer students intellectually ambitious tasks. Tasks did not yet consistently push students to engage in more complex kinds of thinking that resulted in high-quality products and performances. Later in the chapter we discuss how some teachers conceived a more ambitious agenda for their students when they went to the library. Before shifting to some examples of high-quality instruction, we present evidence that in a few cases instruction was even less ambitious than what we have portrayed thus far.

Different Expectations

New Haven, Connecticut's, proposal for funding called for resource-based instruction using rhetoric that was remarkably similar to that offered by other districts. Students should become information users and problem solvers. At the school level, practices did not always seem to follow the implications of the rhetoric. Observers noted that some of the slippage between word and deed could be attributed in part to the pressure educators felt to raise students' test scores. The district had a reputation for low student achievement as measured by the Connecticut Mastery Test. Scores were reported annually as the percentage of students reaching or surpassing achievement goals set by the state. Only 5.1% of the students in grade 4, 3.4% in grade 6, and 4.9% in grade 8 met goals in reading, writing, and mathematics. Statewide about 25% of students in each grade level

met achievement goals in these subjects. In the suburbs success was much higher.

Given these low achievement levels, reports indicated that the New Haven schools were "under enormous pressure" to show that some program, any program, could raise test scores. Two and one-half years into Library Power no one was willing to claim that evidence of such favorable impact from Library Power was yet available, but most educators believed that richer resources and improved instruction would eventually lead to such results. The directors of reading and mathematics for the district pointed to the many new books in the teachers' professional library that could be used to enhance their instruction. It was anticipated that improved instruction would be a major force in closing the achievement gap.

The Library Power director argued that low achievement could be attributed in part to long-standing inequalities in resources that had plagued the system, but that Library Power had helped to address the resource equity issue. He explained the district's strategy as follows: "How do you expect the kids to read when they don't have libraries and books? We think that if we saturate the schools with books and the kids have opportunities to read and are encouraged to read, of course they will learn to read."

Certainly a major accomplishment of Library Power in New Haven was getting books into schools and subsequently spawning a number of reading incentive programs, called by various names: Ravenous Readers, Story Spinners, Rookie Readers, Library Link, Battle of the Books and Quinnipiac Families Love to Read. Concern over low expectations for student achievement led the school board to enact a number of policies encouraging more ambitious instruction and goals. For example, one policy required every student to complete a research paper and science project every year, a mandate that Library Power could certainly help fulfill. But stating a policy was one thing; getting teachers and students to act in accordance with that policy was another.

One elementary school had adopted James Comer's School Development model of reform. This kind of program committed the school to changes that could address the "social, moral, physical and psychological development of the child." The principal summed up the Comer philosophy for her school by saying, "Academics are important, but social and nurturing needs must be met first. We're really looking at what's best for children." Given this view of priorities, an emphasis on instruction of high intellectual quality was not likely to become the main focus at this school any time soon.

In such an environment, it was not surprising that teachers displayed some ambivalence about the instructional goals they should promote. At the same time that the school was committed to addressing non-academic concerns and to raising test scores, a number of staff were trained to offer instruction based on the principles of "constructivist learning" and problem solving. The implication was that teachers should be offering a different kind of instruction; teachers should try for more than improved test scores. Interviews with staff indicated that test score enhancement and the incorporation of the new library resources into their instruction competed for attention. Nevertheless, the school's comprehensive plan for 1995–96 called for incorporating Library Power into classroom learning centers; flexible scheduling for research; and introducing students to report writing, use of reference materials, and note taking. Such goals might have pointed the school toward more ambitious instruction and academic excellence, but a year later a revised plan, while repeating a number of the same goals, inexplicably made no mention of flexible scheduling for use of the library and de-emphasized collaboration, calling for it between the librarian and teachers in grades 4 and 5 only.

One result of an inconsistent educational vision was a lack of clarity and purpose in instruction. When teachers at the school were asked how Library Power had changed their instructional practices, it was reported that the question usually "elicited a blank look." Apparently many staff at the school did not see Library Power as an instrument of instructional change. Yet teachers reported that students were learning to do research and write reports. However, in 1997, the last year of Library Power funding, collaboration logs at the school still reported an emphasis on basic "research" tasks. For example, a seventh-grade unit on the Middle Ages asked students to find five sources on a famous person of their choice. They were to take notes and then write a three-page paper that included 25 facts about the person. A week was devoted to this assignment, a considerable investment of staff and student time considering that it sent students on a fact-finding expedition that resulted in reproducing information that could be lifted from books. We judged the intellectual quality of this task to be low.

"Collaboration" at this school continued to find the librarian scheduling a whole class visit, providing materials for students to complete their assignment, and arranging displays of their finished products. The field observer noted that student reports were mainly filled with direct quotes and paraphrasing. In nearly every instance, reports were limited responses to carefully selected questions similar to those found at the ends of chapters in textbooks. One class that went to the library to do research found all the books on their topic neatly arranged for them on a shelf; the answers were easily found. In sum, students used computers, encyclopedias, and trade books as well as their texts, but the instructional tasks involving these sources constrained the substance of learning markedly. What students learned could not be much different from what they had traditionally learned from textbooks while sitting in classrooms.

As we indicated earlier, the quality of instruction at Library Power sites ranged considerably. In another New Haven school (described in some detail in Chapter 7), instruction was judged as more ambitious. Teachers had adopted the Bank Street model of curriculum and instruction based on a conception of learning that relied on student use of library resources to write reports. In theory, the Bank Street model and Library Power were well matched and teachers could presumably utilize the new resources in their instruction. Practice, however, fell short of rhetorical refrains about teaching students to become inquirers and problem solvers whose critical thinking capacities were stretched and developed. Most tasks asked students to identify a topic of personal interest, go to the library for information, or in some cases use books made available on a cart by the librarian, and then write a report and produce an artifact representing the topic. Based on the CORS standards, most student work at this third school was given a modest, middle-range score by the specially trained observer, despite its emphasis on resource-based learning. Tasks often called for superficial inquiry to "expose" students to a topic. Further, the belief that responding to students' interests was paramount meant that children were often allowed to pursue marginal topics that could produce at best a fragmented understanding of important ideas. For example, in a unit on the Great Depression a student was allowed to study and report on the advent of air mail service in 1939, hardly a topic of importance when considering the momentous events of that period. When compared to the tasks in a number of other schools, student work here was often more intellectually challenging, even though the model of inquiry became routinized and predictable.

The most disappointing evidence about instruction came from another district, where tasks were largely textbook driven and teacher centered. Little rhetoric about resource-based learning was heard from teachers. It was reported that "Children were only rarely given the opportunity to raise their own questions and answer them through a deliberate, systematic and sustained process of inquiry." In fact, in this district the observer concluded that the "goals of Library Power . . . ran counter to general classroom practice." Instruction was based on the assumption that students were incapable of learning except through direct instruction emphasizing basic skills. The case study included the following comment from an interview:

> Parents, teachers, principals, and even children themselves, still have a negative, self-defeating attitude about the capabilities of our children. For so many years children have not had access to real learning opportunities. It is not until recently that the schools have focused on instruction and student learning. It is too soon to see the results of this change.

The norms of the district meant that Library Power was reinterpreted to support what had become unquestioned mainstream practice in the district. Unlike other districts, low-quality instruction was the norm. Given this kind of environment, Library Power could be expected to have only a marginal impact on instruction.

Analysis and Commentary

Data from the collaboration logs, interviews, and direct observations indicated that Library Power was often used to practice what educators referred to as "resource-based" instruction. Considerable variance in the quality of this kind of instruction was found both within and across sites. Contrary to the assumptions held by some educators and reformers, resource-based instruction was not inherently of high intellectual quality. Tasks may or may not have assigned students work that was intellectually challenging. While some teachers may have changed their instructional practice by offering resource-based tasks, by themselves such tasks did not necessarily produce higher-quality teaching. For example, in one school's collaboration log, an eighth-grade science unit was described as having as its main objective helping students develop an "understanding of the scientific method." In pursuit of this goal, students were to use encyclopedias to select a topic of interest and subsequently gather information from three sources for writing a four- to eight-page report. Students could choose any topic that struck their interest. In this class, using information from secondary sources and reference books was sufficient to complete the task and achieve the objective: "understanding of the scientific method." No experiments or testing data for their validity were required. Even though it was considered an example of resource-based instruction, this kind of instructional task asks students only to reproduce knowledge.

Many examples of teachers' tasks exhibited only modest evidence of intellectual quality according to the CORS standards. Tasks were limited in their potential for two reasons. On the one hand, teachers sometimes gave students a highly constrained task based on a list of pre-specified and largely factual questions that were easily answered, sometimes with a single word. Worksheets and end-of-chapter-type questions provided for fact-finding expeditions with librarians laying out the right books for students to skim in their quests for the right answers. Even when students were asked to develop some kind of extended written report about a topic, the framework was dictated in the form of an outline that mainly required students to fill in the outlined sections. One consequence of this notion of inquiry may well have been that students learned that library skills were sure-fire formulas that produced expected answers. To this extent, tasks provided students with an inadequate understanding of inquiry, one that depended on simple questions given by an authority and reinforced the assumption that library resources were sure to hold correct answers. The result was a naive form of routinized and mechanized inquiry.

On the other hand, sometimes teachers went in an entirely different direction; their tasks were very non-directive, letting students choose topics, ask questions, and define the scope of work with only minimal guidance. Almost unfailingly this strategy also produced low intellectual quality in student performance. While the first direction gave students a misguided mechanistic notion of inquiry and how to use information skills, the second was negligent in that it often failed to demand that students develop an in-depth understanding of important ideas and knowledge. Any topic was good enough as long as the student was interested in it. But neither teachers nor students had internalized standards that governed their selection of subjects and issues. Trivial topics were as legitimate as important ones, as long as students were engaged in the work. Students could hardly be blamed for choosing to study topics that they saw as interesting but demanded little effort. The license to pursue this open-ended approach to inquiry failed because it did not insist on rigorous application of prior knowledge and a connection to important ideas and concepts.

How can we explain the practice of asking students to engage in severely truncated forms of inquiry under the label of resource-based teaching? The answer to this question is not altogether clear from data we gathered in this evaluation. Several possibilities are worth further investigation. In some situations it may be that the district's or school's curriculum severely constrains teachers and requires them to teach to the curriculum or test, thus prohibiting more authentic investigations. Another explanation may be that low-level instructional tasks result partly from teachers' limited experiences in conducting their own inquiry. A college degree does not guarantee that a person has had to conduct inquiry using standards similar to those required by authentic achievements. Inadequate tasks may also reflect popular beliefs about progressive education and the natural development of children. A version of such beliefs insists that learning occurs naturally for children, but only if they are interested in a topic. Allowing them to follow their interests and choose what they want to study will result in high engagement and learning. Imposing topics selected by the teacher or demanding that a child deal with difficult ideas is thought to blunt natural interests and interfere with the child's development. But given such a position, how does a teacher also ensure that children learn to test important ideas and construct careful arguments based on information?

Another possible explanation for teachers' highly abridged forms of inquiry involves instruction based on "active learning" and the search for tasks that address what are said to be different "learning styles." These terms reflect a concern for the problem of getting students engaged in their studies. The library was seen as a place that accommodated such instruction. Of course, we have already seen that activity and high levels of engagement can occur without challenging students to use their minds well. One unit in language arts for fifth graders had the students investigating holiday customs of different cultures. The assignment was to read a variety of holiday stories from different cultures, write an original holiday story, and make a hand-sewn book for a gift. Writing an original story called for some construction of knowledge, and making a gift seemed to satisfy another component of authentic achievement: performance having personal, aesthetic, or utilitarian value. Still, a task such as this one may not have much intellectual quality if it is not demanding of disciplined inquiry about important ideas. If the emphasis is placed primarily on producing a gift to take home, without attention to the other criteria, authenticity is diminished. Putting into practice standards of intellectual quality becomes difficult when teachers begin instructional tasks with the assumption that their first priority is to provide children with engaging activities.

At a different school, assignments almost always ended with some kind of group performance or display. A science assignment to research "biomes" resulted in skits, news reports, and puppet shows. A group of five jointly wrote a story about a boy who pollutes the sea. The boy encounters a hermit crab, a turtle, and a shark, each of whom tells him how his pollution harms them. Again, some understanding and analysis of biomes by students was necessary in this performance, but from evidence reported about the science content of the students' work, the task was not demanding. According to the group's own report of their work, interest was focused mostly on making the puppets. Making instruction engaging by employing "activities" is understandable. Hooking students' interests is necessary, but too often these activities appeared to promote relatively trivial pursuits. The "fun" of the activity became more important than helping students use their minds well.

It is fair to say that for many teachers who embraced resource-based instruction their practices were different from their colleagues who relied on the basal reader and textbook. It might be argued that moving away from the traditional classroom of basal reader and text represented a fundamentally important change. Giving children the opportunity to draw on the wealth of sources found in a modern library was an important shift in tone, if not always substance, that was aided and abetted by Library Power. Routinized inquiry that sends kids on fact-finding expeditions may well foreshadow, even if it does not require, that students will learn to construct meaning using disciplined inquiry. Such change in the tone and context of instruction can be viewed as a step in the right direction. The next step requires teachers (and students) to internalize standards for such activities that place intellectual demands on children resembling the demands of authentic adult activities.

Finally, the lack of inquiry requiring more complex intellectual operations and goals might also be attributed to the emphasis Library Power itself placed on collaboration between teachers and the librarian. Collaboration in a number of schools was understood in a limited way. It was construed as a technical innovation only; that is, teachers and the librarian met to plan instruction, but they did not also reconsider instructional goals and tasks. For example, during 1995, one school was given two awards. One was recognition in the state's excellence competition and a second was an award in the state's "pay for performance" program. It was the only school in the district to receive both awards. One criterion for the performance award was that "75% of the instructional staff will meet, collaborate . . . and plan monthly with the school's media specialist." This goal, only one of several, may have been perceived by the staff as quite ambitious, but as stated it reflected only a technical dimension of collaboration. Improving the quality of instruction was not included as a criterion in defining a high-performance school. At the same time, the site's proposal for Library Power funding envisioned qualitative changes in instruction that would help students to become critical thinkers and users of information. It appeared that many other schools also made formal and technical collaboration central to their understanding of how Library Power was to affect instruction.

A district's central office may have used rhetoric offering a chain of reasoning something like the following: Collaboration will change instruction by having children use the library; such change will produce more information-seeking activity by students; engaging in these tasks will raise student achievement. Missing from such reasoning is a set of standards to establish expectations about the intellectual quality of student achievement. Neither the national Library Power initiative nor the individual school districts had developed clear notions of instructional quality. The direct link between Library Power, improved instruction, and higher-quality student achievement was never spelled out in proposals or in official pronouncements from Library Power.

However, some individuals at all levels of the initiative recognized the absence of standards and a clear connection between Library Power, better instruction, and higher-quality student achievement. Staff development efforts offered in several districts began to address questions about standards. But in general, given the lack of consensus about standards and the heavy emphasis on collaboration, it was easy to understand why collaboration often resulted in the repackaging of old instructional units. It seemed to follow that collaboration plus reasonably high levels of student activity and engagement could be viewed as evidence of successful use of Library Power.

We have offered several possible reasons to explain why teachers' practices fell short of providing children with more challenging instruction. In future iterations of Library Power, some thought should be given to how best to raise issues about the quality of instruction. One way is to provide educators with compelling examples of good instruction. In the next section, we present "existence proof" that some teachers succeeded in presenting students with instructional tasks characterized by higher intellectual quality. These examples point out the potential educational effect of Library Power.

Constructing Knowledge Through Disciplined Inquiry

When guided by clear ideas about how students might use their minds well, some teachers developed fairly powerful instructional units using Library Power resources. For example, a fifth-grade Atlanta teacher became involved in extensive collaboration with the librarian and staff at the public library to produce a highly original instructional unit. While participating in the school's summer institute offered by the Library Power initiative, the teacher was encouraged to plan a unit that would have her students be inquirers. She returned to her school that fall and, with other teachers on her team, her students began a study of their neighborhood. Initially they could find little information; their questions seemed unanswerable. Where is information if it is not already in books? The teacher, with the help of the librarians at the school and public library, began to learn about how to conduct primary research.

Students first developed a list of long-term residents and then interviewed them. Their informants gave them tours of local "historic" places and explained about changes in the neighborhood. Old photographs were collected from community members and the students took their own pictures, sometimes showing the same street corners and buildings. Students soon discovered that their neighborhood had a rich and proud past, although currently it was under assault from the problems of illegal drug use. As the children accumulated information, they turned it into historical accounts and stories, artwork, and photo displays.

Objectives for this four-week unit included that students would be able to construct a map of the geographical area, explain the differences among neighborhoods, and explain how and why neighborhoods change. In constructing their maps they had to develop symbols, accurately measure distances, and be able to use the cardinal directions to locate places. They had to learn "to use primary source information (letters, pamphlets, oral history) . . ., learn basic oral history interview techniques for gathering information . . ., [and] use pictures to gain information and to present information." They also had to construct models of buildings, write stories about their own neighborhood, and make graphs depicting numbers of people and buildings. To culminate the unit, they presented their work before an assembly that included the superintendent, district administrators, public librarians, parents, and local residents of the neighborhood. The presentation served as a test of their competence and achievement.

A similar unit was undertaken in a Cleveland middle school, where students undertook to describe one square kilometer surrounding their school. Some historical research was conducted, but the tasks also included creating an inventory of the flora and fauna of the area. Students had to draw maps and sketches of buildings. Collectively they produced a rich description of their urban landscape.

To count as authentic instruction, tasks need not ask children to perform primary research. In New Haven, teachers on one sixth-grade level team recognized that students should pursue important complex topics in depth. They wanted students to learn that research is more than practicing a set of library skills. To avoid the superficiality that often came with open-ended student choice, teachers structured inquiry tasks to ensure that children would have to address specific topics. By the third year of Library Power, the team had developed a unit on the Civil War that required students to use various kinds of information found in the library. For the unit more than 100 books were made available by the librarian. The class worked toward a collective understanding of major events of the war. Some questions were appropriately simple factual ones: When did the war occur? Who fought? How many people died? Other topics were explorations of events such as the incident at Harper's Ferry. Some tasks required analysis and interpretation of information. Students wrote "front page" reports of the war, graphed casualties, developed a timeline, and wrote poems and dramatic readings based on historical events.

Products from this kind of research had a greater degree of coherence, depth, and rigor than was found in classrooms where students could simply follow their particular interest in a narrow topic. The Civil War unit also demonstrated changes over time in teachers' thinking and practices through collaboration and growing awareness of the potential of Library Power resources. Teachers had been prompted in part by their collaboration with the librarian to consider how they might better use library resources to create not only engaging but also more intellectually challenging and coherent tasks for students.

Science instruction at one of the Berea, Kentucky, schools was built around a long-term project that involved a number of phases. The assignment began by focusing on content objectives already outlined in the district's science curriculum. Also included in the unit were objectives in math and language arts, but the main purpose was to have each student develop an experiment and write up the results in a form that was acceptable for presentation at the local science fair. Students were required to use the library's resources to determine what was already known about the topic they had chosen to research. Based on this background, an experiment was to be performed using a specified format for describing the experiment and reporting the results. Included in the required format were an hypothesis statement, a description of steps in the experiment with recorded data or photos, and statements about the "constants" and "independent and dependent variables." Students were encouraged to construct charts, graphs, and tables to report data. Children not only had to describe their experiment but also to orally explain it to the class and to visitors at the science fair.

The "science fair" approach to teaching science and experimentation satisfied a number of criteria for tasks of high intellectual quality. It placed students in the role of constructing knowledge while at the same time providing sufficient structure to prevent them wandering aimlessly off target. By drawing on the district's curriculum framework, attention to important ideas in science was assured. By requiring an extensive write up and explanation of steps and results, students were made to provide elaborated communication. And given that students' products had to be publicly presented and explained, a sense of personal value and investment was likely. A number of other Library Power schools developed similar approaches to science instruction, providing a sharp contrast with tasks described earlier, in which students had only to use a few reference books to list some facts about a topic. In addition to science fairs, a number of schools staged similar events for history, math, and writing. When done well, such public displays push students to work hard in academics just as they do when engaged in public performances of music, drama, and athletics.

A few schools used the library as the center for almost all important instructional units. Using the library as the main environment for instruction required considerable collaboration among teachers as well as with the librarian. A Denver, Colorado, middle school, for example, created a series of major interdisciplinary units that often culminated in student productions and performances. One month was devoted to doing research and preparing for the presentation of Ray Bradbury's play "The Halloween Tree." Different groups of students did the acting, created scenery, and presented the music. Some students wrote original "scary stories" and others studied the literary genre of mystery and horror. It should be noted that because groups of students specialized in the tasks they performed, not all experienced the same kinds of intellectual challenge. Nevertheless, tasks such as these can present a high degree of authentic intellectual challenge because students must understand, interpret, create, and perform their own productions.

In summary, some teachers used Library Power to help construct intellectually challenging tasks for students. That such instruction occurred is exciting and promising. On the one hand, finding these examples argues that high-quality instruction can be given to students regardless of race or class. We found that teachers with students from disadvantaged backgrounds could immerse their students in tasks that produced authentic achievements. On the other hand, it also points to the problem of inequitable educational opportunities. Some teachers used Library Power very well, but when only some use it well, it exacerbates the difference in opportunities offered different groups of students. In the next section, we explore the issue of equity.

Improving Instruction in Decentralized Schools

The American school system is highly decentralized, both politically and administratively. No official or national curricula are mandated, as is the case in many European and Asian countries. The content frameworks offered by most state educational agencies are optional for teachers. Further, no national assessment system holds teachers and schools accountable for students' achievement. While states engage in periodic testing, generally the standards reflect minimal expectations. The upshot of this situation is that schools and even individual teachers are left free to invent much of their own curriculum and choose how best to deliver instruction. Sometimes instruction responds to district-level content frameworks that have been developed locally, but these usually leave much room for adaptation. For a number of teachers, basal readers and textbooks are the main tools of teaching, and assessment of student performance is conducted largely by using the teacher's guide and end-of-chapter questions.

Some see textbook-based instruction as uninspired, but at least providing important structure for teacher and student alike. Teachers who are dissatisfied with such an approach search for alternatives. Out of necessity they become instructional entrepreneurs as they invent their own packages of objectives, materials, and tasks. This situation produces enormous variations in the quality of instruction. Some teachers are extremely creative and their students benefit from the high-quality experiences that are produced. Others are not so inventive, with the result that their instruction is less challenging and stimulating to students' intellectual growth. Thus in any school district, even in any particular school, one is likely to find great variations in the quality of instruction. Some of it is exciting, daring, and intellectually challenging. Some of it seems patronizing and calculated mainly to keep students quietly on task. Much instruction falls somewhere in between these extremes, as we have already documented in this chapter.

The introduction of Library Power into a school provided another significant opportunity to create variation in the quality of instruction. For some teachers, the new resources and ideas contained in Library Power became rich possibilities to invent tasks that immersed children in the processes of inquiring and constructing knowledge. Such teachers saw immediately what could be done with new sources of information and the strength of collaborating with others. They may well have been heading in this direction already; the new opportunities increased their confidence and momentum as they experimented with the new resources. As we have seen in the examples presented above, children in these classrooms had opportunities to learn in ways that other children did not.

Other teachers were not so sure what Library Power could do for them in terms of improving their instruction. They could not always imagine what new possibilities were offered to them and the children now that they had access to Library Power resources. Did the program mean to imply that previous instruction was not as good as it should be? Would it mean inventing new lessons, complicating a teacher's life, perhaps working closely with a librarian in planning and teaching? A few teachers saw Library Power as creating a conflict in goals because, it was thought, a lot of library work would interfere with teaching basic skills and hurt test scores at the end of the year. Nevertheless, many teachers (most in some schools) sought to bend instruction to fit with the new resources. Recasting old lessons to fit Library Power was a natural and sensible response. Instruction that had worked well for a teacher could be made into lessons that had students using the library. Instruction was changed, but mainly because previous goals and methods were reinvented in collaboration with a librarian.

Those teachers and librarians who were best able to provide instruction of high intellectual quality held fairly clear ideas about inquiry and what Library Power implied for such instruction. Teachers whose concept of research was one of requiring students to construct their own knowledge through rigorous application of prior knowledge, concepts, and skills were the ones who made best use of Library Power. The highest-quality instruction using the library occurred in schools where teachers were already fairly experienced in developing instruction using inquiry and constructivist learning principles.

Teachers in several sites—most notably Berea, Denver, and Chattanooga—had the advantage of incorporating Library Power into a relatively strong school reform agenda and staff development program that included ideas about having students construct knowledge. (This topic is explored further in Chapter 7, on school reform.) These reforms offered fairly well-articulated definitions of academic achievement and the instructional role teachers were to play in helping children move toward more complex kinds of learning. Berea was responding to the Kentucky Education Reform Act, Denver had the benefit of the Public Education Business Coalition and the Literacy League program, and Chattanooga schools were influenced by the Paideia and Edna McConnell Clark initiatives. While these reforms differ in a number of ways, they each provided educators with a fairly coherent vision of schooling. Issues about instructional goals and strategies were addressed. Practitioners were given guidance in deciding what content was most worthwhile. Each reform had an identifiable character to it that was missing in most school systems where teachers were asked to become instructional entrepreneurs.

To the extent that teachers understood and embraced substantive school reform initiatives, Library Power took on greater coherence and practicality. In Chattanooga, the three major reform efforts combined their resources to create greater staff development coherence. Similarly, in Berea the line between Library Power and KERA staff development was quickly blurred as the staff for the two programs saw considerable overlap in goals and instructional strategies. In Denver a linkage between the Literacy League initiative and Library Power also combined to integrate their staff development programs. Staff developers found a number of key ideas inherent in both the Literacy League and Library Power programs that helped to direct their common efforts to improve instruction. For example, they agreed that reading, writing, and research greatly overlapped and could not be meaningfully separated for instruction; reading and writing skill development should be focused on content objectives; and collaborative planning should address the goals of instruction and not just create a menu of activities for students. Teachers were helped to see that issues of how to teach, what to teach and who should teach it were variations on one theme, improving instruction, which was the goal of both programs.

Professional Community: The Base of Improved Instruction

The most powerful use of Library Power came not necessarily from the presence of reforms and mandates, as much as they were helpful, but rather from the momentum created by a strong professional community at the school level. Newmann & Associates (1996) described this momentum in a number of schools undergoing reform and restructuring. Research on this set of schools defined professional community as having the following four elements:

1. Teachers establish a set of shared norms and values that promote student learning, the central focus of professional community.

2. Teachers frequently engage in reflective dialogue with colleagues to improve themselves and their school.

3. Teachers de-privatize their practice to promote dialogue and reflection with their colleagues about curriculum and instruction.

4. Staff engage in collaborative activities as a way to ensure continuation and renewal of shared norms and values and to provide occasions for reflection.

Building this kind of organizational environment required the intersection of certain structural and cultural conditions. Structurally, opportunities for de-privatization, collaboration, and dialogue must be built into the organization of the school. It was found that if there was no time or occasion for talking with one's colleagues about issues of teaching, it was unlikely to occur during teachers' "spare time." In a number of Library Power schools, teachers talked about the need for common planning time when they could not only meet with the librarian but with each other as a team. Collaboration on the fly was not conducive to reflective dialogue.

From their research on restructuring, Newmann & Associates (1996) concluded that culture was the key underlying support for successful structural arrangements in an organization. Educators had to be open to the possibilities of discussion and even disagreement with colleagues. Trust in one's colleagues was essential to promote honest and helpful dialogue. People had to trust others enough to allow observations and comments on their teaching.

Our analysis of Library Power data supports a similar conclusion. At one school in Denver, for example, teachers had made considerable progress in developing collaboration among themselves as well as with the librarian. How to organize research-based instruction was a frequent topic of conversation at team and department meetings. The result was to promote a freer exchange of ideas and question some of their regular practices. Helping, too, was the connection between the Literacy League and Library Power, which provided teachers at this school with a common language to discuss instruction. This language also made it possible to be more concrete and less abstract about the school's sense of purpose. Periodic demonstration lessons by staff developers from the Literacy League furthered the common base of experiences that these teachers could use in their discussions of instruction.

The importance of professional community to the success of Library Power has been recognized by the Fund (Public Education Network, 1997). It was understood that Library Power required collective understanding and a high degree of consensus about its value if the program were to function successfully. In addition, the presence of the program's new resources, along with its requirement to engage in collaboration, suggested the hypothesis that Library Power might contribute to the building of professional community. The way in which Library Power helped to strengthen professional community is addressed for the three schools featured in Chapter 7. We present here some evidence that Library Power contributed to building professional community in at least two of these schools.

For the population of Library Power schools, data were collected through questionnaires to principals, librarians, and teachers. Seven questions asked about the extent to which teachers worked together, agreed about what students should learn, felt responsible for ensuring that all students learn, respected each other's ideas, trusted each other to make decisions, were responsible to one another for carrying out school goals, and shared their best ideas with each other. The questions were designed to measure trust, respect, consensus, and a collective effort to teach well, all essential elements in a school's professional community.

Table 6-1 presents the mean scores from the LMS, Teacher, and Principal Surveys of 1997 on professional community for librarians, principals, and teachers from 73 schools. Each of the seven items was scored on a five-point scale indicating the extent to which the respondent disagreed or agreed with a statement. Items b, e, and g were phrased in the negative to control for response bias, and their scores in Table 6-1 have been reflected so that scores for all items are conceptually oriented in the same direction. Principals tended to be the most positive about the professional community status of their schools, but teachers and librarians also saw their schools reflecting trust, consensus, respect, and good effort on behalf of children. The generally positive response to the above items suggest that with a few exceptions many schools contained the basis for building professional community.

Table 6-2 presents the mean score for professional community for teachers only for each of the 73 schools. This table indicates the amount of variance across schools on professional community. The schools ranged from a score of 22.29 at the low end to 33.38 at the high end of professional community. The validity of results from the questionnaire data were confirmed, to some extent, by examining case study data. As it turned out, the three highest scoring and the two lowest scoring schools were also case study sites. Observation and interview data from all five case study sites indicated that the questionnaire data were able to tap the strength of professional community in these schools. The case studies reported evidence that high-scoring schools tended to make much better use of Library Power than low-scoring schools.

TABLE 6-1
Mean Scores on Professional Community Items for Librarians, Principals, and Teachers in Teacher-Sampled Schools (LMS, Principal, and Teacher Surveys, 1997)

	Librarians (Mean)	Principals (Mean)	Teachers (Mean)
a. Teachers in this school generally work together to do what is best for all students.	4.26	4.48	4.30
b. Teachers in this school do not generally agree on what all students should learn (reflected).	3.72	4.05	3.66
c. Teachers in this school generally feel responsible that all students learn.	4.31	4.42	4.46
d. Teachers in this school generally respect each other's ideas about teaching and learning.	4.09	4.20	4.27
e. Teachers in this school do not generally trust each other to make decisions that are best for the staff (reflected).	3.85	4.33	4.03
f. Teachers in this school generally feel responsible to one another for carrying out the goals of the school.	3.99	4.07	3.98
g. Teachers in this school do not generally share their best ideas with each other (reflected).	3.85	4.37	3.93
Number Responding	1,171	415	482

TABLE 6-2
Mean School Sums on Professional Community Items for Teachers in Teacher-Sampled Schools, Sorted by Mean (Teacher Survey, 1997)

School ID	Mean Sum Score	School ID	Mean Sum Score	School ID	Mean Sum Score
RZ	22.29	AK	27.90	W	30.50
SA	22.94	LJ	27.93	GD	30.68
IK	23.27	UM	28.22	DW	30.69
SW	23.80	Q	28.24	CJ	30.70
PU	24.03	VB	28.37	HO	30.72
ES	24.33	FE	28.47	RO	30.75
IT	24.48	N	28.57	X	30.79
OK	24.52	FJ	28.58	IV	30.81
CN	25.08	Total	28.66 Mean	JK	30.88
EQ	25.12	TN	28.83	HD	30.89
RQ	25.81	MI	28.84	GJ	30.93
FS	26.17	GB	28.91	G	30.94
AM	26.25	MV	29.00 Median	JL	31.47
HQ	26.40	DV	29.22	DY	31.58
SI	26.44	SD	29.56	CS	31.87
BH	26.50	U	29.61	DB	32.00
FI	26.67	DQ	29.65	EJ	32.20
TC	27.04	JB	29.65	AR	32.64
AX	27.06	BW	29.70	BU	32.71
MY	27.22	MO	29.79	MW	32.94
GE	27.26	EI	29.80	DO	33.08
LR	27.72	CQ	29.86	T	33.16
SL	27.76	VL	29.89	EB	33.26
A	27.79	HY	30.04	DZ	33.38
JT	27.82	VK	30.44	Number Responding	1,171

The extent to which Library Power fostered trust, respect, consensus, and sharing cannot be determined from the data. It may have been that high-scoring schools had already developed agreement on such issues and that is why they were receptive to Library Power and made good use of it. On the other hand, a reasonable hypothesis is that new resources, a trained librarian, and the structural elements of flexible scheduling and collaboration were contributing factors to strengthening elements of professional community.

Conclusion

Library Power offered teachers an opportunity to change their instruction by using new resources and drawing on the expertise of the librarian. Unlike exhortations contained in some reform efforts that ask teachers to change their instruction by following some ideas, principles, or theories, Library Power provides concrete forms of assistance in new books, a professional librarian, and the innovation of collaboration on collection and instruction. Rallying around such concrete assistance can provide a school with the basis for building agreement about purpose and working collectively to improve instruction.

In almost all of the schools we examined, staff took at least partial advantage of this opportunity by giving assignments that required students to use books and other resources in the library. Librarians provided sets of books to support instruction, and sometimes teachers consulted with the librarian regarding what resources were available and how they might best be used. For many teachers, instruction changed mainly in that they were able to do more research-based teaching, something they had been doing already. However, a good share of such instruction emphasized processes and objectives that did not significantly challenge students intellectually.

Library Power also provided opportunities for some teachers to offer students more intellectually challenging tasks. These teachers had developed a fairly clear understanding of what students had to do to construct knowledge by engaging in disciplined inquiry, problem solving, and critical thinking. Such instruction showed that Library Power could make a qualitative contribution to the education of children.

Consistent with other research, we found that to realize the full potential of any instructional innovation, a strong professional community was important. In the best of all possible worlds, a powerful organizational culture blended with a rich library collection, collaboration with the librarian, and flexible scheduling to produce better tasks for students. In this scenario, culture and structure produced new roles and responsibilities. Librarians saw themselves as teachers and teachers opened their practice to scrutiny by colleagues, including the librarian. Questions were entertained about the adequacy of present practices. When staff engaged in constructive dialogue about their school's educational goals and practices, instruction improved.

Our data supported what other studies have found: that the task of creating a culture and structure in support of professional community is likely to prove difficult. An activity such as collaboration between the librarian and teachers must be more than a formal obligation; it must become a valued component of a school's professional culture. Collaboration may well fail to produce better instruction unless staff believe that an essential part of this activity is a continuing dialogue over ideas about what and how to teach. The school's professional community must include the belief that such dialogue will make teachers and the school stronger; that building a strong professional community is an obligation they need to fulfill to produce the best possible schooling for children.

The task of building a school-wide professional community requires even more than serious conversations among staff. Also required is a public, especially parents, who believe that the kind of education students need is characterized by construction of knowledge through disciplined inquiry. Staff must convey to parents and the public the belief that it is important for students to learn the basics: to spell correctly, to memorize the multiplication table, to use nouns and verbs correctly, to know that Lincoln was President during the Civil War. Then parents and their children must be convinced that it is important to be able to use these basics in thinking and communicating in complex ways.

If educators and parents believe that the central goal of public education is helping students become problem solvers and critical thinkers who can construct knowledge through disciplined inquiry, then the job of teaching will indeed become easier. Efficiency and effectiveness result when the professional and general cultures overlap significantly. Overlap means that everyone, including students, agrees about what schooling should accomplish. Without overlap, confusion and contention result as people push and pull in different directions.

Maintaining a strong professional community is difficult. Some schools are plagued with a high turnover of staff, making it hard to establish and maintain strong professional ties among people. Turnover among principals can be especially detrimental to professional community because of changed agendas and relationships in response to new leadership. Finding a starting point for schools suffering from low levels of community presents another major difficulty. If the level of trust is low among teachers and/or administrators, how can this be remedied? If there is little consensus among staff on the need for changes such as collaboration and de-privatized practice, what can be done to convince them otherwise? Does a school start with organizational restructuring under the assumption that the culture will be modified as people increasingly make use of the new opportunities for dialogue and collaboration? Or is it necessary to first build trust among staff before making structural changes? These are some of the practical questions raised by our findings about the importance of professional community to improving instruction through Library Power.

References

The Fund. (1997, Winter). *Focus: Library Power*. New York: DeWitt Wallace–Reader's Digest Fund.

Newmann, F. M., & Associates (1996). *Authentic achievement: Restructuring schools for intellectual quality*. San Francisco: Jossey-Bass.

Newmann, F. M., & Wehlage, G. G. (1995). *Successful school restructuring: A report to the public and educators*. Madison, WI: Wisconsin Center for Education Research.

Newmann, F. M., Secada, W. G., & Wehlage, G. G. (1995). *A guide to authentic instruction and assessment: Vision, standards and scoring*. Madison, WI: Wisconsin Center for Education Research.

Public Education Network. (1997, Summer). *National Library Power Newsletter, 5* (2).

7 LIBRARY POWER MEETS SCHOOL REFORM

Gary Wehlage

Introduction

Library Power was initially conceived in 1988 as a basic school improvement program. Its intent was clear: to provide selected public schools with modern library collections and professional librarians, two resources that were, and still are, absent from many elementary and middle schools. By 1996, approximately 700 elementary and middle schools in 19 communities had received about $40 million from the DeWitt Wallace–Reader's Digest Fund. Library Power grants provided not only for new books but also for staff development in the Library Power schools to incorporate library resources into the core of their curriculum and instruction. In some communities Library Power remained primarily a school improvement initiative that provided new resources to under-funded schools, but in others it was seen as a way to leverage a broad school reform agenda.

This chapter describes the relationship that developed between Library Power and other school reform initiatives. Three schools were chosen for in-depth study based on preliminary evidence of their success in implementing Library Power and the independent presence of a clearly identifiable, comprehensive school reform program. Studying this relationship was seen as important because Library Power provided its own dimension of reform. To what extent were such initiatives compatible or competing?

Definitions

Before proceeding with the analysis of this chapter, some terms associated with "school reform" require definition and explanation. Terms often associated with reform are *restructuring, change,* and *improvement.* None of these words is used consistently either in the research literature or in the everyday language of practicing educators. In general, however, *restructuring* refers to organizational changes affecting time (for example, the length of class periods), size (for example, the number of students and staff), and role relationships (for example, who makes decisions about teaching responsibilities and use of resources). Restructuring suggests comprehensive, even radical changes. Among the changes suggested by restructuring advocates are shared decision making, multi-age grouping, and teachers in teams with common planning time. Some of the national leaders in such restructuring are James Comer's School Development project (originating at Yale University), Theodore Sizer's Coalition of Essential Schools (originating at Brown University), and Henry Levin's Accelerated Schools project (originating at Stanford University). These initiatives are seen as compatible with Library Power, which called for its own restructuring with flexible scheduling (reorganizing time) and promoting collaboration (new role relationships).

Apart from altering organizational features, questions of *change* are often focused on teachers and teaching. Changes in teachers' beliefs about goals and objectives, instructional practices, use of new materials, and content and resources in instruction are frequently of great interest to reformers. Many of the national restructuring initiatives seek to strengthen teaching and learning on a school-wide basis with new approaches to curriculum. Library Power also is designed to promote new teaching practices through the new structures and the availability of richer, modern library resources. By implication, Library Power also suggests that teachers should act on the value of having students learn to inquire and develop complex skills and knowledge associated with what the popular literature refers to as an "information-based society."

Finally, reform can also be viewed from the perspective of *improvement* in student learning. Here the focus is on students' success in reaching higher levels of achievement or in being able to produce new kinds of performances that demonstrate complex kinds of thinking and knowledge. Taken as a whole, the picture of teaching and learning seems consistent with both the goals of Library Power and a number of major reform initiatives now in place in some of our nation's schools.

Other Reform Efforts in Schools

To what extent were the 700 Library Power schools also engaged in some other reform effort? On the one hand, it appears that most claimed to have some initiative in place that educators considered reform. A canvass of Library Power sites, conducted by the American Library Association, found Library Power schools listing the following discrete programs as reforms: Reading Recovery; Head Start; special education inclusion; self-esteem development; and interventions targeting violence, drug abuse, and dropout prevention. While such programs may be important components of a good school, they lack the characteristics of fundamental change for teachers and students described above. Moreover, while some may be compatible with Library Power (such as Reading Recovery), others (such as drug abuse prevention) seem very marginal to the intent of Library Power. Other reforms listed by a number of schools included Chapter 1 status, having a school improvement plan, membership in a professional development organization, being a magnet school, and having a grant from a foundation. Such school-wide efforts appeared to focus mainly on infusing new resources into the school, but it was not clear that these programs necessarily required organizational restructuring, fundamental change in teaching and learning, or more ambitious outcomes for students.

Relatively rare were reports from Library Power schools that they had implemented broad initiatives that sought to alter the process and outcomes of schooling fundamentally. Only about 10% of the Library Power schools reported to ALA that they had implemented comprehensive departures from conventional practice affecting all students and staff. This chapter reports on the relationship that developed between Library Power and restructuring and reform initiatives in three of the latter schools. We wanted to discover whether there was mutual support for change. We were particularly concerned about whether such a mixture of reforms helped to improve the intellectual quality of student learning.

Focus of the Study

To address such questions, an elementary school, a middle school, and a K–8 school were studied by experienced field researchers for two weeks during the fall and spring of the 1995–96 school year. Researchers made a follow-up visit to these same schools during 1996–97 to assess the validity of earlier findings and the extent to which additional changes had occurred. Researchers spent considerable time in their schools' respective libraries observing students and teachers as they used the new resources. Classrooms were also visited and in-depth interviews were conducted to understand how Library Power was viewed by teachers, administrators, and the librarian. Researchers also learned about each school's other reform efforts intended to improve teaching and learning. Reports detailed how school reform and Library Power worked together, or did not.

Part of the study focused on the intellectual quality of teaching and learning associated with the use of the library. Observers made judgments about the intellectual demands of teachers' assignments and the resulting quality of student work. Such judgments were based on standards developed at the Center on Organization and Restructuring of Schools (CORS) at the University of Wisconsin–Madison as reported in Newmann, Secada, & Wehlage (1995). These standards are particularly appropriate for research on Library Power schools because they were developed to conduct research on the impact of school restructuring on student achievement. As reported in Newmann & Wehlage (1995), schools characterized by a focus on intellectual quality produced higher levels of "authentic achievement" by all groups of students. These standards of intellectual quality can be applied to any grade level and any core school subject. The researchers in the Library Power schools had been trained to use the standards and had recently employed them in conducting research for CORS.

A second major theme of the evaluation examines the professional community in the selected schools. Research conducted by CORS found that the existence of a strong professional community was a key variable in successful school restructuring (Newmann & Wehlage, 1995; Newmann & Associates, 1996). Such schools featured staff that had developed consensus about the meaning and importance of student achievement characterized by high intellectual quality. These schools had developed norms and practices of collaboration among staff that promoted high-quality achievement by students. As indicated above, the CORS program of research had prepared observers of Library Power schools to make judgments about the strength of professional community.

Reform in Three Schools

The three schools chosen were Martin Luther King school, Benjamin Hooks Middle School, and Daniel Boone Elementary. (Note: To preserve anonymity, the school names have been changed.)

Martin Luther King school served 450 students in kindergarten through eighth-grade. The school, located in a medium-sized city, opened in 1990 as a magnet featuring the Paideia approach to education. As a school of choice that was part of a desegregation plan, it served a diverse population: 55% white and 42% African American, with about 12% of the enrollment on free or reduced-fee lunch. In addition to being a magnet, the school also featured site-based decision making that allowed the principal considerable discretion in hiring. This authority was important because it permitted her to assemble a staff that was, for the most part, committed to the school's Paideia program and to Library Power.

The Paideia program, originated by Mortimer Adler at the University of Chicago, was designed to feature a common core curriculum with three traditional goals: acquisition of knowledge, development of intellectual skills, and an understanding of key ideas and values. Instructional strategies to attain these goals included Socratic methods featuring questioning and discussion, as well as coaching and supervised practice of skills by teachers. To develop the core curriculum, teachers focused on themes, integrated subjects, and essential questions. Other innovations at King included alternative assessment tools and exit projects for eighth graders. Organizational restructuring at the school included multi-age grouping in grades 1 and 2, grade-level teaching teams with common planning time, flexible scheduling of library time, and small-group seminars to facilitate dis cussions once a week. The Library Power grant to King provided resources appropriate to serve both the elementary and middle school children.

The second school in the study, Benjamin Hooks Middle School, also was located in a medium-sized city. Originally opened in 1967, the school had moved twice. The school's present site opened in 1988, and at the time of the study served about 320 students in grades 5 through 8. Enrollment was balanced by the district to achieve desegregation; 44% were white, about the same percentage were African American, and the remainder were mainly Hispanic. The school was designated as a magnet featuring three themes: racial, ethnic, and socioeconomic integration; parental involvement; and a curriculum organized around social studies themes developed in conjunction with Bank Street College of Education in New York City.

Hooks's relationship with Bank Street College began some 25 years ago as part of a Head Start program. Bank Street's role in bringing innovation to Hooks was ongoing, and the college had a strong impact on the school; it was called "a Bank Street school." Hooks used the college's multimedia science/social studies integrated curriculum, *The Voyage of the Mimi*. The district contracted with the college to provide two staff members who each spent about one day per month on site; one consulted with teachers in grades 5 and 6, and the other worked with teachers in grades 7 and 8. An important role for these two staff members was to demonstrate teaching strategies and curriculum materials that conformed to the Bank Street philosophy.

Founded in 1916 by the progressive reformer Lucy Sprague Mitchell, Bank Street College devised an early childhood educational model on the principle of "developmental interaction." Ideas about child development were drawn from the psychology of Erikson, Piaget, and Vygotsky, and from John Dewey's views about pedagogy. A central belief at Bank Street is that cognitive development follows a sequence of stages that teachers can recognize and target with their instruction. The interactive part of the theory rests on the belief that cognitive and social development co-evolve through children's explorations of high-interest materials. Hooks's teachers operationalized this philosophy by having students engage in extended group research projects that also included some opportunities for individuals to pursue topics reflecting their own interests. Curriculum almost always culminated in students producing written research reports. For years, teachers at Hooks implemented this instructional strategy by building personal classroom collections of materials, such as *National Geographic* magazines, to facilitate students' research.

Library Power's arrival at Hooks brought rich new resources that had the potential to help staff better implement the Bank Street approach to teaching and learning. The year prior to obtaining Library Power funding, the school had received a small grant from another foundation that allowed them to hire a full-time librarian and begin the processes of collection building and wiring the library for new technology. Our study of Hooks occurred during the first year of Library Power at the school, 1995–96.

The third school for this study, Daniel Boone Elementary, was located in a small but growing suburban community. Boone first opened its doors in 1992 and by the year of the study had 650 students: pre-primary (ages three and four) through grade 5. The student population was 95% white and 4% African American. At the time of our study, Kentucky was the scene of substantial school reform, the consequence of massive state legislation affecting the entire system of public education. The reform legislation, the Kentucky Education Reform Act (KERA), compelled the state to rewrite virtually all of its educational codes.

KERA mandated many changes affecting the organization and governance of schools and the assessment of student achievement. The organizational structure of schools was modified in several ways, including the requirement that each have a governing council comprising parents, teachers, and administrators. In the area of teaching and learning, KERA stipulated that students must be able to build on past learning and apply concepts and principles from academic disciplines to problems they would encounter in life outside of school. Students are to develop skills necessary to become lifelong learners by acquiring new information through a variety of sources.

To support these ambitious learning outcomes, KERA mandated several new forms of assessment of student performance. For example, students were required to assemble portfolios to demonstrate their competence in writing and mathematics. The state developed new student assessment instruments to measure each school's progress in helping students acquire more complex skills and knowledge. "Threshold levels" of student performance were established for each school. Rewards and sanctions were implemented by the state to provide incentives to schools to improve on these measures. It was into this context of comprehensive, state-mandated school reform that Library Power came to Boone Elementary in 1994.

School reform had high visibility in each of the three schools. Library Power was only one of the influences competing for teachers' time and attention. Library Power had an advantage because it was less comprehensive and more focused than some of the reform programs. King and Hooks were guided by explicit theories and practices that represented complex philosophies of education. At Boone, KERA was a mandate that reflected a broad political commitment by the state to improve the quality of public schools.

Given that the three schools were sailing well-defined courses of school reform, how did Library Power fit into the voyage? Could Library Power enhance what was already being attempted? In our research, we were especially concerned to discover whether Library Power could succeed in adding value by providing students with more ambitious curriculum and learning outcomes. We had reason to expect such results from adding Library Power to a school reform, because intellectual quality in student achievement was explicit in the language of the three school reform programs. Three questions guided our study of the relationship between Library Power and school reform and, in the following sections, we explore these issues at each of the schools:

- To what extent did teachers use Library Power resources, implement flexible scheduling, and collaborate with the librarian in ways that enhanced teaching and learning?

- To what extent did Library Power support a school's primary reform, especially in helping teachers promote student learning that was of high intellectual quality?

- To what extent did Library Power serve as a vehicle for building a stronger professional community among staff that increased the organizational capacity of the school to promote further improvements and sustain reform?

Library Use and Collaboration

At all three schools it was clear that teachers and administrators saw Library Power as a valuable, useful tool. Most staff saw that Library Power could support some of their instructional efforts. Some staff also saw Library Power as a support for the more general school reform they had adopted. This mutual support was especially evident at King, where the principal was quick to volunteer that Library Power complemented the school's Paideia vision. She stated that Library Power "fits like a glove" with Paideia. The librarian at King elaborated this view by pointing out that the school was committed to a thematic and conceptual approach to curriculum, teachers used few if any conventional textbooks, and the curriculum was based on teacher-constructed units. The librarian used Library Power funds to build the collection around specific themes or concepts that teachers used. Of the 18 teachers at King, all but 3 or 4 used the library extensively during the year.

Students at King used the library frequently, and about three-quarters of students' observed time in the library involved looking up information in response to their class assignments. The remainder of the time involved some kind of whole group instruction either by a teacher or the librarian. Teachers testified that the new print resources had clearly enhanced their ability to create better units of study, especially interdisciplinary units. They also valued the technology found in the library.

More than at the other two schools in the study, the librarian at King played a leadership role in curriculum development. Teachers and the principal considered the librarian an instructional leader. One example of this leadership was her facilitation of a two-day summer workshop on curriculum mapping for teachers. In curriculum mapping, teachers identify topics by grade level and subject along with resources needed. Following the lead of the librarian, teachers at each grade level developed a chart organized by subject area to guide curriculum development for the school year. For a few teachers, collaboration with the librarian in planning specific lessons became a fairly frequent occurrence. Moreover, aware of what teachers were teaching, the librarian used Library Power funds to buy materials that complemented their curriculum. The Library Power director for the district claimed that the librarian was the person who gave continuity to the curriculum in the school. "There would be no curriculum mapping without her," said the director.

At Hooks, Library Power seemed to fit well with the theory of child development espoused by Bank Street College. In practice, however, the fit proved to be less than perfect. In part, Library Power was new and teachers had not yet figured out exactly how to use it. More important, because no library had existed before, Hooks's teachers had stockpiled their own supply of teaching resources in their rooms. As a consequence, most teachers did not immediately see the new library as critical in building their curriculum. On the other hand, as the school year went by, the librarian began to play an increasingly active role in helping teachers prepare their units, and some teachers began to see the potential of the library. Slowly the librarian was able to increase her involvement with a number of teachers because of her knowledge of the new collection and its possibilities for supplementing and supporting teachers' instructional efforts.

For the most part, teachers at Hooks equated Library Power with the librarian who brought them additional resources. As one teacher said, "She's able to go out and get books based on what we want to do, and that's really broadened our horizon in terms of resources." For this particular teacher, the librarian had researched a unit topic and then assembled resources for students. Similarly, to support the seventh grade's research project on Ancient Egypt, the librarian loaded and indexed three book carts full of materials, including some borrowed from public libraries and a regional library service center. This kind of direct service was highly valued by teachers. It added a dimension to their teaching that was much appreciated. However, although teachers loved it when the librarian pulled together a multitude of materials, it made her a "gopher" rather than a professional collaborating with other professionals.

In the eyes of many teachers at Hooks, Library Power was a wonderful new service provided by the librarian rather than a new resource that teachers and their students could learn to use. Throughout the year at Hooks, the librarian continued to stop into teachers' classrooms to find out what lessons were forthcoming and to provide carts full of materials. But she reported that, except in a few cases, she felt rebuffed by most teachers as a professional colleague because they seemed unwilling to collaborate with her or to learn from her how to use the library's resources. For example, one teacher planned a seven-week unit in which students were to develop their own questions on certain legal issues and then do research to find the answers. The teacher did not consult with the librarian or search the collection in advance to determine its potential to help students address their questions.

However, the librarian at Hooks was not one to give up easily in her quest to work with teachers. She continued to pursue several avenues for joint activity, starting a "Reading to the Outer Limits" program in which teachers helped to select high-interest readings and keep track of the "miles" their classes earned. The librarian also organized an all-school "read-in" and a "Ravenous Readers" club. All of these efforts were well received by the staff and such initiatives helped to give greater exposure to the library and its collection. Gradually over the course of a year some teachers began to see the potential in working more closely with the librarian to use the new and more extensive collection. For example, one teacher worked with the librarian to develop a unit that had students doing research in women's history.

Having pointed out the limited role that Library Power and the librarian initially played at Hooks, it is important to mention that as the year went on, and in the next year, the library was increasingly used by students and some staff. The librarian kept a weekly schedule posted on the door that allowed teachers to sign up on short notice, and usually three to five of the seven periods found teachers and/or students in the library. This flexible approach also allowed for unscheduled use of the facility. No unscheduled period passed without at least some walk-in student traffic to look for recreational reading or pursue some assignment. But such ad hoc use of the library was not always productive from the librarian's point of view. She stated that too often students were sent to the library without clear directions and consequently they engaged in "aimless use of irrelevant books."

The third school in the study, Boone Elementary, was restructuring in response to coincidental mandates: KERA and Library Power. KERA called upon schools to help students achieve six goals:

1. Use basic communication and mathematics skills.

2. Apply basic core concepts from the disciplines.

3. Become self-sufficient citizens.

4. Become responsible members of society.

5. Become problem solvers.

6. Be able to integrate new knowledge with experience.

Through in-service programs, the state and district had provided teachers with some knowledge about how to promote teaching and learning consistent with these goals. Library Power funds were used for staff development to help teachers not only understand Library Power but also see how it could promote Kentucky's reform agenda. The superintendent for Boone's district stated that "KERA and Library Power are symbiotic."

Boone's principal estimated that about one-third of the teachers in his school had become fairly knowledgeable about and committed to the teaching and learning required by KERA. But he also estimated that another third were resisters. And the remaining third of the staff were still ambivalent, taking a wait-and-see attitude in the face of the many changes that teachers were being asked to embrace. Given this division among staff over KERA, Library Power also evoked varying levels of enthusiasm, especially when it was initially implemented. However, by the second year of Library Power, resistance to it had largely disappeared. Still, the use of the library by Boone's teachers ranged widely from not much to considerable. The librarian estimated that all but two or three teachers had availed themselves of at least one opportunity to use the facility in some way. Even among those staff who used it, the skill with which they used the resources ranged considerably. The librarian noted that "some teachers don't have a clear purpose for bringing students into the library, nor do they have a strategy for working with students once they get there." The principal, who was an enthusiastic advocate of Library Power, recognized the problem and attempted to push teachers to use the library better. He reported that when he evaluated a teacher, he always included two important questions: "How much research have you done with your students? And how have you used technology?" Such questions were intended to push staff to use the library.

Even though only a few teachers were heavy users of the library, it was a busy place on most days. During almost every hour some students were there to read, look up materials, or get help from the librarian in writing a report or preparing a speech. From time to time, a teacher would bring in an entire class to work on a project. Teachers, too, used the library for their own research on lessons. Given the steady and fairly heavy usage by some, one wonders what would happen if, in fact, all teachers at Boone had wanted to use the library as extensively.

The librarian at Boone reported that initially some teachers had been reluctant to collaborate with her in developing teaching units; however, by the end of the second year, resistance to collaboration was said to be fading. For other staff, collaboration still reflected some of the same teacher attitude that was found at Hooks: The librarian was an assistant who gathered materials. The Library Power director for the district indicated that while most teachers were seeking help from the librarian, during the first year of our study only six to eight accepted the librarian as a collegial partner in creating curriculum.

A mixed picture emerges from our findings at the three schools. In general, a significant number of teachers saw the library as an important new resource to supplement and strengthen their curriculum. Library Power provided a concrete form of assistance to help teachers address ambitious goals for their students. A wealth of materials could be assembled from the new and expanded collection, often targeting topics already taught at specific grade levels. This service was much appreciated by teachers. All of this concrete, visible help provided teachers with support that exhortations from reformers about improving or changing instruction did not.

At a rhetorical level, each of the schools formally embraced more ambitious learning goals for students. Hooks, using the Bank Street conception of child development; King, using the Paideia philosophy; and Boone, responding to the requirements of KERA, all formally embraced ideas about engaging students in gathering and processing information. For those teachers who wanted to have students engaged in in-depth study, a well-equipped library with a professionally trained librarian was an enormous asset. Some teachers leaped at the opportunity to use new materials and collaborate with the librarian.

However, a few staff found it difficult to see a clear connection between their school's stated goals and the materials available in the library. For these teachers, Library Power meant changing their curriculum from a less didactic and routinized approach to one that was more open-ended and problematic. At the very least, old units would need to be revised in view of the new resources available. Such change is almost never easy, even if Library Power could deliver to teachers new and better materials and more engaging learning opportunities for their students. Working in collaboration with the librarian demanded another kind of change that was even more difficult for some teachers, who were reluctant to embrace Library Power if it required collaboration with the librarian. Collaboration risked exposing one's ideas and practices to questions and implicit criticism. For some, the telling factor was that collaboration with the librarian took more precious time from an already full schedule.

The Issue of Intellectual Quality

The second evaluation question addressed the extent to which Library Power supported reforms that promoted high-quality teaching and learning. To define "high quality," we turn to the criteria developed at the Center on Organization and Restructuring of Schools (CORS) at the University of Wisconsin (Newmann & Wehlage, 1995; Newmann, Secada, & Wehlage, 1995; Newmann & Associates, 1996). A central question for CORS was the extent to which school restructuring improved the achievement and performance of students. CORS developed 14 standards to judge the intellectual quality of teachers' classroom instruction, including both assessment tasks and students' academic performance. The 14 standards were developed from three central criteria that define "authentic achievement" for students. Such achievement requires the following: 1) Students construct rather than merely reproduce knowledge; 2) Students engage in disciplined inquiry in addressing problems; and 3) A student's achievement has some personal, aesthetic, or utilitarian value beyond merely demonstrating to the teacher that the student has learned something. (Appendix G lists the 14 standards developed at CORS.)

The first criterion, construction of knowledge, reflects a belief that learning requires a student to engage in the process of making meaning from facts and other information. Students make meaning by analyzing, synthesizing, generalizing, and drawing conclusions from information. In short, they must do what adults do when they construct knowledge. When a student sees connections, similarities, and differences among phenomena, he or she is engaged in meaning making. Construction of meaning also occurs when a student explores alternatives and explains relationships. In general, schools have been criticized because too little construction of knowledge occurs; far too much time is spent on rote drills and covering vast quantities of information without giving students a chance to become producers of knowledge. Too often children are asked only to be reproducers of what others have discovered.

To engage students in the construction of knowledge, teachers' tasks, assignments, and projects should require the manipulation of information to address an issue, question, problem, or topic. Of course, students cannot be expected to construct knowledge all the time in school, but as a whole their work should reflect this goal. In our study of Library Power schools, observers looked at instruction and the tasks that were assigned to students and made judgments about the extent to which they required the construction of knowledge.

Disciplined inquiry, the second criterion, reflects the need for students to pursue knowledge in a rigorous manner. Rigor is possible if students have a prior knowledge base of facts, concepts, theories, algorithms, and skills that they can use. Disciplined inquiry requires that students use their prior knowledge base to strive for an in-depth understanding of a problem, issue, or topic. Deep understanding increases the chance that students can see the complexity of knowledge, and it allows them to test relationships among facts and ideas. Finally, disciplined inquiry requires that students provide elaborated communication to express findings, interpretations, conclusions, and ideas. The language of communication can be verbal, symbolic, or visual. While the criterion of disciplined inquiry may seem too demanding for young children, it can be applied if age and development are considered as well.

The third criterion for authentic achievement requires that children's work have a purpose or value other than proving competence to the teacher. This criterion rests on two ideas. First, value is established to the extent a student's performance responds to a problem connected to the world; that is, knowledge and skills are used to address some condition that the student understands as a real problem. Second, a student's work or performance has value to the extent it is addressed to an audience. Common examples of student performances for an audience are plays, concerts, and sports events. Much rarer are *authentic academic* performances in which children apply knowledge and skills for audiences at science and history fairs; at museums; and in newspapers, books, and plays.

Constructing knowledge through disciplined inquiry that has value beyond the classroom conveys a picture of students and teachers engaged in activities different from many of those found in schools. For example, conventionally much school work finds the teacher transmitting knowledge in the form of information and skills to students. Typically students are asked to reproduce this knowledge at some later time. Acquisition of knowledge is stressed over learning to use it to address real world situations. Further, many of the cognitive tasks in school require students to show only a superficial awareness of unrelated topics. Finally, much of the communication in schools is truncated and fragmented. Students circle correct answers or offer short phrases. Extended writing, to the extent it is required, is often limited to language arts classes and not required elsewhere.

King School

The King school had a fairly clear vision of student learning based on the Paideia model that entailed a commitment to authentic achievement. Paideia asks students to explore important, persisting questions in some depth through research and discussion. Nevertheless, during our initial visits to the school, observations found that to a large extent the work students were asked to do reflected lower levels of intellectual challenge as measured by the CORS standards. Twenty-two observations of student groups produced the following judgment: Much of the work involved simple fact-finding. Students were primarily asked to find facts by searching encyclopedias or similar sources. This sort of retrieval work is illustrated by the following examples:

> Fifth-grade students used library resources to complete a worksheet on an American colony. The worksheet asked for the date the colony was founded, who founded it, the origin of its name, the reason it was founded, and its major towns and products.

> As part of a study of their state's history, fourth graders were told they would have to know three things about Indians, explorers, and early settlements in the state. The librarian told them where they might find such information, and she read subheadings from the *World Book*.

Sixth graders, in preparation for a field trip to Savannah, Georgia, were given a study guide with the following questions: When was the area settled? By whom? What is the major industry of the area? What is the climate? What is the elevation of Tybee Island and Savannah?

Fourth graders were beginning a unit on electricity. They were told to use three sources from the library to write a one-page summary of what they learned about electricity. One student paper reported the following: "Electricity is energy. You can make electricity out of water. This kind of electricity is called hydro-electricity. . . . Another thing that electricity can make is an electromagnet. Something an electromagnet is used for is to make a door bell."

These examples suggest that students were not primarily engaged in the construction of knowledge using disciplined inquiry. Rather, they were reproducing information by copying material from standard sources. Moreover, the questions were pre-defined by teachers and no problem or issue was presented that might challenge students to investigate and communicate in some depth. The main "problem" was to meet the teacher's requirement of a written report. One word or short answers seemed to suffice, and in some instances it appeared that students got the "right" answer without really understanding what they had written, as in the case of the student who said that "you make electricity out of water."

Having noted the limited use that was often made of the library in the King school, it should be pointed out that a number of more authentic achievement opportunities were also observed. For example, eighth graders were required to complete an "exit" project. Each student was to create a magazine that included 12 articles, with at least one article reflecting each of several subject matter perspectives: language arts, math, social studies, science, music, art, and a foreign language. Also required in the magazine were an interview, a biographical sketch, an editorial, two visuals, and an article featuring a "critique."

This kind of exit project clearly had the potential to be intellectually challenging for students because it required them to construct knowledge using disciplined inquiry. Copying information directly from sources was minimized because the teacher insisted that the magazine articles be written in their own words. However, the observer also noted that because the task required 12 articles using a number of disciplines, most students did not go into depth in their inquiry. What was essentially an authentic task tended to encourage superficial coverage of many topics.

An important structure of a Paideia school is the weekly seminar that is intended to allow students to explore important questions in depth. Often, by their own admission, teachers did not use the seminar as intended. For example, for several weeks students were engaged in career explorations featuring guest speakers, library research, and reports on selected careers. As one person at the school commented, Paideia had been "dumbed down."

Recognizing that Paideia and Library Power could be more effective, the principal urged teachers to use the intellectually rigorous standards of Paideia to build curriculum and assessment "from the bottom up." It was believed that this process should begin by having staff pursue authentic assessment and critical thinking because the two needed to be joined. It was argued that ideally "assessment drives the rest of what you're doing." The hope was that if assessment tasks required students to construct knowledge and engage in disciplined inquiry, curriculum and instruction using the resources of the library would become central to these tasks.

Examples of activities at King that reflected some of the standards for constructing knowledge and disciplined inquiry include the following:

Ten eighth graders worked collaboratively to develop a "newscast" presentation about Valley Forge during the Revolutionary War. Students were to use their own words to report accounts of historical events.

The librarian led a discussion of "Brer Rabbit" stories with primary grade children. The children were challenged to consider how the stories related to conditions on plantations and the hopes of slaves.

A foreign language teacher had students do research on the issue of Quebec's possible secession from Canada. Students then debated the issue, with the librarian serving as judge for the debate.

One King staff member noted that several teachers were developing very thoughtful instructional units in collaboration with the librarian. It was observed that the intellectual challenge of a number of assignment tasks was high. For example, during the second year of the evaluation, teachers were asking fourth graders to demonstrate their understanding of electricity by designing an "operational item" and writing an "owner's manual" that explained how the item worked.

Authentic assessment was seen as central to the Paideia philosophy. Accordingly, work groups discussed the content of essential questions, benchmarks, and rubrics. Using these tools in ways that encouraged intellectual quality in student achievement sometimes proved difficult. Initially rubrics tended to emphasize procedural knowledge, for example, students demonstrated mastery of the process of converting metric to English system measurements. By the next year, however, outcomes suggested more challenging tasks for students. For example, students were to demonstrate their understanding of ratio and proportion by using accurate equations in comparing real-life dimensions and scale dimensions. Primary students gathered information and wrote a brochure explaining living conditions in polar communities; that is, they described daily life and cultural and social activities related to the environment. Students wrote a "tourism brochure" describing their findings. The brochures and videotapes of student presentations were then sent to the Alaska Bureau of Tourism. The number of such examples increased over the previous year and suggested that authentic achievement was increasingly a feature of learning at King.

Many of the staff recognized the need to clarify and operationalize the vision of intellectual quality found in Paideia. One indicator of this awareness was that about 40% of the staff were involved in two study groups that met once a month to explore authentic assessment of student learning. Three topics had been identified by the groups: writing essential questions to guide assessment, establishing benchmarks to guide evaluation of student portfolios, and designing rubrics for the staff to use in scoring these portfolios. The results from the three study groups during the first year of the evaluation sometimes promoted intellectual quality and sometimes did not. Several outcomes focused on low-level thinking and procedures such as demonstrating mastery over the process of converting measurement from the metric system into the English system. For the eighth-grade exit project, only one of the six standards indicated a cognitive challenge by requiring multiple sources of evidence and some demonstration of original thinking. By the second year of the evaluation, however, a number of higher-quality tasks had been developed.

The Library Power director for the district, the principal, and the librarian all testified that they were encouraged that King was headed in the right direction. A new expanded collection, a commitment to Paideia, and an increased understanding of authentic assessment and achievement were moving the school gradually, if unevenly, toward a more intellectually challenging approach to teaching and learning.

Hooks School

At Hooks, where Bank Street's model of interactive development provided the framework for teaching and learning, the level and the amount of intellectually challenging work for students was somewhat less than at King. Much "active" student learning was observed, but its presence did not mean that students were intellectually challenged or that their work was of high quality. Typically, students worked in groups, made choices about what to study, and were generally free to move about and interact with one another. Students used the library frequently to do what the teachers called "research." While teachers talked frequently about their intent to have students engage in research, the process was observed to be rather formulated. Typically, after choosing a topic, students retrieved information (often from standard reference books), sorted it according to the teacher's directions, and almost always produced a written report. Teachers assessed these reports by the following standards: amount of information, quality of organization, and quality of expression. Student reports were usually straightforward presentations that rarely inquired into complex ideas or problems. Some projects included activities other than factual reporting. For example, an eighth-grade class integrated art and geography, with one group painting a large map of North America that depicted important natural resources. Another group made a clay topographical model of the same region. However, these products were basically reproductions of what students found in standard reference books.

Allowing student choice was an important element in the Bank Street approach to promoting child development. Students were encouraged to define their own topics and tasks based on "interest," but this meant that challenging, complex ideas were often not encountered. Moreover, allowing individuals to follow their interests is often at odds with teachers pursuing goals for all students. The librarian, recognizing this problem at Hooks, advocated that teachers establish a "developmental continuum" which would guide all student learning. Such a continuum would frame a common set of expectations for all students to achieve between grades 5 and 8. This suggestion was not popular with a number of teachers because it suggested that they needed to specify in greater detail what students were to learn. Resistance to such specification surfaced because it interfered with allowing the pursuit of students' spontaneous interests.

Nevertheless, the belief that student reports should be assessed using a common set of "rubrics" was generally accepted at the school. Developing a clear set of standards proved difficult, as it did in other schools. Typically rubrics at Hooks assigned a point value for each element of a report. For example, the seventh-grade team used the following rubrics to assess the final report on Egypt:

> The research is complete and adequate.
>
> The student used an adequate number of sources.
>
> The information is adequate.
>
> The report is interesting and creative.
>
> The paper communicates well.
>
> The thesis statement is well supported.

Students could earn extra points by using graphs, charts, and visuals. The rubrics were generally vague in terms of defining criteria or scales to indicate why a score given to a paper on any particular standard might be high or low. Still, the fact that teachers had agreed to public criteria for assessment indicated that they were trying to help students think about what made a better or poorer quality report.

Moving toward more explicit instructional goals was opposed partly because a number of teachers believed that "exposure" was an important instructional goal; that is, they wanted to expose children to a topic rather than expect any particular learning outcomes. Given such a goal, the new library was seen as a boon because children could be exposed to a wider array of topics than before. The Bank Street model seemed to encourage this exploratory view of learning. Teachers talked about "branching off" from main topics when student interest was piqued by something. Lacking a clear vision of intellectual achievement, however, some teachers tended not to be concerned about what such learning should enable students to do. A 10-year veteran said that she adjusted her pace and emphasis according to how the children reacted based on their interests. Student engagement was usually found to be high in most activities in her classes, but the tasks were also judged to require low levels of intellectual work. Most students were busily occupied, but the tasks typically asked them to take notes from a text, fill in the blanks on a data-gathering form provided by the teacher, or respond to questions that could be answered with one word or a short phrase. Eventually these disparate pieces of information were assembled by students working in groups to create a written report, a skit, or a display.

One major curriculum unit that involved extensive use of library materials focused on the Civil War. The librarian said she collected more than 100 books to support this particular unit. The teacher presented her students with a number of questions and reading assignments. For example, questions asked for the two sides in the war, how many people died, and why the war occurred. Text assignments specified readings about the Kansas-Nebraska Act, Missouri Compromise, Dred Scott, and Harper's Ferry. Students were given the task of writing a "front page report" that included pictures, captions, and headlines. They had to construct a timeline of major battles and graph casualties. Each student wrote a poem, and they collectively made a quilt patterned after those made by abolitionists to identify safe houses on the Underground Railroad.

The unit was intended to expose students to major facts and ideas about the Civil War. Students identified a number of key facts; for example, the South was called the Confederacy and Robert E. Lee was its most distinguished general. It is likely that students primarily became more practiced in skills related to basic information retrieval. Some construction of knowledge may have occurred when students assembled information into front page reports about the war, but the majority of their work was dominated by intellectually low-level tasks.

The librarian at Hooks recognized the limitations of this type of research project. She made numerous efforts to nudge teachers to try lessons that could challenge students' thinking more, but her efforts produced only modest change. In the spring she tried a different approach; she wrote a proposal and received funding for a local university-teacher curriculum development institute. The focus was on using primary sources to understand the history and government of the local region. Teachers would be taught how students could use sources such as government databases and recorded oral history. For example, students could study immigration through statistics, and they could encounter the actual words of immigrants. The curriculum using such data was to be developed over the summer and implemented the following year with the intent, according to the librarian, of promoting more "authentic teaching and learning."

In summary, despite the rather progressive philosophy of education espoused by Bank Street College, the model did not offer a clear conception of high-quality student learning. Given the precepts of the model, teachers had not been encouraged to develop a conception of intellectual quality to guide student achievement. Instead, the model tended to promote a relatively superficial approach to research that failed to demand high-quality intellectual work. Even when teachers made use of the new library resources, their goals and instructional practices remained much the same as before. The new library and a thoughtful librarian did not stimulate much discussion of how the intellectual level of learning might be enhanced. Most teachers saw no reason to make substantial changes in what they did; what they were already doing seemed to be working well. On a hopeful note, the librarian had begun to create some dissonance in the thinking of a few staff members, and in the long run this may produce more reflection by teachers and eventually move them to offer more intellectually rigorous learning experiences.

Boone School

At Boone, where KERA mandated a framework of educational goals, the level of intellectual challenge for students was mixed. As noted earlier, use of the library was fairly high. Typically students were engaged primarily in fact-finding expeditions. For example, a unit on the Mayan, Incan, and Aztec cultures focused on answering factual questions about family life, clothing, and customs of these people. Encyclopedias were the main source for many students. Even obvious tasks, such as comparing the three cultures to identify similarities and differences among them, were not part of the assignment. Teachers emphasized activities that were interesting and engaging for students, such as "tall-tale heroes" and storytelling. The latter was a major emphasis at the school and involved the librarian in helping to select stories and then coaching students to be good storytellers. Some children became involved in a storytelling club and presented their tales to audiences in and outside the school. Such activities were engaging but fell short of challenging students to use their minds well, at least as defined by the higher levels of our standards.

A few teachers were found to offer intellectually challenging tasks. A unit on Spanish, French, and English explorers of North America presented students with questions beyond fact-finding, such as: "What was and is today the influence of the explorers? How did the coming of the explorers change Indian cultures?" Depending on the sources, these questions may have required students to think about the consequences of events. They may have synthesized information from several sources into their own conclusions. Other projects that appeared to challenge students to construct knowledge based on disciplined inquiry included a science fair and a play written by students based on their understanding of Southwest Indians and their desert environment. Overall, the quantity of writing required of students at Boone was substantial, and in some cases its quality was judged to be very high.

Conclusions

Looking at all three schools, Library Power can be seen as a valuable resource ready to support more challenging and ambitious learning, if such learning is understood by teachers as the goal of school reform. What we found was that those teachers already aiming at such learning responded almost immediately by tapping the new resources and expertise offered by the librarian. Students of these teachers were provided with opportunities to construct knowledge and engage in disciplined inquiry. But other teachers who were not already trying to help students to think and write in complex ways were not prepared to immediately pursue a more challenging curriculum. At least initially, these teachers used the library to continue the kind of teaching and learning with which they were comfortable.

Building Professional Community

Why are some schools more successful than others in making effective use of innovations such as Library Power to increase the intellectual quality of student performance and achievement? To a large extent, the answer appears to lie in the strength of a school's organizational capacity (Newmann & Wehlage, 1995). A number of factors make up organizational capacity, including a school's technical facilities and its human resources, but the most important is the strength of professional community among a staff. To create such a community, staff must establish a clear vision of teaching and learning for the school. They must share norms and values such as accepting collective responsibility for helping all children achieve academic success. Finally, a professional community is also a learning community in which teachers help one another to better understand and master the more complex dimensions of teaching. In our study, we looked for evidence that Library Power helped a staff to build professional community.

We have already discussed the extent to which collaboration occurred between the librarian and teachers. Collaboration in the technical sense of meeting to jointly plan curriculum is an important element in building a professional community, but face-to-face meetings are not sufficient. Professional community is essentially a cultural construct requiring a community of shared beliefs and expectations. Collaboration between teachers and the librarian can help to promote such a culture if it is part of a larger set of relations that includes interdependent work structures, reflective dialogue, commitment to a collective responsibility for student success, and shared beliefs that teachers can make a difference in students' success (MacMullen, 1996; Newmann & Wehlage, 1995). Teachers need to participate in continuing discussions in their teams and departments to establish trust and provide constructive criticism. Dialogue about the intellectual quality of teachers' tasks and student work is essential if teachers are to establish common goals for teaching and learning. Discussions by teams, grade levels, and the librarian can establish trust that allows the participants to give and accept constructive criticism. Dialogue involving issues of intellectual quality are necessary if the school is to move toward a more challenging curriculum that reflects intellectual quality. Such dialogue requires teachers to be open to reconsidering their assumptions and practices. In our study we looked for evidence that Library Power had begun to play a role in creating conversations about educational purpose. We found that collaboration as defined by Library Power was a main vehicle for promoting professional conversations in all three schools.

At King, the librarian met with teachers to plan lessons, make selections for the collection, and schedule use of the library. She was involved with teachers in at least 12 major curriculum units during the school year. She estimated that a typical week involved four to eight meetings with teachers. The amount and frequency of librarian-teacher contact varied across the entire staff; according to the librarian's log, she met almost daily with one teacher, but much less frequently with a few others. But more important than the amount of contact was the quality of ideas that emerged from collaborative sessions. The librarian noted the following: "P., for example, comes in having done some planning already on topics, themes, concepts for a unit and we go from there. But with others, planning takes so long, or doesn't go anywhere because they look to me for those ideas when that's their responsibility." One of the teachers agreed that preparation is important to productive collaboration. She said, "It's up to the teachers and the team to take the initiative, to take advantage of the opportunity to plan with [the librarian]." Some teachers came to a planning session with only vague notions about learning objectives and activities. In such cases, the potential of collaboration was stunted. For example, the librarian met with two teachers who were scheduling a unit on Native Americans. Most of the planning time was consumed figuring out how to help students prepare for a debate in which they were to argue the relative merits of being a Cherokee or Iroquois. The purpose of the unit, expected student outcomes, and the value of the debate itself could not be addressed given time constraints.

In contrast, another teacher had thought carefully about collaborative planning. She and the librarian had engaged in numerous successful planning sessions, and they agreed that given their experiences they could offer a presentation on unit planning for the faculty of another Library Power school. The presentation emphasized ways to get the most out of a collaborative session, the role of essential questions in bringing focus and purpose to a unit, and the best ways to utilize library resources in carrying out a unit. To the extent that this kind of shared understanding produces a school culture, a powerful force for teaching and learning can be established.

Another way in which Library Power contributed to building professional community was through mini-grants to teachers. Five grants totaling $4,200 funded projects that involved 18 staff members and the librarian. The result was to increase dialogue among staff as teachers collaborated in designing curriculum. Library Power money was also used to support faculty study groups: two on assessment and one each on multi-age grouping, multiple intelligences, and writing across the curriculum. Such work by faculty sometimes (certainly not always) produced serious dialogue about significant educational issues. Several of these groups succeeded in establishing enough agreement to develop some assessment standards and create new curriculum.

The emerging professional culture at King was built partly on collaboration and flexible scheduling found in Library Power and partly on the vision of teaching and learning found in Paideia. Central tenets of Paideia, such as the importance of essential questions, gave guidance to the structure and process offered by Library Power. The culture at King was building on a commitment among the faculty to use Library Power structures and the habits they engendered to enhance the quality of teaching and learning. Library Power mechanisms created a norm of collective work and decision making. Paideia and Library Power combined to help staff see the need to jointly plan new curricula that were intellectually more challenging for students. To achieve this goal, teachers saw the need to develop new assessment strategies in response to new student outcomes, write grant proposals consistent with these new expectations, and advise the principal about hiring new staff who could support the direction in which the school was heading. These kinds of tasks had increasingly become the shared vision and responsibility of the staff. The principal credited such activities, along with collaboration between the librarian and teachers, with drawing staff into a school-wide conversation. Still, as promising as these indicators were, it would be an exaggeration to say that a strong professional community existed.

At Hooks, magnet status and a long history of association with Bank Street College contributed to a fairly well-developed sense of school mission. However, it was observed that two separate communities divided the school by grade-level teams. Fifth/sixth grade teams had by far the strongest sense of community because teachers shared students and planned around a common curriculum, Bank Street's *The Voyage of the Mimi*. As a result, they frequently talked to one another and shared ideas about teaching. Seventh/eighth grade teachers, on the other hand, exchanged students for some subjects only. No common curriculum existed; instead, teachers developed their own units, with one or two becoming entrepreneurial about their curriculum. Consequently the upper grade teachers were more independent and communicated with each other less often; the result was somewhat less collegiality among these staff members. Further, the organizational difference between the two sets of grades produced a degree of isolation between them that impeded dialogue and the development of deep, school-wide professional community. For example, the split between the two sets of teams was reinforced by an annual migration of white students to private schools after grade 6. This phenomenon was the focus of much discussion at one faculty meeting. It was clear that a difference of views held by the two sets of teachers was based partly on the claim that parents of seventh and eighth graders wanted a more subject-centered curriculum that would prepare students for high school. Teachers in the earlier grades could continue with their interdisciplinary thematic approach to curriculum, which seemed successful with younger students.

Despite its emphasis on collaboration, Library Power had limited impact on professional community at Hooks given the organizational constraints that existed. Well-established patterns of relationships among the staff did not mesh particularly well with the assumptions of Library Power. A few teachers began to work more closely with the librarian but, by the second year of our study, the seventh grade as a whole made collaboration with her less of a priority. After two years the librarian was still seen by many staff members primarily as someone who could fetch carts of books and materials for them. Some inroads on this view were made as the librarian began offering her own staff development opportunities. For example, she offered the "Gaining the Online Edge" workshop, which was developed by *Technology and Learning* magazine. Curriculum units (for example, on solar energy) were presented to supplement the *Voyage of the Mimi* units. Eight teachers eventually took the "Edge" workshop, but in the eyes of most teachers the librarian remained something less than a collegial partner capable of helping staff members consider different goals and instructional processes. The staff's commitment to Bank Street was strong, and teachers tended to see Library Power as useful to the extent that it supported what had become ingrained practice. Bank Street's conception of teaching and learning was clear in the minds of teachers; Library Power was seen as subservient to this vision. Teachers also had the benefit of a staff member from Bank Street College who came to the school regularly to help in planning curriculum. To some extent this person competed with the librarian for influence in the school. Furthermore, because Library Power did not create dissonance or prompt challenges to the conventional wisdom of the school, the professional community that existed at Hooks did not include enough intellectual openness or doubt to rethink many of the practices that had become conventional wisdom. Instead, Library Power worked on the margins of the teachers' belief system.

The character of professional community at Boone falls somewhere between what was found at King and Hooks. Like Hooks, Boone lacked a strong school-wide sense of professional community, at least partly because it was a relatively new school; staff simply did not know each other well. Moreover, the demands made by KERA created tension among the staff as they struggled to respond. For example, fourth-grade teachers were under stress because their children were the first to be assessed by the state. The librarian at Boone tried to make Library Power a vehicle for bringing people together. For example, Library Power sponsored two "roundtables" at which teachers could voice their views and concerns about life at Boone. At these discussions, teachers shared their concerns about implementing new techniques such as portfolios and helping children to become problem solvers as mandated by KERA.

Near the end of the school year, Boone's teachers began to report that collaboration among staff had contributed to greater collegiality. Collective responsibility was emerging. One teacher reported that Library Power helped "us have a sense that all the children are *ours*, not just *my* class and *your* class. As we collaborate we share ideas that spark a synergy. We feed off each other. I feel Library Power has drawn many of our teachers together." More teachers came to see the library and the librarian as resources that supported the school's efforts to meet the demands of KERA. Teaching a more ambitious curriculum and obtaining higher student achievement were possible if all staff pulled together. While the vision of what they were trying to accomplish needed a lot of sharpening, it appeared that the staff were on the right track to building professional community.

In summary, Library Power succeeded unevenly in promoting a greater degree of professional community in each of the schools. Without question, the librarian played an important role in all three schools. At Hooks, a central problem was an already strong commitment to the Bank Street model; the staff had already developed a set of norms around a vision that guided practice. At Boone, a growing confidence in the librarian suggested that Library Power and KERA might yet contribute to building a common professional community around challenging intellectual work for students. King had developed the strongest professional community. The principal and the librarian succeeded in articulating a clear vision of how Library Power meshed with Paideia. Such leadership and vision allowed and encouraged teachers to explore ways of using Library Power resources to promote the school's mission.

Conclusion

What happened when Library Power met school reform? Our study was generated by three questions about this relationship. The first addressed the extent to which Library Power was implemented according to the vision developed by the Fund. The second inquired about whether the integration of Library Power with a major reform initiative promoted student learning of high intellectual quality. Finally, we explored the extent to which Library Power contributed to building a professional community that promoted and sustained reforms, particularly in teaching and learning.

Answers to these questions were mixed. The degree of implementation of Library Power varied across the schools. Teachers' understandings and uses of Library Power varied. King appeared to have most successfully implemented and used the program, and Hooks made the least use as envisioned by the Fund. Observation and staff testimony indicated that Library Power was more supportive of the primary reforms underway at King and Boone. Intellectual quality of student performance was clearly mixed at the three schools. When teachers already had a clear vision of such quality, they were able to capitalize on the resources of the new collection and the skills of the librarian. School-wide professional community also varied both within and between schools. Again, King appeared to have moved further in developing the characteristics of a shared vision and norms toward teaching of ambitious content to all students.

How do we explain the uneven use and impact of Library Power? At this point in the evaluation we can offer only a speculative answer, but one that can serve as a hypothesis to guide further investigations.

Explanations for educational change, or the lack of it, are numerous. We do not propose to test even a few theories of change to explain our findings. However, one straightforward explanation draws upon theory found in the literature on innovation diffusion in education (Miles, 1964; Berman & McLaughlin, 1978; Hall & Hord, 1987; Fullan & Stiegelbauer, 1991; Knapp, 1996). According to this literature, innovations are defined as discrete programs and practices that are introduced by experts, leaders, or policy makers from outside the school. School staff are instructed on the use of an innovation by change agents who offer a combination of dissemination and training. In general, this model fits the dissemination of Library Power.

The literature also argues that an educational innovation such as Library Power is adopted and adapted slowly as individual teachers take slow, imperfect steps in its use. The literature reports that some teachers resist changing their practices, while still others simply adapt aspects of the innovation to their practice without embracing a whole program as envisioned by its developers. Resistance, it is argued, is generated by the complexity and asymmetry of the innovation when juxtaposed with teachers' existing practices. The more complex an innovation, the more likely that teachers will resist its adoption. Some research found that teachers go through stages of concern about an innovation; initial resistance is followed by increasing acceptance and adoption as teachers become more familiar and comfortable with new practices.

Innovation diffusion theory tends to explain some of what we found in the three case studies. Technically, Library Power was not a terribly complex innovation. To the extent it was viewed by practitioners mainly as a set of concrete resources to support instruction, Library Power was not controversial. In our study of the three schools, we found very little resistance to the idea that teachers should use new library resources. Also, restructuring the use of the library through flexible scheduling, although introducing a little more complexity, seemed not to be disconcerting to most teachers; most adapted to it easily. According to innovation theory, general acceptance of the new resources and flexible scheduling was a predictable result.

Innovation theory suggests that resistance to a particular practice can be overcome with continued external support and reinforcement of teachers' use. Accordingly, teachers will gradually become more comfortable with the new expectations and practices. However, Knapp (1996) pointed out that innovation theory does not do a good job of explaining how cultural change problems can be overcome. He argued that innovation theory assumes a rather discrete, clearly defined practice or process that can be easily prescribed. Flexible scheduling, for example, fits this criterion. More problematic for educators was the requirement of collaboration between teachers and the librarian. Collaboration can be viewed as both a form of restructuring, because of its call for new role relationships, and as a form of cultural change involving teachers' beliefs and practices. As the latter, collaboration introduced much more complexity and ambiguity than flexible scheduling. To the extent that an innovation is ambiguous and not entirely specified, practices remain somewhat unclear to teachers, the principal, and the librarian. Correspondingly, we found more doubts among teachers about the meaning, practice, and value of collaboration. Teachers were asked to accept the premise that the librarian's professional expertise could add significant value to curriculum and instruction, arenas normally reserved for the teacher. Viewed as cultural change rather than as organizational restructuring, collaboration called for new beliefs and new behaviors such as engaging in thoughtful dialogue about what goals were appropriate for students and how best to use library resources. This new culture was not easy for some to accept or practice.

Whereas reforms such as Paideia, Bank Street, and KERA advocate ambitious learning outcomes, it is not obvious which practices will succeed in promoting intellectual quality. Promoting student work characterized by high intellectual quality is more ambiguous than either flexible scheduling or collaboration. Teachers are to have students engage in complex intellectual processes that lead to relatively weakly specified goals. Moreover, the absence of clear and accepted standards for judging the intellectual quality of student achievement makes it even more difficult for educators to agree on a course of action. While certain principles and standards can be specified for intellectual quality, as found in the CORS standards, teachers need to give them personal meaning, internalize them, and make them operational through a process of discussion and reflective practice. Building a professional community around shared and internalized understanding of high intellectual quality is a cultural process that takes time and other organizational support.

Innovation theory has only limited value in explaining the success of Library Power and comprehensive reforms because it does not conceptualize schools as organizations with cultures. Instead, it tends to address schools as collections of individuals who accept or reject ideas about how to improve their practice. The theory says little about the organizational capacity of schools to address collective problems such as the implementation of innovations. But staffs are more than collections of individual teachers who practice their craft. Professional community among staff produces a whole that is greater than the sum of the parts. A school is an organization that creates a unique culture based on collective experience. This culture tends to sustain particular norms, values, and expectations that underlie practice. Cultures encourage some teacher practices and discourage others. Goertz, Floden, & O'Day (1995) described "communities of practice" that can either enhance or inhibit an individual teacher's ability to act on personal intent.

A school culture can be receptive or hostile to central ideas contained in a vision of learning characterized by high intellectual quality. For Library Power to promote school-wide student achievement of high intellectual quality presumes a collective vision and organizational knowledge that may not exist. In fact, many teachers in their own education have not experienced learning that meets our standards of intellectual quality. While some teachers have had such experiences, collectively many schools have not acquired a critical mass of teachers who can help establish a school-wide culture of learning focused on intellectual quality. In the absence of a strong professional community that endorses, legitimizes, and reinforces such a goal, it is difficult to imagine Library Power's being used to promote this kind of student achievement.

How might a school move toward a stronger professional culture that focused on intellectual quality as the most important goal of schooling? We are not sure, and research only suggests some strategies. One important element appears to be the leadership offered by a school's principal. We saw in the three case studies variations in strength of leadership in pushing and helping faculty grapple with issues surrounding the improvement of teaching and learning. A central role for a principal is prompting and facilitating staff dialogue over key issues of the kind this chapter has raised. While a principal alone may not move a faculty toward a strong professional community, that person's efforts probably make a great difference. Teachers, too, can be leaders, and when they have clear ideas about where their school should be headed, they should seek opportunities to lead. Structural features are another element that can make a difference in creating a professional culture. Opportunities for dialogue can occur through formal mechanisms, such as in teacher teams and departments, and also by establishing regular times when staff can address substantive issues. But structure is limited to providing opportunities; the will to address tough questions collectively must also exist. Finally, formal staff development provides another setting for bringing staff together to build shared understandings of a school's purpose. Again, leadership is required to focus such opportunities on issues of intellectual quality.

In the absence of a good theory about how to build a strong professional culture around intellectual quality of student achievement, strategic policy might be aimed at finding schools with such a vision and investing Library Power resources in them. This would maximize the possibility that limited resources would be used in the most effective way.

References

Berman, P., & McLaughlin, M. W. (1978). *Federal programs supporting educational change, Vol. VIII: Implementing and sustaining innovations.* Santa Monica, CA: Rand Corp.

Fullan, M., & Stiegelbauer, S. (1991). *The new meaning of educational change.* New York: Teachers College Press.

Goertz, M. E., Floden, R. E., & O'Day, J. (1995). *Studies of education reform: Systemic reform, Vol. I: Findings and conclusions.* Newark, NJ: Rutgers, the State University of New Jersey, Center for Policy Research in Education.

Hall, G. E., & Hord, S. M. (1987). *Change in schools: Facilitating the process.* Albany, NY: State University of New York Press.

Knapp, M. S. (1996, July). *Between systemic reforms and the mathematics and science classroom: The dynamics of innovation, implementation, and professional learning.* Paper prepared for the National Institute for Science Education.

MacMullen, M. M. (1996). *Taking stock of a school reform effort.* Providence, RI: Annenberg Institute for School Reform at Brown University.

Miles, M. B. (1964). *Innovation in education.* New York: Teachers College Press.

Newmann, F. M., & Associates. (1996). *Authentic achievement: Restructuring schools for intellectual quality.* San Francisco: Jossey-Bass.

Newmann, F. M., & Wehlage, G. G. (1995). *Successful school restructuring: A report to the public and educators.* Madison, WI: Wisconsin Center for Education Research.

Newmann, F. M., Secada, W. G., & Wehlage, G. G. (1995). *A guide to authentic instruction and assessment: Vision, standards and scoring.* Madison, WI: Wisconsin Center for Education Research.

PROFESSIONAL DEVELOPMENT

Dianne McAfee Hopkins
Norman Lott Webb

Introduction

Library Power is a cohesive, large-scale initiative to stimulate student inquiry, build information literacy, and reinforce libraries' centrality to instruction. It embraces the goals of larger systemic education reforms to advance effective organizations and instruction for all students to authentically understand concepts and ideas beyond memorizing lists of facts and replicating specified algorithms. Library Power makes a unique contribution to the host of national education reforms seeking improved student learning. It is the only one that focuses on transforming school libraries from outdated archival repositories into active, real-time learning centers that complement, strengthen, and amplify students' classroom instruction. Releasing the power of information is important for students' knowledge development. The theory is simple. When librarians become more knowledgeable about teachers' classroom efforts, they are better able to build a library collection more aligned with learning goals. When students and teachers have more access to the librarian and a contemporary library, students have more opportunities to engage in meaningful research, inquiry, reading, and resource-based learning. These learning activities, across the full curriculum spectrum, then help advance literacy among students and increase students' ability to use higher-order thinking skills, both highly desirable goals for education.

Although easily stated, Library Power's strategy to develop schools' capacity to educate students to become effective users of information and productive researchers across all curriculum topics places great demands on librarians, teachers, school administrators, and district staff. How effectively Library Power's theory can be put into practice depends overwhelmingly on these participants and how they build the required knowledge base to effectively structure engaging learning activities for students. How well schools and districts become environments where students can delve deeply into a range of resources, do research, and become empowered learners will depend on what librarians, teachers, and administrators do.

Librarians have to become very knowledgeable about the curriculum across all grade levels and in all content areas. They have to understand interdisciplinary learning. They need to learn how to become collaborators with teachers and educators of teachers. They have to become more effective teachers and instructional leaders. They must learn new skills such as collection and curriculum mapping, and they have to continually grow in their knowledge of collection development, technology, and evaluation techniques.

Classroom teachers need to be more knowledgeable about resource-based instruction and how to use the library and its staff effectively. Instruction needs to be structured to take advantage of the resources in the library and the librarian as a fellow teacher. Teachers must develop their pedagogical knowledge so they are able to monitor closely each student's learning and to select from expanding alternative experiences, including a highly functioning library, what will most effectively increase each student's understanding. They need to become collaborators with other teachers and the librarian, learn new skills such as curriculum mapping and using interdisciplinary approaches to learning, and update continually their knowledge of content areas to stay current with ideas their students will gain through using contemporary resource materials.

School administrators need to understand how to build and manage effective instructional teams of collaborating teachers and librarians. They need to know more about resource-based instruction, inquiry learning, and indicators of their effectiveness. They should be able to distinguish between an illusion of reform activity and actual improved student learning under reform goals, and they need to learn what is required to finance and sustain school-wide change for effectively integrating library-based and classroom-based instruction.

The Library Power Program positioned its reform strategy for school change in the contexts of networking among schools and partnerships with district and community agencies. Critical to the program's vision for successful change was developing the organizational capacity within schools. Through fostering collaboration among teachers, administrators, and librarians and strengthening the instructional role of librarians, Library Power sought to change the culture in schools. The initiative promoted forming new relationships among school staff centered on student instruction and learning. This required teachers, librarians, and administrators to change their views about the division of instructional duties, address what activities lead to important learning, and grapple with establishing common professional norms for student learning.

When Library Power was inaugurated in the early 1990s, what the program proposed to do on such a large scale was largely untested. However, since its initiation, an expanding body of research adds validity to its approach to strengthen collaboration among staff and provide in-depth and sustained professional development. O'Day, Goertz, & Floden (1995) found in a three-year study of systemic reform that boosting organizational capacity required expanding teachers' and staff's capacity on multiple dimensions, linking development of teacher capacity with organizational capacity, and providing external input and assistance. Traditional professional development devoted to expanding a "teacher's repertoire of well-defined classroom practices" (p. 2) was too limiting in achieving significant outcomes. In their study of restructuring schools, Newmann, King, & Rigdon (1997) found that strong external accountability tended to be related to low organizational capacity. Schools that developed strong internal accountability by staff joining together to develop explicit school-wide standards for student performance and a culture of peer support achieved more valued learning. Organizational capacity was enhanced by a school's achieving more consensus about professional norms, collaboration, and "stimulated inquiry and a search for additional professional knowledge among staff." (p. 63) The authors also found that an infusion of ideas from outside the immediate organization is important to move beyond current practice.

A growing body of research identifies the complexity of teacher change and the variety of perspectives for thinking about reforming instructional practice (Fennema & Nelson, 1997; Webb, Heck, & Tate; 1997; McLaughlin, 1993). One important characteristic distinguishing current reforms, including Library Power, from earlier reform attempts, is the recognition that teachers and others who work directly with students have a critical role if significant improvement is to be attained (Webb, 1997; Goldsmith & Shifer, 1997). However, teachers—and librarians as teachers—vary greatly both in approaches to instruction and in belief as to what is right. It cannot be taken for granted that teachers, librarians, and administrators will advocate for students to become more effective users of information and researchers at the "expense" of learning the "basic skills." There are many reasons for teachers and others not to change, including entrenched beliefs; long-term uncertainties; possible or actual loss of status, influence, or power; and redefinition of their posts. Frequently, reform efforts will create a "time warp" because teachers and staff within a school or district will embrace change at different rates, and some will either passively or actively resist change (Huberman, 1997, p. 162). Some teachers could change fully along the lines of Library Power while others in the same school remain traditionalists or even actively resist change.

Library Power's principle of ongoing, school-wide, and sustained professional development in concert with the other core principles is compatible with the AASL/AECT national school library media guidelines, *Information Power* (1988), that call for continuing education throughout the librarian's career, ongoing self-assessment, and professional growth through both academic and non-academic experiences. This principle of professional development also is attuned to the understanding that teacher change encapsulates multiple elements of professional growth, including a sense of disequilibrium in current practice, exposure to a better way, the existence of proof that the new way will work, modeling, support, experimentation in one's own setting, and reflection (Webb, Heck, & Tate, 1997).

Professional Development

Professional development for educators offers opportunities to develop new knowledge, skills, approaches, and dispositions to improve their effectiveness in their classrooms and organizations. The emerging common vision of effective professional development is addressed by seven principles (Loucks-Horsley, Hewson, Love, & Stiles, 1998, pp. 36–37):

- Effective professional development experiences are driven by a well-defined image of effective classroom learning and teaching, for example, an emphasis on inquiry-based learning, investigations, problem-solving, and applications of knowledge; an approach that emphasizes in-depth understanding of core concepts and challenges students to construct new understandings; and clear means to measure meaningful achievement.

- Effective professional development experiences provide opportunities for teachers to build their knowledges and skills.

- Effective professional development experiences use or model with teachers the strategies teachers will use with their students.

- Effective professional development experiences build a learning community, for example, continuous learning is a part of the school norms and culture, teachers are rewarded and encouraged to take risks and learn, and teachers learn and share together.

- Effective professional development experiences support teachers' serving in leadership roles, e.g., as supporters of other teachers, agents of change, and as promoters of reform.

- Effective professional development experiences provide links to other parts of the education system, e.g., links with other district or school initiatives.

- Effective professional development experiences are continuously assessing themselves and making improvements to ensure positive impact on teacher effectiveness, student learning, leadership, and the school community.

Professional development occurs in many different forms to produce professional learning. Teachers, librarians, and school administrators can develop new knowledge through immersion in inquiry in a content area, curriculum development or implementation, case discussion, examining student work and thinking, coaching and mentoring, and professional networks. Educational changes of value require individuals to act in new ways and to think in new ways, but can be attained from many different types of experiences. Even though conventional wisdom holds that changing teacher beliefs should be the primary work of professional development, research on teacher change indicates that changes in attitudes often result when teachers use a new practice and see students benefiting. Changes in ideas and attitudes occur in a mutually interactive process (Loucks-Horsley, et. al., 1998). Teachers and others require multiple opportunities to learn, practice, interact, and reinforce new behaviors.

Professional Development As an Important Implementation Strategy

Effective professional development for Library Power had to be molded to fit the needs and context of each site. Some sites were more successful than others in developing an overall strategy for identifying what experiences teachers, librarians, and administrators needed for their schools to transform into learning communities with the library central to instruction. A common characteristic of these sites was strategic thinking and planning by a director or a central group.

In East Baton Rouge Parish, the four-member Library Power management team, including a visionary full-time director, saw that any gathering of those participating in Library Power served as an opportunity to learn more about the principles of the program and its implementation. This included meetings, in-services, and interschool visitations. A range of topics was covered, including thematic units, flexible scheduling, storytelling, resource-based learning, information processing skills, conflict resolution, collaborative planning, curriculum frameworks, and whole language instruction. Professional development began with the beginning of the grant and expanded as the number of participating schools increased. In the second school year of the grant the number and types of Library Power professional development activities were already numerous:

2	general meetings
6	area meetings
24	cluster meetings

234   faculty meetings

8   breakfast meetings

3   advisory board meetings

38   parish-wide in-services

1   summer institute

In addition, during that year, 121 people attended state or national conferences. The central library office staff learned more about what professional development teachers, librarians, and administrators needed as the program evolved and responded to this need. The one-week summer institute was refined over the four years as the attendance grew from about 100 to 250, including those in all positions. During the week, a range of experiences was offered, such as using a planning web to develop thematic interdisciplinary units, collaborating, and using trade books in teaching science and mathematics. The program was rich enough that those who attended during more than one summer could still find relevant and different learning experiences. Library Power provided professional development to school staff in a district where school-based professional development or funding substitutes to release teachers received very little budget support from the district, supplemented by PTA fundraising. The Library Power director, with the help of part-time staff, made at least monthly visits to schools that were having more difficulty putting in place flexible scheduling, collaborative planning meetings, and other tenets of the program. Librarians in some schools where not all teachers were convinced that Library Power was the best for their situation took the responsibility to work individually with teachers to encourage them.

Professional development was the central focus of Library Power in the Denver area, a multi-district site. The Public Education and Business Coalition (PEBC), fiscal authority and headquarters for the Library Power grant, applied a model of on-site professional development it had developed over a number of years. One librarian or a team of one teacher and one librarian was assigned to each Library Power school. These staff developers, serving as mentors to librarians, spent about one or two days per month at their assigned schools providing 20 to 25 days of staff development support per school during the year. The focus of the staff development was on-site demonstrations and hands-on work with teachers, principals, and librarians. Usually, staff developers did not serve another school in their own district. In addition, specific schools were identified as demonstration sites that staff from other schools could visit.

Forward in the Fifth (FITF), a regional center, administered Library Power in a multi-district area in Kentucky. Library Power had to fit within the massive statewide reform that imposed censures and rewards based on school performance. School staffs were under heavy pressure to improve student learning. Within this context, professional development was conceived as hands-on training that participants could use immediately. Each year institutes and workshops, generally day-long events held at a resort or motel, were offered on the major themes, including the major components of Library Power, advanced collaboration, literacy, technology, and literature research. Forward in the Fifth staff shaped what professional development experiences were offered from the feedback they received on what librarians, teachers, and principals needed. Network meetings with required attendance were held for librarians to share their experiences about what worked and what did not. Mentoring relationships were established between librarians at model sites and those at the expansion sites. New ideas were infused into the program by supporting school staff's attendance at national conferences and meetings.

Professional Development Across the Library Power Sites

Funding

Library Power enabled districts to provide multiple professional development opportunities to promote the full use of the library program in teaching and learning. The importance attributed to professional development can be seen, in part, in expenditures for it during the Library Power years. In addition to any other sources of funds for professional development that might have been utilized, on average, Library Power sites spent approximately $307,800, or 26% of their total Library Power allocation of $1.2 million, on professional development activities (see Figure 8-1).

Site expenditures on professional development ranged from a low of 13% to a high of 45% of the overall program budget. A multi-district Library Power site allocated the highest percentage of its budget to professional development, which then became the local program's centerpiece. A one-district site with a well-established library program and a district-level library media supervisor allocated the lowest percentage of its Library Power funds to professional development. The majority of sites (12) spent between 20% and 30% of their Library Power funds on professional development. Sites that joined Library Power in the later rounds allocated more of their funds to professional development than did the first group of sites.

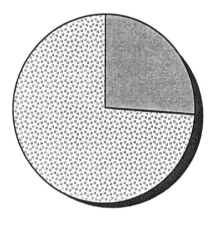

26%—Professional Development
74%—Other Expenditures

FIGURE 8-1 Library Power average allocation for professional development.

Sites in Round 2 and Round 3 spent on average between 27% and 28% of Library Power funds on professional development, compared to only 22% by Round 1 sites (see Table 8-1).

TABLE 8-1
Professional Development Expenditures by Round*

Round 1 average	22%	or	$263,400
Round 2 average	27%	or	$325,200
Round 3 average	28%	or	$334,800
Overall average	26%	or	$307,800

*These figures do not include the New York Library Power site. That site's pattern did not conform to the Round pattern.

For some communities, there was little or no funding available for professional development prior to the receipt of the Library Power grant. In these instances, the professional development funds enabled the school library to become a focal point for professional development for the first time in years. Other communities added the Library Power funds to the existing professional development budget available from the district or through other initiatives. When Library Power resources were merged with other funding, the source of money for professional development activities became more difficult to trace.

How sites allocated funds for professional development varied greatly. Library Power funds went toward materials development; mini-grants; expert speakers; teacher stipends for summer institutes and workshops; compensations for district teachers, principals, and librarians who led area workshops; and travel expenses for staff to attend professional conferences and meetings. Librarians and teachers also engaged in significant professional development experiences, that had no monetary costs, through interacting with each other.

Professional Development Opportunities

All Library Power sites used a variety of professional development methods to reach the primary audiences of librarians, principals, and teachers, including institutes and workshops, school visits, networking, mini-grants, videos, coaching and mentoring, and annual meetings. Librarians were the major focus for professional development opportunities at all sites, although principals and teachers were targeted as well. According to survey data, librarians across the initiative attended, on average, 19 professional development programs, for an estimated total of 76 hours. Of these programs, librarians reported that 88% had been vital. Teachers who were part of the school-level Library Power team were more likely than other teachers to be invited to participate in Library Power in-services, particularly in-services held outside the school. This participation was important because one of the roles of the school-level Library Power team was to promote Library Power activities and, in some cases, to work with the librarian in providing in-school staff development programs. In some instances, parents and students were invited to participate in in-service opportunities.

Institutes and Workshops

Annual summer institutes were very popular staff development opportunities among the sites. Repeated institutes at a site in subsequent summers frequently varied their main theme to address numerous areas of interest. In addition to featuring outside experts, many summer institutes also featured local school district talent and offered time for school groups to plan instruction and prepare instructional materials such as interdisciplinary units for the coming school year. Institutes and workshops serve the primary purpose of building knowledge, along with developing awareness and translating what is learned into practice (Loucks-Horsley, et al., 1998).

Library Power sites regularly held workshops and in-services. A few of the sites incorporated workshops on specific topics into their summer institutes, but generally sites used this form of staff development during the school year. Sites held workshops at all times during the day including before school, during the school day (with substitute teachers usually provided so that teachers could attend), after school, in the evenings, and on Saturdays. Like the summer institutes, they featured outside speakers as well as school district teams and often included planning time.

School Visits

Principals, teachers, and librarians took time from their schedules to visit other schools with operating Library Power programs. School visits allowed the visitor to see a library program in action. These experiences gave those thinking about participating in Library Power and beginning their own program an existence model of the effectiveness of Library Power. The visits helped observers visualize how Library Power could be realized in their own environments.

Sometimes in-service programs on Library Power were planned at different schools to give librarians and teachers in the district a better understanding of different physical arrangements for the library, posters, and other equipment. In these cases, tours and speeches about the activities of that school's library program were critical components of the learning experience. At other times, the school library facility was more in the background, used primarily as a meeting place. Even these situations encouraged professional learning by having librarians and others at least experience the physical layout of a Library Power library.

While most school visits were likely to occur within the district itself, some sites chose to visit Library Power sites outside their communities. Baton Rouge and Chattanooga were among Library Power sites that hosted visitors from all over the United States. The sites of Library Power annual meetings also provided opportunities to visit other schools. Nashville, Philadelphia, and Providence were among sites hosting national Library Power meetings and school visits as part of conference opportunities. Multi-district sites in the Denver Public Education Business Coalition (PEBC) area and the Forward in the Fifth (FITF) Kentucky area also hosted national Library Power annual meetings and provided school visits.

Although the emphasis of most school visits was on Library Power schools, non-Library Power districts that advanced student learning opportunities while embracing *Information Power* concepts were also visited. For example, a Paterson team of district-level and building-level administrators and school faculty traveled to Blue Valley, Kansas, to observe effective library media programs that made full use of information technology for teaching and learning. That visit was important in motivating central office staff to collaborate in promoting student learning through technology and library partnerships.

Networking

Regular meetings with groups of principals and groups of librarians were a common form of staff development at Library Power sites. Leaders and directors recognized the importance of networking among educators with similar responsibilities. Such networking helped participants learn that they were not alone, others had succeeded with similar obstacles, and there were strategies to help ensure success. For these reasons, a popular feature of these meetings was a sharing time in which participants informally discussed Library Power practices that worked or that needed suggestions or special attention.

Most sites reported having monthly meetings of librarians and periodic meetings of principals. The frequency of the principal gatherings, sometimes breakfast meetings, varied from monthly to twice a year, depending on the site. These meetings tended to include both discussions on administrative details about the operation of Library Power in the district or school and short programs on a variety of topics. Meetings of the school Library Power team afforded other networking opportunities. School teams, usually consisting of the principal, the librarian, selected teachers representing different grade levels or grade ranges, and occasionally a parent, met to plan, share information, and solve problems.

Mini-Grants

A number of sites offered librarians and teachers mini-grant awards of $500-1,000. A very popular Library Power feature, mini-grants gave the teachers access to much-needed discretionary funds to acquire library materials and other materials for special projects. Some sites required the librarian and teachers to write applications as a team, thus furthering collaboration and group learning. Other sites required mini-grants to support specific efforts. Chattanooga, for example, required that a unit plan or other instructional activity be described. As participation progressed, subsequent proposals showed emphasis on student involvement in evaluation, portfolio assessment, and expectations of student reflection on the learning process. Teachers, librarians, and principals also could apply for mini-grants to extend their professional development opportunities, including professional meetings.

Videos

Another formal staff development program utilized instructional television. In Kentucky, Forward in the Fifth produced three 90-minute professional development programs for teachers, librarians, and administrators. The major focus of these programs was on collaboration: beginning collaboration, advanced collaboration, collaboration within the school, and collaboration with others outside the school. Featured speakers included Forward in the Fifth site leaders, area classroom teachers, and area school librarians, as well as state Department of Education officials and area public librarians.

Coaching and Mentoring

A few Library Power sites hired staff developers, or the director and staff assumed the responsibility to work individually with librarians and teachers. On-site staff development enabled the librarian to gain useful information while remaining in the school library and encouraged specific consultations with the staff developer that related directly to the needs of that particular school. A very focused staff development model was developed by the Denver area's Public Education Business Coalition (PEBC). In Denver, staff developers worked as mentors for several days each year with librarians and teachers in Library Power schools, observing, encouraging and guiding collaborations, demonstrating lessons, guiding evaluations of activities, and debriefing faculty. In Baton Rouge, the Library Power program operating out of the district administration building hired a teacher and a librarian to lead workshops and work individually with librarians and teachers in their thematic unit planning and collaborations. Both the Library Power director and district-level library supervisor in Baton Rouge made regular visits to schools to work with librarians and teachers and to confer with the school principal. Similar activities were repeated at other sites. In New Haven, for example, the Library Power director made it a point to visit at least one school a day. In the course of a month the director was able to visit each Library Power school.

A similar support for school personnel was pairing. Pairing was a one-on-one relationship that encouraged learning in mentor/mentee relationships or collegial relationships focused on topics of greatest interest or need. Several Library Power sites paired experienced staff with less experienced ones. This pairing usually occurred between librarians within a site, but sometimes included classroom teacher teams as well as principals. Atlanta teamed school classroom teacher and librarian groups so that they could work jointly on instructional projects over a year. Principal teams were among Forward in the Fifth teams. One paired principal said, "The resource people helped us plan. The other principal and I talked several times. We still talk. A lot of the time, we talk about libraries. Making available those resources to us—having someone from outside this school help us plan for the future—what a library should look like and what a library should be doing, was immeasurable."

Annual National Meetings

The National Library Power Program required site-level team members and key school team members, including librarians and teachers, to attend annual meetings. These gatherings afforded leaders at the different sites an opportunity to "calibrate" what they were doing with other sites, an important learning experience for leaders. Annual Library Power national meetings were jointly planned by the American Library Association's American Association of School Librarians (AASL) and the Public Education Network (PEN), both providers of technical assistance for Library Power sites. Held annually during the years of the Library Power initiative, these programs offered a wealth of support and ideas. The programs featured outside experts as well as Library Power participants. Annual meetings were attended by Library Power participants from school and district levels and included parent representatives as both presenters and participants. The meetings offered formal and informal opportunities to plan and network with others within the Library Power site, as well as with those in similar positions at other sites. Written materials and site programs also were shared through displays.

Library Power annual meetings focused on areas designed to achieve the goals of Library Power. These were areas of common interest to all sites. In 1995, for example, topics included collaboration, school reform and restructuring, and professional development. The 1997 annual meeting had the theme "Celebrating Learning." The program featured unique aspects of Library Power from each of the sites centered around essential questions. Topics included advocacy for strong instructional programs through collection mapping, community involvement efforts of Library Power schools, and institutionalization of an integrated information literacy program. Additional features of each annual meeting included "role-alike" meetings, where individuals with similar roles met with others from the various sites; tours of several Library Power schools in the host community; and reports from the University of Wisconsin–Madison national evaluation team. In addition to the National Library Power Program annual meetings, Library Power site members attended other national meetings. These included the American Association of School Librarians' national conferences and other national conferences such as the International Reading Association Conference.

Professional Development Content

Many Library Power sites offered staff development that featured common topics. These topics included those that related specifically to the philosophy and operation of Library Power as well as those that focused on concepts for teaching and learning that embraced Library Power goals. Among topics common to the sites were the role of the librarian in promoting student learning opportunities, collaboration or collaborative planning, flexible scheduling, facilities, collection mapping, and institutionalization. Because of Library Power's emphasis on providing a collection that reflected each school's curriculum, collection mapping workshops were offered in Round 2 and Round 3 site communities by collection mapping creator David Loertscher. Other topics receiving emphasis included thematic or interdisciplinary units, information literacy, resource-based learning, information processing skills, and research.

In addition to such programs relevant to teaching and learning, some Library Power professional development topics centered on district publications. Examples were *The Guide for Thematic Units* in Baton Rouge, and *The Guide to Integrated Information Literacy Skills* in Lincoln, Nebraska. Numerous other topics were featured to varying degrees at the sites and included authentic assessment, cooperative learning, multicultural literature, connecting the library to science and math, storytelling, the role of technology in instruction, team building, and whole language instruction. Finally, topics that were covered but did not appear to be emphasized as much as those previously cited included reading aloud to students, poetry, multi-age groupings, multiple intelligences, writing across the curriculum, community connections, and critical thinking.

Among the outside speakers listed by case study researchers as presenting professional development programs in several locations were library educators Dr. Michael Eisenberg, Dr. Ken Haycock, and Dr. David Loertscher; Library Power Director Barbara Stripling; and reading educator Dr. Jim Trelease.

Stages of Professional Development in Library Power Case Study Sites

Throughout the Library Power years, some areas of professional development received constant attention. Networking among site leaders at different Library Power sites was begun early and continued throughout the Library Power years. Networking among librarians within districts was actively encouraged through regular meetings, as well as shared projects and mentoring. During the Library Power grant years, outside speakers were also periodically used to further Library Power aims and to extend and expand the knowledge of Library Power leaders and participants throughout the district. In addition, as discussed earlier, Library Power participants actively attended national conferences to broaden their perspectives.

Although some aspects of professional development were ongoing, study of Library Power case study sites reveals six stages in professional development. While these stages were common, in general, to the case study sites, the degree and order of their occurrence may have varied. The stages are the following: needs assessments, communication of Library Power principles through district-wide emphases, model school identification and the emergence of leaders within the district, school-based professional development, the need for expanded professional development, and institutionalization.

Needs Assessments

As part of the grant proposal, Library Power sites were engaged in overall needs assessments. Sites used formal as well as less formal strategies to assess the need for professional development emphases, but all engaged in strategies to determine the focus of professional development programs. Lincoln provides an example of formalized needs assessment that addressed teachers' engagement with their school library. Working with the district's evaluator and the district's director of staff development, the Library Power district leadership surveyed elementary school teachers to find out the level of their library use using the eight steps of David Loertscher's "Teacher's Taxonomy of Resource-Based Teaching" (Loertscher, 1988, p. 23) The steps are as follows:

- Step 1: Self-contained teaching (no need for library)

- Step 2: Teaching with a private collection (permanent room collection)

- Step 3: Teaching with a borrowed collection (materials borrowed from school and other libraries for use in the classroom)

- Step 4: Using the library media staff as an idea resource (for materials and training suggestions)

- Step 5: Using the library media center staff and resources for enrichment of a unit (to supplement content)

- Step 6: Using library media resources as a part of unit content (materials and activities integral to unit content)

- Step 7: Teacher and librarian partnership in resource-based teaching

- Step 8: Curriculum development (advance planning and content development)

The results of this assessment clearly showed that most teachers operated at Step 3 or below, indicating that at best, only a few library materials were borrowed on occasion and that the librarian was not engaged in collaborative activities. Professional development programs were then planned based on these findings.

When Lincoln teachers involved in Library Power were surveyed a year and a half later, after having participated in planned professional development programs, results showed that the majority of teachers had moved to Step 6, consulting with the librarian on student learning activities and using library materials in thematic learning units. One-third of the teachers had moved to more interactive planning and teaching with the librarian as a partner and with the library collection critical to the implementation of instructional activities.

Communicating the Library Power Concepts Through District-Wide Emphases

Initially, it was important that district-level administrators, as well as school-level principals and faculty, understood and embraced the requirements of Library Power and school librarians' potential impact on learning opportunities. Thus, initial professional development opportunities focused on outside experts and programs provided by site-level leadership on a district-wide basis. During this time, schools were introduced to Library Power and given the opportunity to apply to be among the first schools in the district to participate in Library Power. Among the early topics introduced were collection development, flexible scheduling, facilities, and collaboration.

Model School Identification and the Emergence of Leaders Within the District and School

Several case study sites selected schools within their district to serve as model schools from which others could learn. This often happened either officially or unofficially with the first schools selected for participation as Library Power schools during the first year of the three-year grant. Baton Rouge, Kentucky's Forward in the Fifth district schools, and the Denver Public Education Business Coalition were among sites that had model or lab schools from which others learned. Regardless of the formal or informal designation, the networking among librarians in the districts encouraged school visits and sharing.

A clear by-product of involvement with the Library Power initiative was the emergence of school librarians as leaders within their schools. Viewing the librarian as an instructional leader was a transformation for many, including many school librarians. In case study after case study, this leadership trend is supported through interviews and observations. Case studies offer many rich examples of ways in which librarians emerged as leaders. The Library Power initiative in most instances, by design, centered around the creativity and productivity of the school librarian. This was most often borne out in collaborative relationships with principals and with teachers. Many librarians developed a partnership with their school principals, attending in-service programs together, developing a shared vision of the library program's role in learning, and designing programs for teachers and students alike that provided opportunities to use the library's human and material resources. By association as well as program implementation, then, the librarian began to be viewed as a school leader.

In collaborative relationships with teachers, the librarian was viewed as a knowledgeable team member. A case study researcher in Chattanooga described the librarian's role in unit planning meetings: "In all of the planning sessions, the librarian was accepted as a full member of the team. At times her opinion was specifically solicited. In all cases, it was evident that she knew the curriculum, the materials, and the students as well as the teachers." Here, and in many case studies, teachers learned to expect the librarian to play a key role in determining learning objectives, co-delivering instruction, and sometimes evaluating student performance on information literacy skills.

Professional development programs, the strong backgrounds most librarians brought as classroom teachers, and librarians' advanced degrees were important in promoting the librarian as an instructional leader in schools. As an instructional leader, one of the roles that the librarian assumed was that of coach. Librarians provided constant encouragement and reassurance that changes in the library program, like flexible scheduling, were best for teachers and students alike. One teacher said, "I found out that I was scared to death to think of sending first and second graders to the library alone to do research." The librarian functioned as a coach to guide the teacher in the effective use of flexible scheduling.

The librarian was also viewed by some case study researchers as a leader who understood the varied ways in which students learned and the importance of acknowledging and building upon the diversity of learning styles. A Denver-area case study researcher noted a new librarian's hope that she could prod teachers to move away from the assumption that all students at a grade level or even in a single class had to be working on the same thing at the same time all at once. The librarian believed that there were many situations where it was appropriate for small groups of students within a grade level or class to work on projects that the others would never do, or work on them at a different time from the rest. Library Power gave the librarian opportunities to explore individualized student learning approaches with teachers.

Most Library Power schools had school advisory committees, usually made up of the school principal, the librarian, and teachers representing various grade levels. Librarians either chaired these committees or worked with the chair of the committee. This too was a time for demonstrating leadership as well as gaining information that was important to the librarian's leadership in the school. A Denver-area case study researcher described it in this way: "It would be difficult to overstate the importance of these meetings. They provided the structural mechanism by which librarians gained an appreciation of the broader objectives of classroom instruction and brainstormed with teachers about what kind of library instruction made the most sense. This led to deeper integration of the library into the instructional program of the school."

Librarians regularly planned, and sometimes conducted, in-service programs for teachers in the school. This was important because most Library Power professional development programs located away from the school involved only a few of the teachers in a school. It was important that the librarian, along with the Library Power advisory committee, plan and often provide in-service programs for entire school faculty. Collection mapping workshops conducted by librarians, discussed in Chapter 2, were among the opportunities for leadership that librarians assumed.

Several librarians, often with fellow teachers and principals, also provided workshops about their programs to other school faculties in the district. In Lincoln, a cadre of Library Power teacher and librarian teams presented professional development programming. In 1997, these teams made presentations to every school in the district plus presentations at four state conferences and at the American Association of School Librarians national conference held in Portland, Oregon.

Thus, not only were librarians active in planning and/or leading professional development programs in their districts, but they also provided similar leadership at state and national levels. The type of leader capable of providing leadership at school, district, state, and national levels is probably like the librarian described in this Denver case study:

> The librarian brought to the project a genuine desire to learn. She also brought high regard for teachers' knowledge and expertise. And, she brought her own set of skills and knowledge in resources, in use of technology, in the ability to work collaboratively and her genuine enjoyment of and respect for children. She exhibited a high degree of flexibility, fitting her teaching around the schedule and style of each teacher. She exhibited initiative in reaching out to teachers to help them understand the benefits of the library for their students. She exhibited excellent organizational skills; she invested a high level of energy in her work. Perhaps her most important attribute was that she was an eager learner and wanted each child to be also.

School-Based Professional Development

While district-level professional development programs like the summer institutes were popular throughout the Library Power years, there was a natural and, in many cases, planned movement to focus staff development opportunities at the school level. Although districts like Baton Rouge encouraged the broad participation of principals and teachers in summer institutes along with their librarians, some sites were only able to accommodate a team from each school, and thus, did not directly reach all teachers in this way. Also, many of the major components of Library Power such as collaboration and flexible scheduling were building-based and required a shared vision on the part of the entire school community to succeed. Lincoln was a Library Power site that already embraced a philosophy of school-based staff development. Others, like New Haven, Forward in the Fifth, and Chattanooga, recognized the value of a school emphasis and built that into their planning.

School-based professional development often focused on many of the same topics that might be emphasized in larger professional development programs. Major differences were that school-based professional development programs enabled all school faculty to participate, were tailored to needs of the specific school, and included faculty from that school as planners and/or presenters, especially the librarian. Thus, the school-based professional development programs were likely to be seen as being directly and immediately applicable to the school's needs.

Expanded Professional Development

At many sites, initiating the Library Power program required professional development to concentrate on introducing the potential role of librarians and libraries in instruction. It soon became evident, however, that expanded professional development programs were needed, as were introductory programs for those new to Library Power concepts and those hesitant to embrace the initiative. Forward in the Fifth was mindful of these differences in its instructional television programming, for example, and offered a program on "Advanced Collaboration," as well as earlier programs on beginning collaboration. The Denver Public Education Business Coalition offered special staff development programs, sometimes with outside speakers, for its staff developers who provided leadership for Library Power schools on an individualized basis.

There was recognition, however, of the need to develop more advanced or more challenging programs on Library Power topics originally offered at introductory levels. There was also recognition that different programming was required. The Chattanooga Library Power director noted that while the new librarian needed staff development related to teaching and curriculum, she also needed administrative staff development related to management, leadership, and collaboration. The director noted that librarians needed to become curriculum specialists so that they could lead others in the development of curriculum and instructional units. They needed to be able to incorporate thinking, decision-making, production, and expression skills into units they planned with teachers. The new roles of librarians required them to serve as curriculum developers, instructional leaders, process specialists, chief collaborators, assessment gurus, and school reform catalysts in their schools. As one Chattanooga principal said, "Library Power has helped focus the role of the librarian as central to school reform. It brought libraries directly into the middle of total school reform and created a legitimate role for the librarian as an instructional leader. In some schools, the librarian is now perceived more as an instructional leader than the principal."

Institutionalization

The question of how to maintain the momentum of the Library Power years from the standpoint of professional development was a real one for Library Power sites. Many strategies put in place during the Library Power years were designed to build on and continue professional development programming. Among the strategies were the following: ongoing networking among site leadership of the various sites; ongoing networking among school librarians to be encouraged through regular meetings as well as through continuing school visits and informal communications; the nurturing of leadership within the district among librarians, teachers, and principals; and the natural movement toward school-based professional development. The Public Education Network provided network opportunities through its own annual conference as well as periodic telephone conference calls for local education fund Library Power leadership. At local levels, networking was promoted through regular meetings held with librarians as well as pairings within the district. Networking was promoted in natural ways through the ongoing relationships that librarians had with each other. They were motivated to communicate and found such interactions to be informative and personally and professionally rewarding.

Baton Rouge and Chattanooga provide examples of institutional efforts. By design, Baton Rouge had a goal of reaching all 63 of its elementary schools with the Library Power initiative. This plan, and the professional development efforts that were developed to ensure that it occurred, meant that when the 1996–97 federal desegregation plan requiring bussing was lifted, nearly all elementary school principals and faculties were knowledgeable about Library Power, and made it more likely that the Library Power principles would be continued throughout the district. In Chattanooga, an ambitious staff development strategy was used in 1996–97, the last full funding year for Library Power. There, the responsibility for professional development gradually was being turned over to the schools. Each school was encouraged to develop a school plan in 1996 to evaluate the status of the library in the instructional program and to create tailored staff development plans to enhance the use of the library. As a special incentive, schools had the choice of using their annual Library Power staff development allotment or applying for a $1,500 staff development grant available from the Public Education Foundation. Twenty-seven out of twenty-eight schools that applied received the $1,500 grant. The schools were ready to implement their own staff development programs.

Value of Professional Development

When surveys and case studies are analyzed, three findings about the value of Library Power professional development programs stand out.

For Librarians

The case studies provide many examples of changes in librarians that were evident as a result, in part, of their participation in the many professional development opportunities that were available to them. As discussed earlier in this chapter, the work of the librarian changed. For many, the role of the librarian changed to include roles as a teacher, coach, mentor, instructional leader, co-planner with the school principal, curriculum specialist, staff developer, and leader in the district and the community. One community college librarian said:

> Before, the school librarians were the weakest link in the entire library structure in this community. Now we see them at the front end of the curriculum. We see a different, more profound understanding among librarians about the type of role they play. This shows me that the Library Power training has had an impact over time on the knowledge and framework of the librarians. I can picture one librarian specifically who has had a great metamorphosis. She is now chairing the school's entire self-study committee, and the principal relies a great deal on her for advice about the curriculum. She has emerged as a real curriculum leader in the school.

For Staff

Through the emphasis on modeling, Library Power principals and faculties had formal and informal professional development experiences. Pairing beginning schools and staffs with more experienced ones, and featuring teacher/principal/librarian teams to provide in-services based on their own school successes, were only a few of many professional development programs that were evident in the schools. These programs, using in-district educators in leadership positions, served to acknowledge successful Library Power programs and encourage other educators to emulate these practices. It is likely that such public acknowledgment of these programs encouraged those doing well to strive to do even better.

For Advancement of Goals

At least five of the Library Power goals were addressed directly through various professional development at the sites. They were the following:

1. To create a national vision and new expectations for public elementary and middle school library programs and to encourage new and innovative uses of the library's physical and human resources.

2. To create model library programs that are an integral part of the educational process.

3. To strengthen and create awareness of the role of the librarian as a teacher and information specialist who assists teachers and students.

4. To encourage collaboration among teachers, administrators, and librarians that results in significant improvement in the teaching and learning process.

5. To demonstrate the significant contributions that library programs can make to school reform and restructuring efforts.

Whether focusing on the role of the librarian as a teacher and information specialist, creating model library programs, or encouraging collaboration among teachers, administrators and librarians, the primary key to addressing these areas both initially and continually was through staff development. Thus, professional development contributed to flexible scheduling and collaboration. Professional development was a vehicle for mentoring, not only librarians, but some teachers and principals as well. The dialogue encouraged through professional development promoted team and school planning among the various professional communities. In so doing, professional development was important in bringing the library into the instructional arena with school reforms. In these ways, professional development was an important vehicle in promoting student learning opportunities through the library.

The role of professional development in moving the library program into the instructional arena can be seen in the case studies of the Denver Public Education Business Coalition area and Chattanooga. In the Denver area, a professional development model using school-based staff developers was already in place. This model was used especially with Literacy League, a school reform that emphasized a literature-based rather than a basal or textbook approach to reading and writing instruction. The Denver PEBC saw Library Power as reinforcing key concepts of Literacy League. Library Power staff developers worked with Literacy League staff developers to guide and encourage collaboration among teachers and the librarian.

In another example in Chattanooga, Paideia and Edna McConnell Clark Foundation school reforms were present in many of the schools at the time that the Library Power grant was awarded. Initially, the reforms were isolated, with each reform having a staff development component. One of the school reform heads described the collaboration that developed and the positive professional development plans that resulted in the following way:

> Library Power, McConnell Clark, and Paideia used to operate in isolation. There was not as much communication as needed. Each of the programs wanted to offer staff development to teachers. This created confusion for teachers. The same people were bumping into each other as all these grants tried to get teachers and principals involved in change. As the Library Power, McConnell Clark, and Paideia heads became more familiar with each other and began talking with each other, we found out that teachers were too busy to buy into any of these projects because they had to be involved in different activities for each project. This was confusing. So, we decided to cooperate and developed an integrated plan for staff development. Now we can parlay our staff development funds and also help teachers see the connections between our projects. We try to look for common themes that cut across our projects, themes like resource-based instruction, interdisciplinary units, and curriculum mapping. Our biggest accomplishment has been the summer institutes collaboratively offered for all teachers in the middle schools, any Library Power school, and any Paideia school.

These sentiments about the value of cooperatively developed professional development programs were echoed by each of the heads of school reform initiatives. There were plans in place to invite the National Science Foundation district coordinator to be part of summer institute programs as well.

Challenges

Professional development was highly valued and emphasized during the Library Power years. The Chattanooga Library Power director summarized it by saying: "Staff development caused more change than anything else we did." Professional development was not without its challenges, however. The Library Power case studies describe four of them.

Need for a Common Vision

To achieve the Library Power goals to the fullest extent possible and at the earliest time possible, a common vision or understanding of the potential role of libraries and librarians is needed. Library Power school faculties varied in the degree to which they began the initiative with a shared vision of their school community role in promoting student learning. Additionally, where a shared vision existed, it was important that it be compatible with the concepts promoted by Library Power. Those schools that embraced inquiry-based learning, for example, were probably more ready for changes promoted through Library Power than those schools that embraced basal learning and standardized testing. Depending on school community background, professional development efforts might bear fruit sooner in some locations than others.

Change Takes Time

Library Power sought to improve teaching and learning through library programs. Resistance to change is a natural occurrence. The degree to which schools and individuals were ready to embrace Library Power concepts varied. No change occurs overnight, and there is a need to nurture individuals engaged in the change process. All those involved in Library Power were involved in change. Librarians were thrust into leadership roles where previously many had been at best, in roles supporting the curriculum. Teachers were asked to collaborate with the librarian when they may have had no experience in doing so or previous motivation to do so. Principals were asked to provide leadership in making the library an integral part of the curriculum when this concept was quite new to them. Although change was a challenge, Library Power was promoted through a variety of professional development opportunities that occurred throughout the Library Power years.

Needs Exist on Many Levels

An ongoing professional development challenge concerned the various professional development needs that occurred within one site or even within one building. Teachers who already had a history of collaborating with the librarian might not need the same staff development programs as teachers who never had collaborated with the librarian. Librarians new to the school or district might have needed an introductory Library Power staff development program although they were working in a school with veteran Library Power teachers. One of the ways that this challenge was addressed was through the use of experienced librarians, teachers, and principals who had been successful in the Library Power initiative. These school and district educators presented in-service programs, served as mentors, and provided visitation sites for those new to the initiative.

Another ongoing challenge concerned how to address the more sophisticated staff development needs of experienced Library Power participants. Sometimes, these needs were met through in-service programs provided by outside experts. The question of providing advanced staff development for those who had been greatly involved in Library Power over several years while meeting the needs of those new to Library Power, even within the same building, was indeed a challenge for Library Power professional development programs.

Sustaining Beyond the Grant

Continuing to promote professional development in the use of the library for teaching and learning is a challenge. The Library Power years offered funds that could be used for outside speakers, as well as support for in-district leaders and incentives for faculty participation in staff development. Maintaining a sufficient level of interest in Library Power principles in the midst of the many educational reforms that compete for support will be an ongoing challenge for the Library Power sites since the completion of the

$1.2 million grant period. This grant paid not only for professional development programs but also for the services of the Library Power director, the primary site-level Library Power change agent.

Library Power Professional Development Reviewed Through Framework

At the beginning of this chapter, seven principles of professional development were listed. These principles will be used as a final framework to examine Library Power professional development.

Effective Professional Development Experiences Are Driven by a Well-Defined Image of Effective Classroom Learning and Teaching

The Library Power initiative focused on the difference that school libraries and librarians could make to the teaching and learning in schools. Many districts, but not all, had a primary emphasis on inquiry-based learning and problem solving. Many schools, but not all, embraced authentic pedagogy, requiring students to think, to develop in-depth understanding, and to apply academic learning to important, realistic problems. These concepts are fully discussed in earlier chapters on instruction and curriculum. While most Library Power professional development programs focused on student opportunities for learning through school libraries, initial emphasis for some Library Power programs was on strengthening the library collection, particularly during the early years when the Library Power goals were being defined. Some, but not all, Library Power sites began with a well-defined image of effective classroom learning and teaching and how Library Power could support this image.

Effective Professional Development Experiences Provide Opportunities to Build Knowledges and Skills

A review of the variety of Library Power professional development programs shows that librarians had many opportunities to build their knowledges and skills. Librarians averaged almost 20 Library Power in-service sessions per person during the Library Power years. They participated in workshops and institutes, participated in professional networks with other librarians, and visited other libraries to learn about Library Power in action. Many teachers also had similar opportunities. Several represented their schools at workshops and institutes and visited other Library Power schools. Other teachers had opportunities to learn through workshops held at their own schools. For the librarian, in particular, there were opportunities to build knowledges and skills.

Eꜰꜰectiᴠe Pʀoꜰessioɴaʟ Deveʟopmeɴt Expeʀieɴces Modeʟ Stʀateɢies

There were many examples of modeling strategies to present Library Power concepts to librarians and teachers. Some library modeling, such as observing flexible scheduling and its promotion of student access, came through visits to library programs. Other modeling occurred when teaching led by both the librarian and teachers was observed. In a few Library Power sites, some modeling was formalized through the use of staff developers who demonstrated collaborative teaching with students for librarians and teachers alike. Whether formal or informal, many professional activities were modeled.

Eꜰꜰectiᴠe Pʀoꜰessioɴaʟ Deveʟopmeɴt Expeʀieɴces Buiʟd a Leaʀɴiɴɢ Commuɴity

Continuous learning, a trait of a learning community, was promoted in Library Power schools. Learning was both formal and informal through the many types of professional development programs offered. Tangible results of professional development, such as collaborations between the librarian and teachers and on-site mentors, encouraged faculty members to grow together. A related way in which the promotion of a learning community was evident was through mini-grant awards. Mini-grant awards ranging from $500 to $1,000 represented one widely used strategy that rewarded teachers and librarians for working together by providing resources for particular instructional units. Some sites also rewarded teachers and librarians with stipends for attending some institutes and workshops and planning instructional strategies collaboratively during that time. These and other opportunities helped to promote a learning community.

Effective Professional Development Experiences Support Educators in Leadership Roles

There were many examples of librarians, teachers, and principals serving in leadership roles in their schools, in the district, and beyond. In most instances during the Library Power years, librarians led in-service programs for teachers in their schools. Some librarians participated as part of a team with other teachers and principals to provide numerous in-service programs. An example of this occurred in Lincoln, where teams provided programs to all schools in the district, as well as at state and national meetings. The Library Power sites evolved to place a primary emphasis on professional development leadership from within the district.

In addition to leadership roles in in-service programs, professional development programs were designed to promote changes in how teachers taught and how students learned with the library central to instruction. Librarians were given many opportunities, with guidance, to expand their roles in the schools. The primary emphasis of these roles was on instructional leadership.

Effective Professional Development Experiences Provide Links to Other Education Parts

Because of the interdisciplinary nature of library efforts to impact the curriculum, several links to other education parts were evident. Baton Rouge, for example, linked to many subject areas through its emphasis on thematic units. Chattanooga linked to other district school reforms and provided consolidated professional development programs. The Denver PEBC linked the Library Power initiative to the Literacy League school reform, and Paterson linked its information processing Library Power focus to 4MAT, a program that linked student learning styles to teachers' individualized instructional plans. Forward in the Fifth linked its professional development program to the Kentucky Educational Reform Act (KERA). As Wehlage notes in Chapter 7, Library Power was more likely to be embraced when it was linked to a compatible school reform.

Effective Professional Development Experiences Continuously Assess Themselves and Make Improvements

There is evidence that throughout the Library Power years, assessments of the professional development programs took place. Many of these assessments were informal observations of staff development programs as well as written evaluations by participants of programs. The Forward in the Fifth professional development program, a key to the Library Power initiative in the Kentucky site, was known for excellence in professional development, in part as a result of its constant reassessments. The levels of staff development at advanced as well as introductory levels at some sites is also credited as resulting from staff development assessments that showed growth in Library Power concept implementation.

Conclusion

The Library Power initiative used a variety of approaches to introduce and sustain professional development programs embracing Library Power concepts. Professional development was an important ingredient in achieving the goals of Library Power, and its effectiveness was enhanced by the professional development's direct connection to the initiative taking place in the schools. There were multiple opportunities to learn, practice, interact, and reinforce new behaviors. The elements of professional development that were found most often among the sites studied were opportunities to build knowledges and skills, modeling strategies, and opportunities for educators to serve in leadership roles within their district and beyond. Using a variety of professional development programs and stages, the role of the librarian in teaching and learning was promoted through shared staff development and school-wide implementation of teacher-librarian collaboration.

References

American Association of School Librarians and Association for Educational Communications and Technology. (1988). *Information power: Guidelines for school library media programs.* Chicago: American Library Association.

Fennema, E., & Nelson, B. S. (Eds.). (1997). *Mathematics teachers in transition.* Mahwah, NJ: Lawrence Erlbaum Associates.

Goldsmith, L., & Shifer, D. (1997). Understanding teachers in transition: Characteristics of a model for developing teachers. In E. Fennema & B. S. Nelson (Eds.), *Mathematics teachers in transition* (pp. 19–54). Mahwah, NJ: Lawrence Erlbaum Associates.

Huberman, M. (1997). Assessing the implementation of innovations in mathematics and science education. In S. A. Raizen & E. D. Britton (Eds.), *Bold ventures: Vol. 1. Patterns among U.S. innovations in science and mathematics education* (pp. 155–200). Dordrecht, The Netherlands: Kluwer Academic.

Loertscher, D. (1988). *Taxonomies of the school library media program.* Englewood, CO: Libraries Unlimited.

Loucks-Horsley, S., Hewson, P. W., Love, N., & Stiles, K. E. (1998). *Designing professional development for teachers of science and mathematics.* Thousand Oaks, CA: Corwin Press, Inc.

McLaughlin, M. W. (1993). What matters most in teachers' workplace context? In J. W. Little & M. W. McLaughlin (Eds.), *Teachers' work: Individuals, colleagues, and contexts* (pp. 79–103). New York: Teachers College Press.

Newmann, F. M., King, B., & Rigdon, M. (1997). Accountability and school performance: Implications from restructuring schools. *Harvard Educational Review, 67* (1), 41–74.

O'Day, J., Goertz, M. E., & Floden, R. E. (1995). Building capacity for education reform. *CPRE Policy Briefs.* New Brunswick, NJ: Rutgers, Consortium for Policy Research in Education.

Webb, N. L. (1997). The changing roles of teachers. In S. A. Raizen & E. D. Britton (Eds.), *Bold ventures: Vol. 1. Patterns among U.S. innovations in science and mathematics education* (pp. 73–96). Dordrecht, The Netherlands: Kluwer Academic.

Webb, N. L., Heck, D. J., & Tate, W. F. (1997). The Urban Mathematics Collaborative Project: A study of teacher, community, and reform. In S. A. Raizen & E. D. Britton (Eds.), *Bold ventures: Vol. 3. Case studies of U.S. innovations in mathematics education* (pp. 245–360). Dordrecht, The Netherlands: Kluwer Academic.

9 INSTITUTIONALIZATION

Gary Wehlage
Douglas L. Zweizig

Introduction

As with any effort at school improvement and reform, questions are naturally raised about the extent to which Library Power will leave a permanent mark on teachers' practices and students' achievement. Such permanent impact is construed as *institutionalization* in this chapter. Institutionalization raises at least two important questions: What is meant by this term? What elements of Library Power need to be institutionalized to achieve long-term impact? Answering these questions can help the Fund, local educational funds, and schools focus on essential elements that can sustain Library Power in current sites and eventually spread it to a larger number of schools.

Institutionalization suggests that a reform or innovation has become a regular practice, one that is part of a school's routine. An institutional routine is by definition a regular, ingrained practice because in the case of schools, for example, it has been found to be a compelling, effective, and generally appropriate way to organize and conduct teaching and learning. In its most complete form, institutionalization represents unquestioned and taken-for-granted automatic practice. If we search for practices that already meet these criteria in schooling, several come to mind. For example, five days make up a school week; students and teachers have a three-month summer vacation; teachers are certified by a university and licensed by the state. Further, it is assumed that children should be age-graded; that is grouped by age because this practice facilitates efficient and effective teaching and learning. According to conventional wisdom, how else could a school organize large numbers of children that range in intellectual and social maturity, skills, and learning requirements? It is true that occasionally one hears about alternatives to such routines, but in public education the practice is nearly universal and largely uncontested.

Another institutionalized practice is subject matter specialization. Teachers teach and students study biology, algebra, and American history. This kind of practice is especially apparent in the higher grades, but even in elementary schools it is common to identify the study of subjects such as mathematics, music, and geography. Textbooks are published by subject; districts and states test children by subject. While some professionals advocate interdisciplinary curriculum, they usually justify such departures from conventional practice by pointing to their success in conveying to children the fundamentals of subject matter previously identified as mathematics, language arts, science, and history. In summary, institutionalization refers to routines that are generally (although never totally) unquestioned practices and goals.

In this chapter we explore the extent to which Library Power has the potential to take on the characteristics of habituated, natural practice. Conducting such an analysis is somewhat speculative, but there are some data about the extent to which core Library Power practices have already taken root. Core practices necessary for institutionalization of Library Power include flexible scheduling and collaboration. Collection development and mapping also appear to be key to establishing a library program that can support collaboration, flexible scheduling, and improved instruction. Interdisciplinary curriculum and resource-based instruction, while not mandated by Library Power, nevertheless are identified by many teachers and principals as desirable practices that flow from a thorough implementation of the initiative. Underlying the desire to see these practices institutionalized is the assumption that they collectively enhance the quality of instruction and ultimately increase children's learning and achievement. In the final analysis, the justification for institutionalizing core practices of Library Power rests on evidence that they in fact produce better learning outcomes for children.

In the next section, we explore the extent to which core practices of Library Power have been implemented in schools. Unless core practices have been implemented with some fidelity and embraced widely by staff, institutionalization is highly unlikely. The analysis of implementation draws on survey data from teachers, librarians, and principals, who indicated the degree to which Library Power practices have taken root in their schools. The evidence they provide is the foundation for a number of our judgments about the potential for institutionalizing Library Power. In a subsequent section we draw from case study testimony and opinion offered by educators and field observers regarding a number of factors that they predict will affect institutionalization. Five factors are identified that tend to either support or inhibit the institutionalization of Library Power. First we assess the depth of the roots put down by the initiative.

Adoption of Practice: Roots of Institutionalization

Surveys of principals asked a number of questions pertaining to the degree of adoption; that is, whether certain practices associated with Library Power had been adopted in their schools and the extent to which Library Power was perceived as responsible for newly adopted practices. Table 9-1 summarizes the principals' responses. Flexible scheduling of library use, a central practice advocated by Library Power, was reported as completely adopted in 64% of the schools. Most of the remaining principals, 29%, reported that flexible scheduling of the library had been adopted by most of the faculty. These data indicate that flexible scheduling of library time for teachers is a practice that is generally accepted and practiced, suggesting a strong basis for institutionalization in many schools.

In 1997, 95% of the librarians who were directly asked about the pattern of scheduling for their libraries reported that their libraries were fully or partially flexibly scheduled. Continuity of this practice is found in the report, from 82% of libraries whose formal funding for Library Power had ended two years earlier, that flexible scheduling was continuing either fully or partially. Full or partial flexible scheduling was continuing in 97% of libraries whose funding had ended a year earlier.

TABLE 9-1
Principals' Attribution of Library Power Practices (Principal Survey, 1997)

	Degree of Adoption				Already Existed?	Attribution			
	None at All 1 %	2 %	3 %	Full Faculty 4 %	% Yes	Mostly Library Power %	Mostly School Reforms %	A Mix %	None %
Flexible scheduling of classes in the library (vs. regular weekly visits)	0.8	6.3	29.3	63.6	28.9	58.0	8.3	31.6	2.1
Total Responding	404				412	383			
Collaboration among teachers and librarians to plan instructional units	0.3	12.5	51.8	35.5	20.6	59.8	4.8	34.3	1.0
Total Responding	392				413	393			
Collaboration between teachers and librarians on developing the library's collection	0.3	12.0	44.5	43.2	28.6	52.5	6.5	38.4	2.6
Total Responding	391				413	385			
Collaboration among teachers to plan instruction	0.2	12.2	50.8	36.8	38.5	26.0	16.3	54.5	3.2
Total Responding	394				413	380			

A second central tenet of Library Power was that teachers and librarians should engage in collaborative planning of instructional units. Table 9-1 reports that principals in almost all schools saw this practice as adopted to some extent. Thirty-six percent of the principals reported that all faculty in their schools were engaged in collaboration with the librarian. Another 52% indicated that many or most teachers and the librarian were so engaged. In addition to reporting collaboration on instruction, about 88% of the principals reported collaboration between teachers and the librarian to develop library collections. Further, 88% of the principals indicated that most or all teachers regularly engaged in joint planning of instruction among themselves. Data from Table 9-1 indicate that collaboration is a widespread practice, and like flexible scheduling, fairly well rooted in Library Power school practice. Principals reported that the practices advocated by Library Power already existed prior to the initiative in only 20% to 39% of the schools. They also indicated that, in most schools, the influence of the Library Power initiative was significant in moving the school toward broader and more complete adoption of this practice. In an additional one-third to one-half of the schools, principals perceived that Library Power worked as part of a mix with other school reforms to move the school toward adoption of the Library Power practices.

Table 9-2 illustrates responses from librarians regarding the extent of collaboration with teachers in planning and providing instruction. The median response from librarians was that they collaborated with just over half (53%) of the teachers in their school. At the upper end of collaboration, the top 10% of the librarians indicated that they collaborated with all teachers in their school. The level of collaboration between librarians and teachers that can be attributed to the introduction of Library Power appears to be significant, because half of the librarians reported almost no collaboration prior to the initiative.

An examination, by funding round, of the percentage of teachers collaborated with shows that librarians whose funding had ended a year or more before the data collection occurred were continuing to collaborate, with percentages at levels greater than those whose funding was only concluding at the time of the data collection. This sustaining or increasing of levels of collaboration gives reason to believe that a core practice of Library Power was becoming institutionalized and that this practice, in some settings, can become self-sustaining.

TABLE 9-2
Collaboration Between Librarians and Teachers
(LMS Survey, 1997)

Distribution of collaboration with teachers	Percentage of teachers that librarians collaborated with in planning or providing instruction	
	Before Library Power	In School Year 1996–97
Upper 10%	58%	100%
Upper 25%	32%	77%
Median (50%)	14%	53%
Lower 25%	0%	32%
Total Responding	342	425

A third perspective on collaboration is provided by teachers' responses to questions about the frequency of their collaboration with librarians and other colleagues. Table 9-3 shows that about 17% of teachers indicated they collaborated "very often" with the librarian in planning and designing instruction. About the same percentage indicated that they did not collaborate at all with the librarian, and about two-thirds of the teachers indicated a little or some collaboration. Collaboration by teachers with other teachers in the planning and design of instruction was somewhat greater than with the librarian; 29% of the teachers indicated that they engaged in this practice with other teachers "very often." Teachers also reported that Library Power was instrumental in promoting collaboration with the librarian and other teachers. Forty-six percent said that Library Power was responsible for increasing collaboration with the librarian, and 22% said that Library Power produced increased collaboration with other teachers.

TABLE 9-3
Collaboration Between Librarians and Teachers
(Teacher Survey, 1997)

How often do you participate in the following types of collaboration:

Collaboration with a librarian for the planning and designing of instruction

Not at all	1	2	3	4	Very often	Mean	% saying LP increased collaboration	n
	17.5%	31.0%	34.1%	17.4%		2.51	45.9%	1,152

Collaboration with a librarian in delivering instruction

Not at all	1	2	3	4	Very often	Mean	% saying LP increased collaboration	n
	31.2%	31.3%	27.2%	10.2%		2.17	34.0%	1,143

Collaboration with other teachers for the planning and designing of instruction

Not at all	1	2	3	4	Very often	Mean	% saying LP increased collaboration	n
	10.8%	23.4%	36.5%	29.4%		2.85	21.9%	1,152

Collaboration with other teachers in delivering instruction

Not at all	1	2	3	4	Very often	Mean	% saying LP increased collaboration	n
	23.3%	33.7%	26.9%	16.2%		2.36	14.9%	1,150

*The column "n" indicates the number of respondents to each category.

Library Power schools were to arrange access to the library so that individuals and groups of students could use it in a manner best suited to their needs. Table 9-4 demonstrates that teachers arranged for their students to use the library in a variety of ways. By a slight margin they still favored sending students as a whole class, but more than half sent students in small groups, and two-thirds sent them as individuals. This pattern is substantially maintained by teachers in schools whose Library Power funding has ended.

TABLE 9-4
How Teachers Report Students Visit the Library
(Teacher Survey, 1997)

Please indicate how your students visit the library:

	% Yes	n
As a Class	70.4%	1146
In Small Groups	57.0%	1146
As Individuals	67.7%	1146

* The column "n" indicates the number of respondents to each question.

A central feature of Library Power was the improvement of library collections, and evidence of such improvement is an important indicator of Library Power implementation and the potential for institutionalization. Table 9-5 reports indicators of improvement of collections as reflected in teachers' views about how well teachers' and students' needs were being met. About 72% of the teachers indicated that the collection served them "well" or "very well." In supporting students' needs, about 77% of the teachers responded with "well" or "very well."

TABLE 9-5
Teachers' Report of Collection Support
(Teacher Survey, 1997)

Overall, how well does the school library collection support your needs as a teacher and the needs of your students?

	Very Well 5	4	3	2	1 Not Well	n
Supports Needs of Teacher	41.6%	30.3%	20.0%	5.1%	3.1%	1,143
Supports Needs of Students	44.7%	32.0%	17.6%	3.9%	1.8%	1,145

Table 9-6 presents librarians' ratings of different categories in the collections. Only foreign language and mathematics materials stand out because of their somewhat poorer ratings in comparison with others. The encouraging news is that there is consistent improvement in librarians' ratings occurring over three years in both "currentness" and "quantity."

TABLE 9-6
Percent of Librarians' Ratings of Collection Areas
As "Adequate" or "Excellent"
(Matched LMS Surveys, All Rounds, 1995 and 1997)

	Currentness		Quantity	
Collection Area	**1995** %	**1997** %	**1995** %	**1997** %
Reference	83	95	86	93
Science/Technology	81	95	61	90
Mathematics	51	77	38	63
Geography	61	86	57	80
History	70	85	62	81
Biography	88	91	88	92
Social Sciences	73	93	71	88
Fiction	75	95	82	91
Picture Books	88	96	82	91
Literature	75	91	72	83
Fine Arts	62	81	53	74
Foreign Language	42	70	26	58
Careers	48	61	37	53
Health	65	85	52	77
Total Responding	221	221	221	221

The data in Table 9-6 came from a matched set of Library Power schools responding in the years reported. For each survey year, the schools are a mix, with some near the beginning of their three-year projects and some further along. In 1997, a number of the schools reporting had completed their Library Power projects as much as two years earlier, while others were completing their grant period at that time. Some of the librarians rating collections in 1995 had already upgraded collections in their libraries. The evidence about collection improvement becomes clearer when a subset of comparable schools from Round 3 is examined; collection ratings from this group were gathered close to the beginning of the schools' three-year involvement in the initiative (1995) and close to the end (1997). Table 9-7 provides longitudinal data about collection improvement for schools during the first and third years of their funding. These data indicate that all categories in the collection were given substantially improved ratings over the grant period for these libraries.

TABLE 9-7
Percent of Round 3 Librarians' Ratings of
Collection Areas As "Adequate" or "Excellent"
(Matched LMS Surveys, Round 3 Only, 1995 and 1997)

	Currentness		Quantity	
Collection Area	**1995 %**	**1997 %**	**1995 %**	**1997 %**
Science/Technology	48	95	36	94
Mathematics	31	72	23	59
Geography	44	94	39	87
History	55	89	49	84
Biography	67	98	61	97
Social Sciences	64	94	61	89
Fiction	78	95	73	92
Picture Books	82	96	71	91
Literature	64	85	47	80
Fine Arts	47	87	37	82
Foreign Language	20	61	5	48
Total Responding	64	63	64	63

Teachers also reported greater satisfaction with their libraries. Table 9-8 presents teachers' responses to questions about improvements in the collection since Library Power began. Eighty-five percent of the teachers reported that the library "much better" or "somewhat better" supported their instructional needs, and a slightly larger percentage gave the same responses about the collections' ability to support the needs of their students.

TABLE 9-8
Teacher Ratings of Change of Collections
Since Library Power Began
(1997)

	Much Better	Somewhat Better	About the Same	Somewhat Worse	Much Worse	n
Supports needs of teachers	50.9%	34.0%	13.4%	1.3%	0.4%	1,072
Supports needs of students	56.7%	30.8%	10.4%	1.4%	0.7%	1,072

*The column "n" indicates the number of respondents to each question.

Finally, survey data were collected from all school-level personnel to directly address the issue of institutionalization. Table 9-9 reports responses from librarians, principals, and teachers based on a series of questions about whether they believe aspects of Library Power "will continue" and "should continue." With only one exception, responses overwhelmingly indicated that flexible scheduling, collaboration, collection development, and an enlarged role for the librarian in teaching and learning both *will* and *should continue.* The only irregularity in the responses was from librarians who exhibited some skepticism about whether their schools would continue to add large quantities of new materials to the library. While 98% of the librarians said such additions should continue, only about half believed that it would happen. This response probably reflects past experiences in which libraries have been among the first areas to receive cuts in funding or where previous initiatives have not been sustained. Nevertheless, the highly positive endorsement of Library Power found in these data, coming from different perspectives, suggests that the foundation has been laid for institutionalization. If collection development continues, institutionalization of other practices is more likely.

TABLE 9-9
Continuation of Library Power Practices
(1997)

	Respondents					
	Librarians		Principals		Teachers	
	% Yes	n	% Yes	n	% Yes	n
Flexible scheduling of classes in the library (vs. regular weekly visits)						
Will continue	92.2%	403	96.4%	363	93.1%	851
Should continue	98.2%	405	97.8%	362	85.3%	1,006
On-demand use of the library by individual students or groups (vs. at preset times)						
Will continue	93.2%	404	96.9%	360	90.7%	830
Should continue	97.0%	403	98.0%	355	90.0%	1,008
Addition of large quantities of new materials						
Will continue	49.6%	383	72.2%	339	82.9%	794
Should continue	98.0%	415	98.1%	370	98.6%	1,040
Collaborative planning with librarian on instructional units						
Will continue	95.8%	404	98.6%	363	93.5%	814
Should continue	99.7%	408	99.4%	356	97.7%	1,028
Integration of new technologies into the school's curriculum						
Will continue	95.8%	402	95.8%	361	90.3%	803
Should continue	98.8%	413	99.4%	361	97.6%	1,042
Enlarged role for the library as a resource for teachers and students						
Will continue	94.3%	405	98.4%	368	90.4%	806
Should continue	99.3%	408	100.0%	359	97.8%	1,035
A full-time librarian in the school						
Will continue	96.8%	413	94.5%	365	94.8%	833
Should continue	98.3%	406	97.2%	364	96.5%	1,036
Collaboration between teachers and librarian on developing the library's collection						
Will continue	95.3%	411	98.6%	360	94.1%	814
Should continue	99.8%	408	99.5%	361	99.1%	1,028

In summary, substantial evidence exists that central features of Library Power have been extensively implemented. Survey data from principals, librarians, and teachers all generally support the claim that the innovations of flexible scheduling and collaboration are widely, if not universally, practiced by staff. All parties appear to value these key practices and want them continued.

Most significantly, Library Power has enhanced the quality of school libraries, the bedrock of the new practices. Collection improvement has been nearly universal, and this fact appears to be crucial in bringing about institutionalization for two reasons. First, the addition of significant amounts of new collaboratively selected materials in libraries means that teachers have a personal investment in their library. Second, to the extent that these new resources support their instruction and student needs (as the survey data indicate), teachers are likely to continue demanding new and high-quality materials and seeking the advice and guidance of the librarian. The initiative has given schools a standard to better judge the value of a good library as teachers engage in curriculum development and instruction. While the freshness and adequacy of materials in the collection will decline over time if it remains static, a process of collection development has been established that can be institutionalized. Thus the combination of good library resources and new practices to make better use of the resources suggests that a firm foundation for institutionalization has been laid. However, there is more to institutionalization than the initial implementation of innovations. A number of long-term factors must also be considered.

Supports for and Impediments to Institutionalization

Survey data are useful for viewing the impact and status of core Library Power practices at the conclusion of the initiative. Such information is, however, only suggestive of the future course of Library Power. To provide another perspective on institutionalization, we turn to the views of participants and field observers as they reflect on their experiences and what they believe the future holds. This information comes from a variety of observers, a number of whom are seasoned reformers who have wrestled with the problems of implementation and the politics of maintaining the integrity of programs.

Five factors emerged from testimony about the possibility of long-term use and development of Library Power: 1) external support, 2) policy, 3) leadership, 4) staff development, and 5) funding. These factors are supporting elements when positive and impediments to institutionalization when negative. Each factor is a more specific aspect of the overall culture and structure of schools, both of which are necessary to sustain and institutionalize an innovation such as Library Power. By culture we mean the beliefs, values, goals, and typical practices that characterize day-to-day school life. For example, one cultural trait is a belief by faculty in the practice of collaboration to develop curriculum. Commitments to a coherent and consistent approach to instruction (for example, having students regularly engage in inquiry) and to specific kinds of outcomes (for example, learning to apply knowledge to the analysis of real-world problems) also reflect cultural traits. Combining a number of these traits produces an identifiable school culture.

Structure refers to a school's organizational mechanisms, which are pivotal in shaping the ways in which people interact. Daily interactions (or their absence) generate a particular set of human relationships. Schools can vary substantially in the richness and quality of these relationships; they can be dense and supportive, or sparse and isolating. Variations in school structure include age-grading, teaching teams, and subject matter departments. Some schools have received considerable autonomy through the mechanism of site-based management that allows for rearranging structure. Some faculty have the authority to make decisions about many important areas affecting the allocation and use of a school's resources, such as finances, time, and space. As a reform, Library Power sought to affect both the structure and culture of schools by requiring changes in how the library was used and the practice of collaboration between teachers and the librarian.

The theory of institutionalization for Library Power rests on the following premise: The vision of Library Power includes the belief that a high-quality education requires students to learn to inquire using the information and technological resources of a modern library. Institutionalizing Library Power means that the school culture is built around beliefs that collection development, collaboration, and flexible scheduling are core practices that promote the larger vision. Acting on their beliefs, teachers, librarians, and principals search for useful structural variation to support Library Power practices; that is, to achieve the valued end of student achievement, educators will design policies and structures that facilitate best practices such as collaboration, flexible scheduling, and new uses of library resources.

In describing each of the five factors we explore how they might contribute to or inhibit the building of a culture and structure that would institutionalize the goals and practices of Library Power. Although we separate these factors for purposes of analysis and explanation, it will quickly become apparent that they are often inextricably related and nested within each other. For example, state or local policies often affect funding used to hire staff or to provide staff development programs. In the following sections, we draw selected examples from case study reports to illustrate specific aspects of how these factors support or impede the institutionalizing of Library Power.

External Support

Generally schools need help from beyond their own walls if they are to succeed in establishing innovations in practice. To provide some of this help, the Library Power initiative created a network to support schools in carrying out innovations. This network of external support included AASL and PEN, providing staff development and continuous consultation. Support generated at the site by local education funds proved highly significant when it came to implementation. Parents, educators, business groups, and in some cases even the local public library worked in coalitions to steer Library Power through the school system and give it legitimacy.

If teachers are to transform their teaching in significant ways and then sustain this transformation, they must have the support of external interest groups from the larger community. No reform, no matter how compelling to professionals, can survive unless the larger community also believes that its goals and practices are legitimate and important. In a number of sites, the clout of the local educational fund made the difference in marshaling political, intellectual, and material resources to bring about changes in teachers' practices with regard to using the library and more generally in the culture and structure of schools. In the final analysis, one of the great strengths of Library Power was its acceptance and active support by local educational funds, which represented important segments of the larger communities.

A number of sites stand out in their success at generating local political and intellectual support for Library Power. Chattanooga benefited enormously because the local education fund provided, among other things, a powerful voice for the initiative. The local education fund was able to articulate a convincing rationale and justification for implementation of Library Power. Not only did the local fund convince educators, but the larger community was also persuaded about the value of Library Power. Another example of strong external support was Forward in the Fifth, a regional organization with its headquarters in Berea, Kentucky. Forward in the

Fifth provided support for the multiple school districts within this area. It was responsible for writing the Library Power proposal and subsequently managing grant activities for the schools. Significant also was that Forward in the Fifth succeeded in legitimating both Library Power's and the state's efforts to implement the Kentucky Education Reform Act (KERA), which educators saw as mutually supportive. The political authority of KERA helped to give some momentum to Library Power innovations.

Another example of strong external support for Library Power came from the Denver site. The Public Education and Business Coalition (PEBC) was quickly attracted to the concept of Library Power. This organization recognized that its own initiative, the Literacy League, and Library Power were complementary. The Literacy League promoted resource-based teaching, but without a strong library component in the schools this strategy was limited. Therefore, support for Library Power by PEBC was natural. This message was carried to the school level, where the Literacy League's program was generally well received. Principals, teachers, and librarians clearly understood the supportive relationship between the two initiatives, and at a number of schools testimony indicated that a major reason for joining Library Power was that it meshed so well with Literacy League efforts. Such external support was particularly effective in helping to implement the components of Library Power and, if continued for the long run, will help to institutionalize the reform.

Policy

Another important support (or possible impediment) for institutionalization is policies that flow from national, state, and local agencies. Some policy is produced by federal legislation, such as laws affecting the education of children with disabilities, but most educational policy in this country is generated by state and local authorities. For Library Power to succeed in the long run it is crucial that at the very least policies not inhibit, and ideally support, its goals and practices. Perhaps the clearest example of the potential for policy to support Library Power was in Kentucky.

The story of the Kentucky Education Reform Act and its subsequent impact on many aspects of the state's schools is now well known. In Kentucky, state policy has been relatively effective in bringing about real changes in practice in many schools. The sweeping legislative mandates addressed most of the key leverage points in the educational system, including, among others, goals, staff development, assessment of educational outcomes, site-based management, and support of upgraded technology.

Schools in this state are held relatively more accountable for helping students learn to use communication and math skills, apply knowledge to real problems and life situations, become self-sufficient adults, and learn how to acquire new information through a variety of sources.

Having state policy mandate that schools help students learn to inquire and to apply acquired knowledge in solving real-world problems turned out to be a challenge for which Library Power was made to order. To quote from the proposal written by Forward in the Fifth, Library Power "will be a tool that schools and teachers will use to help students achieve objectives outlined in KERA." It would appear that as long as KERA remains a vital force, schools will have to respond by building a culture and structure to implement its intent, an intent that is closely allied with Library Power. To the extent other states, or even individual districts, implement similar policies, the goals of Library Power will be enhanced at the school level and institutionalization is more likely.

Not all state policy so clearly meshed with Library Power. A more ambiguous case was found in New Jersey, where the state recently provided that each district receive a comprehensive funding allocation of $7,200 per pupil. Among other things, this new formula eliminated categorical allocations for guidance staff, librarians, and nurses. Funding such staff positions became a matter for local decision. School districts could receive a state supplement to the base level allocation by presenting evidence of "demonstrably effective programs," a category of additional funding that might well be used to support Library Power practices and collection enhancement.

How will the Paterson district respond to the new state policy? Several possibilities come to mind. One strategy is to establish district policy to use part of the per pupil allocation to permanently fund Library Power practices and/or to continue developing school collections. A second strategy is to make a case to the state that Library Power was "demonstrably effective" and that the district should receive additional funding to continue building libraries and implementing new practices. Fundamental to implementing one of these strategies is a strong belief in the value of libraries and the kind of instruction that can occur if teachers and students use them well. Given the difficult circumstances for public education in Paterson and the inability to involve all schools in Library Power, whether such beliefs are well entrenched in Paterson has not been clear to observers. At this time, it is too early to be sure what direction Paterson will take, but certainly the new funding policy has created an opportunity for the district to institutionalize the program.

Leadership

Systemic leadership—aligned leadership at all levels—is most likely to promote Library Power institutionalization. Such leadership comes from national and state agencies as well as the local district and staff at individual schools. Several sites produced leadership through strong teamwork among local organizations. For example, Chattanooga benefited from the combined efforts of a strong Library Power director and local education fund director. Lincoln's success was partially due to the close personal ties between the Library Power director, the district's library media supervisor, and the library education fund director. Progress down the long road of library improvements at the Paterson site was due primarily to the close-knit relations between the Library Power director and the district's library media supervisor. Chattanooga, Lincoln, and Baton Rouge had Library Power directors who were able to conceive of and implement district-wide plans, including effective staff development programs, that maximized buy-in from educators in most schools.

Local education funds provided significant leadership, especially during the planning period. Forward in the Fifth was responsible for writing the initial proposal for the Berea site. This organization was repeatedly cited by a variety of sources as crucial not only in generating a visionary proposal but also in carrying out a strategy that successfully implemented the program. As pointed out earlier, Forward in the Fifth provided leadership to integrate Library Power and KERA staff development programs. It took the initiative in developing a successful mini-grant program that stimulated teacher initiative at the building level and made Library Power a high-profile program that captured public support for improving library resources; its leadership proved essential in bringing multiple communities and school districts into a common effort.

As many observers have noted, the principal is often key to whether a reform or innovation becomes a school-wide agenda. In a number of reports from the field, the point was made that the principal determined whether teachers made Library Power a central component in their instruction. In several sites, it was noted that a number of Library Power schools underwent a change of principals during the course of the initiative. In some situations, such a change meant de-emphasizing the program. In still others where Library Power had not been on the agenda, a new principal put it on the agenda, and the school joined the initiative. Unfortunately, the luck and chance of such leadership changes often determined which schools became thoroughly engaged in Library Power. Promoting widespread and consistent leadership for Library Power among principals is an agonizing problem. The most reasonable strategy is to ensure that teachers, their principal, and the central office above the principal are all committed to Library Power. In such an environment, principal leadership on behalf of the program is likely. A number of sites established Library Power as a district-wide practice; these sites experienced much less difficulty with internal staff changes and presented a more aligned leadership, greatly enhancing the likelihood of institutionalization.

Staff Development

The topic of staff development was described in detail in Chapter 8, but it is reviewed here because it is one of the key steps on the path to institutionalization of an innovation. Teachers, librarians, and principals need an initial understanding of the intent of Library Power and how to practice it, and staff development programs need to evolve as educators become familiar with core practices. As staff become more sophisticated and as new issues arise, good staff development programs respond accordingly. Shaping this evolution for experienced staff while at the same time bringing new staff into the community of practice central to Library Power suggests a tension for schools. How can both tasks be accomplished? Institutionalization suggests a continuous socialization process to bring new staff into the fold. At the same time, staff veterans will likely benefit from exploring new issues and some old issues in greater depth as they build on their experiences. This expansion of staff development programs in both range and refinement is fundamental to institutionalization. How did the sites fare in meeting this challenge?

The panoply of staff development activities offered by Library Power sites included almost every conceivable strategy. Summer institutes were held at almost all sites. Workshops and in-service programs were numerous. More specialized meetings for librarians and principals were held at many sites to address aspects of particular concern. To see how Library Power worked, teachers and librarians visited schools with Library Power already in place. Many sites used mini-grants (Chattanooga and Lincoln typically gave $1,000) to help teachers develop their own suggestions about how best to use Library Power resources and ideas. Several sites combined Library Power staff development with other school reform efforts: Berea integrated Library Power with KERA; Chattanooga did this with Paideia and the Edna McConnell Clark middle school program; and Denver used the Literacy League initiative as a springboard for Library Power.

The range of topics covered included the core practices—collaboration, flexible scheduling, collection mapping—as well as many other techniques and topics. In response to other reform efforts and staff interests, topics such as information processing skills, resource-based learning, multicultural literature, technology, and storytelling were all given attention. The variety and frequency of staff development offerings indicated that this component was considered important to the implementation of Library Power by the sites. But what impact did such an investment have on staff?

Reports from librarians and teachers repeatedly lauded their staff development experiences. In particular, librarians claimed that staff development helped them enormously to take on their new role as teacher and in collaborating with other staff in curriculum development. In some cases, librarians took on the role of staff developer as they worked with teachers or with other librarians in schools just getting started with Library Power. For librarians, these experiences were powerful in shaping their beliefs, expectations, and practices. To the extent that librarians became the repository of Library Power culture and used their position to reinforce its practices, institutionalization was promoted. When librarians, and certain teachers who had acquired leadership roles, left a school, the strength of this culture and practice seemed to diminish. Staff turnover was and remains one of the critical problems facing any school in its attempts to develop a strong professional community and institutionalized practice.

Staff development was critical for this initiative because preprofessional education programs for librarians, teachers, and principals have not emphasized the contributions of library resources and collaboration to quality of instruction. At one site, the presence of a library educator on the site-level advisory committee led to close collaboration between the Library Power project in the schools and the instruction provided for librarians in that graduate program. Such arrangements would go a long way to promoting institutionalization.

Funding

A typical query from teachers concerned the fate of the program once DeWitt Wallace–Reader's Digest funding was gone. It should come as no surprise that educators were often concerned about the adequacy of continued funding, especially for staff development and collection improvements. Such concerns appeared more acute in some districts than others. Lincoln's educators pointed to recent state legislation that placed a cap on property taxes. In the short run, the result was almost sure to mean reduced funding for education unless other non-property tax revenue could be generated. It was reported that about one-third of the elementary school principals in Lincoln expressed some doubt about the relative value of Library Power when compared with other needs in their schools. The prediction was that allocations for the school library would be cut. In danger also were supports such as staff development, clerical staff, and time for planning and collaboration. On the other hand, most principals in Lincoln Library Power schools claimed to value the process of collection development and a continuation of the basic philosophy and practices of Library Power. Given this tension, it was unclear which aspects of Library Power, if any, will continue and become institutionalized.

The Denver site was an amalgam of districts with quite different funding situations. Some were financially more secure than the city system, which was concerned because the state legislature had recently voted to restrict spending on education. Instructional programs considered ancillary, such as libraries and music, were hardest hit by these cuts. Hard choices were made, often at the school level through site-based management decisions, about how and whether to support the library. On the other hand, schools in the Cherry Creek district could respond to changes in funding by making their own budget decisions. In this case, the library and the Library Power practices did not have to suffer, especially with creative use of external resources such as parent and community volunteers. In some schools, however, the principals decided to cut paraprofessional help in their libraries; the result was to start a downward spiral of reduced collaboration and use of the resources.

New Haven was a third site where concern about funding was paramount. In general, the district epitomizes many of the urban school problems in this country. These problems have some of their origins in the district's low financial resources and become visible in the district's low human resources and low student achievement. Staff provided for libraries was significantly below that for the state as a whole; the percentage of tested students meeting state goals was less than half the level for the state. A central problem in New Haven is how to obtain the financial resources to hire and train quality staff who can perform the difficult task of teaching large numbers of disadvantaged children. Library Power itself requires high-quality, well-trained staff to act on its purposes and implement its structures. Teaching children to use complex information technology and resources is difficult work, much more difficult than having children read a textbook and answer the questions at the end of the chapter. In a system like New Haven, the financial resources required to train staff and sustain them in new practices are substantial.

Observers noted that in New Haven neither Library Power funding nor new financial commitments from the district were capable of making up for years of neglect. Schools were without libraries and served by itinerant librarians responsible for 9 or 10 schools. Budgets for library materials and equipment were less than one-half the state average. In too many schools, basic facilities such as air conditioning and up-to-date collections were still missing. The average copyright date in history, science, and geography books was 1968. General neglect of the schools prepared people for what they foresaw as inevitable: with the disappearance of external funding the program would also vanish. One principal offered a pragmatic strategy. He had seen programs come and go, and he assumed Library Power was no different, but he hoped to keep the library as a central piece in the instructional picture. Others were not so sanguine. One librarian said there was no substitute for money to buy new books. Another person pointed out that while she was "tremendously pleased" with what Library Power had accomplished, she had seen many fine programs leave no trace after the money ran out. If the basic financial support for the libraries disappears, the best librarians will leave, taking with them the expertise and commitment needed to keep the spirit of Library Power alive.

Even districts not faced with new funding obstacles inevitably encountered tough decisions with the conclusion of their Library Power grants. Baton Rouge is a prime example. Reports on this site from two seasoned observers noted the same problems. As a site thoroughly committed to the initiative and quite successful in broadly implementing it in many schools, the district faced difficulties with continued funding of staff development programs and library collections. The staff development challenge was to fund programs that went beyond the initial stages of Library Power implementation to introduce more sophisticated uses of library resources. Leadership for such efforts was questionable because the position of Library Power director was eliminated.

The Baton Rouge site had re-allocated textbook monies to help build the library collection. Would schools be able to maintain the per pupil allocation for collection development once the Library Power grant was terminated? It was suggested by some in the district that these monies should again be allocated for new textbooks. While the core processes of Library Power were likely to continue in some form at many schools, it was feared that collection development might come to a halt. One librarian summarized the problem:

> If we had more funds, I would spend them on books—in
> fiction, in biography . . . , science, the new Russia. . . .
> Other things we can continue without money—collaborative
> planning, thematic units, flexible scheduling—but you
> can't keep your collection current without money.

The Berea site seemed one of the best prepared to continue funding aspects of Library Power. Forward in the Fifth was a well-established external organization with the ability to generate funds to support a variety of projects in the schools. For example, Forward in the Fifth was prepared to continue funding some Library Power staff development activities that teachers had identified as extremely valuable in helping them make use of the new resources. Highly significant also is the fact that KERA continues to push for improved schooling and, as noted at several points in this book, its intentions are consistent with and reinforcing of Library Power goals and practices. Given this symbiotic relationship, it is likely that funding for collections and help for teachers in using the new resources will continue.

As a general rule, one can expect funding to be less of a problem at sites that have strong external support for Library Power goals. To the extent that state, community, and parental leaders and the local education fund believe that the kind of schooling envisioned by Library Power is what they want for their children, funding will be directed to continuing and strengthening collections and the instructional processes that make good use of them.

Conclusion

Institutionalization of Library Power requires that its core practices become routine. A culture is established in which teachers, students, and the community believe that such practices are valuable because they provide for high-quality student learning. In Library Power schools, the accepted belief is that students must learn to use modern library resources and that collaboration, flexible scheduling, and collection development are important components in promoting this kind of education. Such beliefs and structures combine to institutionalize Library Power.

Evidence from a number of sites suggests that the core practices have been genuinely accepted for their success in providing students with a richer variety of resources. Educators and the public at the sites have come to see value in the structures and practices of Library Power and hope that they can be institutionalized. To the extent that communities, especially through their local education funds, can continue to demand that schools offer the practices and resources associated with Library Power, it will become institutionalized. Long-term factors such as continued funding, staff development, leadership, and support from state and local policy directives each has a role to play in reinforcing the impetus to institutionalize Library Power.

10 FRAMING THE LIBRARY POWER EVALUATION

CURRENT AND FUTURE Implications

Adam Stoll

A New Paradigm for Research

Library Power presented the rarest of opportunities—an opportunity for leaders in a field to implement their vision of practice on a national scale.

The vision articulated by the school library field in *Information Power: Guidelines for School Library Media Centers* (1988), was a call to action. It identified the mission of school library programs as that of ensuring students and staff are effective users of ideas and information. *Information Power* suggests that this mission is achieved by:

- providing intellectual and physical access to materials in all formats;

- providing instruction to foster competence and stimulate interest in reading, viewing, and using information and ideas; and

- working with other educators to design learning strategies to meet the needs of individual students (*Information Power*, 1988, p.1).

This vision of practice places the library media program at the center of teaching and learning. It identifies significant roles for the library media program in the design and delivery of instruction. For this vision to be realized, library media programs have to be thoroughly and thoughtfully integrated into schools' mainstream teaching and learning activities.

This vision of "integrated practice" changes the expectations for practice. As we can see in the years since the vision was articulated through its implementation in Library Power, it's no longer acceptable to think of a school library program as a stand-alone entity that supplements classroom teaching and learning. Under the integrated practice envisioned in *Information Power*, high performing school library programs are fully integrated into the schools' instructional and curricular activities.

This vision of practice also changes the ground rules for program evaluation in ways that are profound and full of promise. It's no longer sufficient to focus on traditional indicators of the health of the library program, such as the currency and quantity of a collection; book circulation rates; number of books read in a library-sponsored book competition; or amount of learning that takes place in the library. Under this new paradigm it becomes necessary to study the fuller incorporation of library program resources in instructional and curricular activities.

Over 10 years, the $45-million Library Power initiative became the largest national demonstration project ever launched in the school library field. Its evaluation, which gathered information from teachers, principals and library media specialists from across 456 schools represents the largest, most comprehensive applied research project ever to examine the role school library programs can play in enhancing teaching and learning in schools. It focused on a large-scale effort to implement the integrated practice envisioned in *Information Power*.

The evaluation engaged leading researchers from the education and school library fields in a sustained effort to consider, under this new paradigm, what's important about school library programs. This chapter summarizes the major lessons that subsequently emerged from this four-year dialogue about what needs to be studied to capture the importance of integrated practice and the implications of these lessons for future inquiry in this area.

The Unnatural Divide

To begin this discussion, it's helpful to examine the existing state of practice and the connections between the school library community and the larger education community. How much has *Information Power* and consequently Library Power shifted the paradigm? How common is integrated practice?

One would imagine that schools nationwide would spend $828 million a year on school library collections and materials alone only if they were intertwined with curriculum and instruction (NCES, 1998).[1] In reality, this is not the norm.

For decades, categorical funding streams, separate professional training programs, and separate professional communities and vocabularies have combined to create distance between the school library and broader educational community. This distance is confirmed in recent national studies.

The national evaluation of Library Power is one such study. It shows that prior to Library Power, library media specialists collaborated with only 22% of the teachers in their schools on planning and providing instruction. Furthermore, it shows that teacher involvement in helping to develop collections and select the information resources being purchased to support instruction was practically unheard of in 71% of the schools.

Another study, the National Center for Education Statistics's Schools and Staffing Survey (SASS) confirms these findings. The SASS data were drawn from a nationally representative sample of teachers, principals and librarians surveyed in the 1993–94 school year. SASS data show that when asked if they plan with librarians to integrate library services into instruction, only 24% of teachers strongly agree. SASS data also indicate that 16% of principals feel librarians have a great deal of influence over establishing a curriculum, whereas 64% of the principals felt teachers had substantial influence on the curriculum. Additionally, SASS data show that only 44% of librarians report helping plan units of instruction related to reading with some classroom teachers on a weekly basis, and librarians reported being much less involved in weekly collaboration with classroom teachers in other subject areas.

Additional evidence of the distance between the school library and education fields surfaced over the course of the national evaluation effort. In dialogues involving more than 30 researchers and advisors, hailing in equal proportions from the two fields, it became evident that very few of the scholars from the education field were aware that in most states, school library media specialists are certified teachers who go on for additional training to become specialists in information resources. Once they discovered this, it changed their outlook on school libraries. The notion of having a certified teacher in buildings with expertise in the acquisition and utilization of information resources piqued their interest in the project and the potential of school library programs.

Similarly, researchers and advisors from the school library field were consistently surprised to learn that the phrase "information literacy" was not well recognized by representatives from the broader education field. Information literacy is the phrase used by many in the school library field to depict the essence of what school libraries are all about—helping students to become effective locators and users of information. It is the central concept around which the updated version of *Information Power* (1998) is organized. Once this phrase was explained to representatives from the broader education field, it too piqued their interest because it embodies many of the concepts that an emerging body of research indicates are central to how people learn (Bransford et al., 1998).

In light of this divide, the Library Power initiative embarked on an important undertaking as it attempted to promote integrated practice. The evaluation of Library Power also embarked on an important undertaking as it attempted to measure progress toward achieving integrated practice and as it attempted to capture the importance of integrated practice.

Evolving Practice and Perspectives

As teachers, library media specialists, and principals worked together to advance integrated practice in schools, their understanding of what could be accomplished through integrated practice evolved. Generally, participants came to understand that original expectations were too low. Through integrated practice, the school library program had the potential to contribute to curriculum development and the design and delivery of instruction in ways that exceeded original expectations.

As the evaluators watched the practice unfold, their understanding of what needed to be captured grew. This required the evaluation to evolve as well. At the outset of the research effort, it was clear that a focus on traditional indicators of the strength of a library media program as a stand-alone resource would not be enough. It was evident that it would be necessary to focus on the ways teachers and library media specialists work together under integrated practice. The extent to which it would be necessary to capture the effects of integrated practice on the quality of teaching and learning and the development and awareness of curricula became increasingly evident as the work unfolded.

As the initiative and the evaluation evolved, researchers realized that to fully understand the effects of integrated practice they would have to focus inquiry on the following core issues:

- How well do library resources support the needs of instruction?

- How are library resources used?

- How do library program resources influence the design of instructional units?

- How does integrated practice contribute to the quality of teaching and learning?

- How does integrated practice affect student achievement?

These issues, identified through this research effort as being central to understanding integrated practice, will be discussed in the remainder of this chapter. In the discussion of each, an effort will be made to highlight ways in which the integrated practice implemented through Library Power required evaluators to stretch their investigation beyond the typical approaches used to examine school library programs, and where appropriate, thoughts about issues that might be tackled in future research will be offered.

Understanding Integrated Practice

How Well Do Library Resources Support the Needs of Instruction?

School libraries' holdings provide rich resources to support reading instruction, student research and inquiry, and deeper content coverage in instruction. Library resources work in concert with other information resources located throughout a school, such as textbooks, technological resources housed outside of libraries, and teachers' classroom collections. Libraries are not capable of being all things to all people. They are never likely to be financed at a level that will enable them to be broad and deep in all areas. At their best, libraries' holdings are strong in areas that align well with the priorities of instruction, and they thereby extend teaching and learning opportunities.

Traditionally, efforts to study the quality of library collections and other holdings have focused on assessing the currency and quantity of materials. This approach attempts to establish whether a library possesses a rich enough set of resources to support a wide array of teaching and learning activities. Traditional indicators provide important information on a collection's quality and breadth. They include:

- average copyright date of materials;

- number of materials held within certain subject areas; and

- librarians' ratings of the adequacy of their collections and other holdings, across subject areas.

It became clear, under Library Power, that additional measures are needed to understand the value of a collection within the context of integrated practice. It's necessary to gather information on the extent to which users value the collection as well. In particular, it's important to understand whether collections are sufficiently deep in the areas in which teachers would most like them to support student learning. For instance:

- If fifth-grade teachers want materials that will enable them and their students to explore the Civil War, does the library possess sufficient depth and range in materials for them to explore social, historical, political, economic, scientific, and biographic material to support this priority?

- If first-grade teachers want to rely heavily on literature to support reading instruction, does the library possess sufficient depth and range in materials to support this priority?

Integrated practice calls for greater connections between library holdings and the priorities of instruction. To gauge whether these connections exist, it's necessary to gather information on:

- the extent to which teachers feel library resources support instruction; and

- the extent to which the collection meets students' needs.

To truly understand the connections between library holdings and instruction, it's important to inquire into the processes used to forge these connections. It becomes important to understand:

- the extent to which teachers and librarians work together to assess the quality of information resources and identify acquisition priorities; and

- the linkages between collaborative work on design and delivery of instruction and the collection development process.

Integrated practice places new demands on library holdings and the collection development process. It requires the collection to place emphasis on areas where teachers want to go beyond the textbook, to deepen content coverage and promote student inquiry. It requires strong awareness of teachers' instructional priorities. The extent to which the collection is being developed to meet the needs of users becomes a core measure of the collection's quality.

How Are Library Resources Used?

Library resources, when used, offer a rich array of literature to promote reading comprehension and students' interest in reading, as well as resources to promote inquiry and deeper exploration of topics. Having strong resources that are well aligned with instruction is important, but library resources are only of value when they're used.

Many of the indicators that have long been used to study the frequency and nature of use of school library media resources remain relevant to the study of use likely to occur through integrated practice. However, integrated practice adds new challenges and presents new opportunities for capturing valuable information on the use of resources.

Typically, in larger existing studies, more emphasis has been placed on capturing data on the frequency of use than on the nature of use. The following indicators have been used to capture information on the frequency of use of library resources:

- Number of visits to the library per student per week

- Book circulation rates

- Types of groups visiting the library per week (e.g., whole class, small group, individual student)

To understand the effects of integrated practice, it's important to understand how resources are used and how often they're used. Integrated practice involves a substantial investment of time and effort on the part of teachers and library media specialists, and it only has payoff if it facilitates the improved use of information resources. One would expect to see increased research, greater use of library holdings to deepen content coverage, and greater use of literature to enrich language arts instruction.

Under integrated practice, to gather insights on how meaningfully resources are being used, it becomes necessary to gather information on:

- the extent to which resources are being used to support student research;

- the role information resources are playing in instructional units;

- the ways in which library resources support language arts/reading instruction;

- the relationship between frequency of use and nature of use; and

- how materials are used in the library and in classrooms.

It's assumed that integrated practice can only really thrive in a system that allows for flexible access because fixed scheduling places too many constraints on both the amount and nature of library use available to teachers and students. Flexible access creates an open-market system under which equitable access to the library resources is no longer guaranteed. Hence it's important to study how equitable student access is to its resources to fully understand the effects of integrated practice.

How Do Library Program Resources Influence the Design of Instructional Units?

School library programs have the potential to make important contributions to the design of instructional units. Libraries possess materials, in multiple formats, that can be used to extend lessons and deepen content coverage. Libraries' material resources are rich enough to support a broad array of student research and inquiry-related activities. Libraries also possess library media specialists, who can play important roles in shaping the content of instructional units and designing learning activities that enable students to advance their skill in locating, evaluating, and utilizing information resources.

Research on the contributions school library programs make to the design of instructional units has been pretty limited to date. While national data exist on the level of collaboration occurring between library media specialists and teachers across subject areas, not much is known about the nature or value of the contributions being made to instructional design by school library media programs.

The integrated practice envisioned in *Information Power* and implemented in Library Power asks schools to put considerable time and effort into incorporating the school library media program more centrally into the instructional design process. To understand whether meaningful incorporation of the library program resources in instructional design has occurred under integrated practice, and whether this yields benefits, it's important to explore the issues discussed below.

The Form and Substance of Collaborative Relationships: How to Optimally Draw on the Expertise of Teachers and Librarians

One important dimension of collaborative relationships is form. Teachers enter the relationship with primary control over the design of instructional units. In the integrated practice adopted at Library Power sites, this control was generally retained by teachers. However, library media specialists were afforded the opportunity to identify ways library program resources could extend lessons and learning activities. In some instances, library media specialists became quite entrepreneurial and actually assumed a leadership role interpreting state or district student academic standards and suggesting ways the library program could help move students toward achieving those standards. In these instances, library media specialists were full partners in instructional design.

Substance is another important dimension of a collaborative relationship. In the integrated practice adopted through Library Power, collaborative work centered on content, pedagogy, and assessment. Library media specialists were most involved in decisions related to content, somewhat involved in pedagogy, and rarely involved in student assessment.

Under the new paradigm outlined in *Information Power*, library media specialists are striving to become fuller partners in instructional design. To understand integrated practice and its potential for contributing instruction, it's important to understand:

- how different types of collaborative relationships affect instruction;

- how thoroughly collaboration is occurring; and

- how to make the best use of the expertise both teachers and librarians possess related to the design of instructional units.

How Instructional Units Are Enriched by the Contributions of the School Library Media Program

The Library Power experience shows that an essential indicator of the extent to which integrated practice exists is whether the library program's human and material resources are being incorporated into the design of instructional units. One would expect instructional units that draw heavily on library resources to look substantially different than those that do not. To test this hypothesis, it's important to examine:

- the extent to which library program resources (human and material) are actually incorporated into lessons; and

- the extent to which there's value added by incorporating library resources into instructional units.[2]

*Broader Ways in Which Curriculum Development and Awareness
Benefit from the Incorporation of the School Library Program
into Instructional Design Activities*

Under the integrated practice occurring in Library Power
schools, teacher and librarian collaboration often happens in groups within
grade level or subject. An unanticipated benefit of this has been the resulting conversations related to the ways different teachers use information.
This has been helpful to all instructors as they trade insights on the ways to
derive maximum benefits from information resources. Another benefit has
been the development of a shared awareness of the schools' "implemented
curriculum." For the first time, many teachers acquired an in-depth understanding of what their peers are teaching. In light of this development, a key
area of inquiry related to integrated practice becomes the extent to which
school-wide curricular development and awareness are advanced through
integrated practice.

How Does Integrated Practice Contribute to the Quality of Teaching and Learning?

School library media programs have the potential to promote
content-based improvements in teaching and to create new opportunities
for student inquiry. Where this potential is fully realized, one would expect
to see a school library program playing a central role in enriching students'
content knowledge; enhancing students' problem solving abilities; and improving students' abilities to effectively locate, evaluate, analyze, and present information.

As Wehlage points out in Chapter 6, however, providing access
to high quality information resources does little to guarantee that these
resources will be used in service of high quality learning activities. Students
may be asked to use library resources to provide factual responses to a
limited set of predetermined questions. This type of assignment is not apt
to help students become proficient locators, evaluators, analyzers, and
presenters of information. Hence, to understand the value of integrated
practice it's important to extend the analysis beyond the quality of available
materials and how they're used and to also examine the quality of teaching
and learning activities generated through integrated practice.

A number of studies and scholarly works within the school library field provide valuable insights about the nature of student learning that occurs in the libraries (Kuhlthau 1993, 1994, Callison 1986). Where the Library Power evaluation may be instructive is in its focus on learning in the classroom, as well as in its application of a scale used to assess the intellectual quality of teaching and learning occurring as a result of integrated practice. The Library Power evaluation employed Newman and Wehlage's framework for assessing the quality of student work produced through integrated practice. This framework can be used to measure the quality of teachers' assignments and the quality of student products by a scale that looks for work to demonstrate the following:

- Construction of knowledge

- Disciplined inquiry (critical analysis of prior knowledge, in-depth understanding, elaborated communication)

- Value beyond school (discourse, products, or performances that have meaning beyond success in the class)

This inquiry moves the analysis beyond access and nature of use of library resources, to quality of teaching and learning produced through the full incorporation of library resources in instruction. It also uses criteria that align well with many districts' academic standards.

The type of integrated practice promoted by *Information Power*, and implemented in Library Power, rests on the assumption that value is added to teaching and learning through the full incorporation of library program resources in teaching and learning. The adoption of integrated practice involves financial costs associated with appropriately resourcing a healthy library program. It also involves opportunity costs as it posits that time spent on learning activities devised through integrated practice is more beneficial to students than other uses of that time. For schools to invest in this, they'll need to be convinced that integrated practice improves the quality of teaching and learning.

How Does Integrated Practice Affect Student Achievement?

Under integrated practice, school libraries have the promise of becoming centers of instruction—where students engage in research and inquiry, library media specialists design and deliver instruction, and seamless coordination exists between learning in the classroom and learning in the library media center. Under this vision of practice, school libraries are at the center of teaching and learning.

Should this vision become realized, it's likely that the school library investment would be expected to produce student achievement results. This is the expectation that's increasingly being placed on all education programs receiving substantial public investment.

Much of the existing research that has attempted to examine the relationship between school library programs and student achievement has looked at the relationship between healthy library programs (as measured by staff, strength of collection, and collaboration with teachers) and student achievement, usually using scores on reading exams and sometimes on tests of research-related skills.

Existing studies that attempt to measure school library programs' impact on student achievement rely on correlational analysis. Correlational analysis allows researchers to examine whether relationships exist between measured variables such as student reading scores and the quality of a library collection. However, correlational analysis says nothing about the reason for this relationship, and it certainly doesn't establish that a cause and effect relationship exists. A limitation of correlational analysis is that it's always possible that an omitted variable—one that has not been captured in a correlational analysis (such as time spent on reading instruction or type of reading curriculum)—may be the variable that actually has the important or "causal" relationship with another.

The fundamental question being addressed through these studies is whether strong library programs contribute to student achievement. This is not the fundamental question that would be addressed through a study on the impact of integrated practice.

Integrated practice calls for a different tack toward examining effects on student achievement. Under integrated practice, the aim is to fully integrate library program resources with a school's primary teaching and learning activities. It challenges teachers and library media specialists to work together to identify ways of fully exploiting their collective resources to support improved curriculum, instruction, and assessment. Under this scenario, it doesn't seem fitting to try to isolate the effects of the school library program. The appropriate focus is on the effects integrated practice has on student achievement.

There is reason to believe that many of the current leading education reforms and popular approaches to teaching and learning would benefit from integrated practice. Many of the capacities they try to promote are the same ones that integrated practice would likely promote, including the following:

- Inquiry

- Critical thinking skills

- Problem solving

In instances where integrated practice aligns well with the aims of a district's educational philosophy or primary reforms, there may be valuable opportunities to assess the effects of integrated practice on achievement. Optimally, the effects of integrated practice could be tested in a setting where many schools were involved in a common reform such as the Kentucky Educational Reform Act (KERA). If some KERA schools adopted integrated practice and others did not, comparisons could be constructed to assess the value added by integrated practice.

If properly designed, such a study could compare the performance of schools using integrated practice with control schools not using integrated practice. This type of "experimental" research design using carefully matched control schools would enable researchers to test the effects of an innovation in an applied setting. It would enable researchers to attribute outcomes to integrated practice if the schools using integrated practice outperformed otherwise comparable schools that did not use integrated practice.

This would be a more rigorous study than those that have typically been applied to school library programs and would produce findings that would be viewed as more credible. It would also likely be of more interest to school districts and funders, particularly if it's framed as a study on ways a reform like KERA is apt to achieve its goals, as opposed to a study on the effects of the school library program. This study would speak to the district's core educational priorities.

It's also important to note that with increased rigor comes increased risk. As recent research shows, very few educational reforms have been able to generate convincing positive impact results when exposed to rigorous study (American Institute for Research, 1999).

The fundamental question being addressed by this inquiry would be: Are there instructional philosophies, approaches to teaching and learning, or particular education reforms that, when accompanied by integrated practice, generate additional benefits for students? The answer to this question is of great importance to the school library community and would be of great interest to education policymakers.

Implications for Educational Technology

The Library Power Evaluation Project and the entire Library Power experience have generated many insights that are relevant to the present discourse on educational technology. At present, there is substantial concern that growing sums are being invested in educational technology to provide access to high quality materials, while there is a paucity of systematic approaches for integrating these materials into mainstream teaching and learning activities (President's Committee of Advisors on Science and Technology, Panel on Educational Technology, 1997).

The vision articulated in *Information Power* seems prescient and highly applicable to this situation. Educational technology potentially offers schools expanded access to information resources. The model for integrating library resources more centrally into teaching and learning activities presented in *Information Power* and implemented in Library Power has many facets that seem relevant to this challenge. These facets include:

- an on-site change agent with expertise in teaching and information resources; and

- systematic collaboration on the selection of information resources, incorporation of information resources in instruction, and delivery of instruction.

In the same way that the vision and program model may inform that discourse, the insights generated through the evaluation effort regarding how to frame inquiry about the incorporation of information resources in schools may be quite valuable. The insights generated through the experience of examining the incorporation of information resources more centrally into curriculum and instruction may offer useful insights on how to study the increasing use of educational technology in schools.

Alerting the educational technology community to the Library Power initiative and evaluation effort may be advantageous to the school library and educational technology fields. Both fields may be able to benefit from exploring synergies.

The Audience for Research on the Incorporation of School Library and Information Resources in Teaching and Learning

Research on integrated practice should always be of value to the school library field. However, since such research will want to investigate the effects of integrated practice—not the isolated effects of the school library program—it should be conducted in a manner that's valued by school superintendents, principals, and teachers. It's important to recognize that if teachers don't have an interest in drawing on library and information resources, integrated practice is unlikely to make it into the classroom. Superintendents and principals are the decision-makers, and even if others buy into a program, superintendents and principals have to support it. Integrated practice presents an opportunity to conduct and present research that doesn't limit itself to examining the benefits of a library program. Integrated practice presents an opportunity to examine ways in which extra instructional resources and materials can be used to support a district's top instructional priorities.

Conclusion

This chapter has presented reflection on a multi-year research effort that sought to capture the implementation of a bold and ambitious new vision of practice articulated and implemented by library media specialists. The Library Power evaluation observed as library media specialists took dramatic steps toward redefining their roles in schools.

The evaluation captures many important lessons about integrated practice and its significance. At the same time, many important issues related to integrated practice were beyond the reach of this evaluation. This chapter has presented insights about important new ways of looking at practice that were uncovered as the research effort unfolded. It also suggests some lines of inquiry that were beyond the scope of this study but which may be particularly valuable areas for future inquiry.

Notes

1. No national data exist on total expenditures on school library programs. However, SASS data indicate that the cost of librarians' salaries alone are nearly four times the amount spent on collections and materials (NCES, 1998).

2. This is an area where the standards' movement may be of considerable assistance. Given that increasingly clear goals for what students must be able to know and do in various content areas, it becomes easier to map out how various units cover content that aligns with standards.

References

American Association of School Librarians and Association for Educational Communications and Technology. (1998). *Information Power: Building Partnerships for Learning.* Chicago: American Library Association.

——. *Information Power: Guildeline for School Library Media Programs.* (1988). Chicago: American Library Association.

American Institute for Research, Pelavin Research Center. (1999). *An Educators' Guide to Schoolwide Reform.* Project Director, Rebecca Herman. Arlington, VA: Education Research Service. Web address: www.aasa.org/reform/

Bransford, J. D., Brown, A. L., & Cocking, R. R. (1999). *How People Learn.* Washington, D.C.: National Academy Press.

Callison, Daniel. (1986). "School Library Media Programs and Free Inquiry Learning." *School Library Journal, 32* (6).

Kuhlthau, C. (1993). *Seeking Meaning: A Process Approach to Library and Information Services.* Greenwich, CT: Ablex Publishing.

Kuhlthau, C. (1994). *Teaching the Library Research Process.* 2nd ed. Lanham, MD: Scarecrow Press.

President's Committee of Advisors on Science and Technology, Panel on Educational Technology. (1997). *Report to the President on the Use of Technology to Strengthen K–12 Educational in the United States.*

U.S. Department of Education. National Center for Education Statistics. (1998). *School Library Media Centers: 1993-94,* NCES 980-282, by Bradford Chaney. Project Officer, Jeffrey Williams. Washington, D.C.

Appendix A
Evaluation Personnel, Researchers, Documentors, and Coordinators Involved in the National Evaluation of Library Power

Library Power Evaluation Personnel

Co-principal Investigators

Dianne McAfee Hopkins, School of Library and Information Studies, University of Wisconsin–Madison

Douglas L. Zweizig, School of Library and Information Studies, University of Wisconsin–Madison

Consultants

Debra Wilcox Johnson, Johnson & Johnson Consulting, Waunakee, WI

Carol Kuhlthau, School of Communication, Information, and Library Studies, Rutgers University

David Loertscher, School of Library and Information Science, San Jose State University

Norman Lott Webb, Wisconsin Center for Education Research, University of Wisconsin–Madison

Gary Wehlage, National Center on Effective Secondary Schools and Center on Organization and Restructuring of Schools, University of Wisconsin–Madison

School of Library and Information Studies Project Staff

Beth Beuch, Student Assistant

Joan Braune, Research Assistant

Miriyam Espinosa, Project Assistant

Eliot Finkelstein, Student Assistant

Susan Fuzard, Project Assistant

Charles Hitt, Project Researcher

Priya Kamat, Student Assistant

John Larson, Student Assistant

Betsy Lawrence, Program Assistant

Kim Merchant, Student Assistant

Jolen Neumann, Student Assistant

JoAnn Tiedemann, Editor

Patricia Young, Research Program Manager

Persons Providing Advice to the Evaluation

Don Adcock

Nancy Beck

Evelyn Conerly

Eliza Dresang

Ginny Eager

Carrie Glenn

Phyllis Heroy

Clarence Hoover

Ellin Keene

Kelly Langford

Beth Lief

Jane Lindsay

Martha May MacCallum

Cathie May

Vivian Melton

Bill Miles

Donna Peterson

Steven Prigohzy

Mary Richter

Robert Saffold

Shiela Salmon

Trixie Schmidt

Patti Geske Schultz

Barbara Stripling

Jo Ann Tiedemann

John Witte

Case Study Researchers

Susan Malone Back, Research Consultant, Denver, Colorado

Suzanne Barchers, Adjunct Faculty, University of Colorado–Denver

Kay Bishop, Assistant Professor, School of Library and Information Sciences, University of South Florida, Tampa

Daniel Callison, Associate Professor/Director of School Media Education, School of Library and Information Science, Indiana University, Bloomington

Nancy Curran (retired), Coordinator of Instructional Materials, Decatur School District #61, Charleston, Illinois

Kenneth Doane, School Partnership Coordinator, Partners in School Innovation, San Francisco, California

Carol Doll, Professor, Wayne State University, Detroit, Michigan

Jean Donham, Associate Professor, School of Library and Information Studies, University of Iowa, Iowa City

JoAnne Smart Drane, Independent Consultant, Raleigh, North Carolina

Jean Jolin (retired), Research Associate, Wisconsin Center for Education Research, University of Wisconsin–Madison

Bruce King, Researcher, Wisconsin Center for Education Research, University of Wisconsin–Madison

Zina Lawrence, Consultant, Selkirk, New York

Carole McCollough, Library Media Consultant, Southfield, Michigan

Joy McGregor, Associate Professor, School of Library and Information Studies, Texas Women's University, Denton

Dianne Oberg, Associate Professor, School of Library and Information Studies, University of Alberta, Canada

Eric Osthoff, Project Assistant, Wisconsin Center for Education Research, University of Wisconsin–Madison

Richard Podemski, Dean, School of Education, University of St. Thomas, St. Paul, Minnesota

Caroline Schmalz, Consultant, Oak Park, Illinois

Greg Smith, Associate Professor, Department of Education, Lewis and Clark College, Portland, Oregon

Susan Snider, Library Media Specialist, Londonderry Middle School, Londonderry, New Hampshire

Leslie Talbot, Consultant, New York, New York

Phyllis Van Orden (retired), Professor and Director, Graduate School of Library & Information Science, University of Washington–Seattle

Donald Wachter (retired), School Superintendent, Decatur, Illinois

Sarah Wachter, Independent Consultant, Decatur, Illinois

Gloria Waity, Freelance Library Consultant, Madison, Wisconsin

Norman Webb, Senior Scientist, Wisconsin Center for Education Research, University of Wisconsin–Madison

Lynda Welborn, Library Media Specialist, Denver Academy, Denver, Colorado

Anne Wheelock, Educational Consultant, Jamaica Plain, Massachusetts

Patricia Young, Independent Consultant, Madison, Wisconsin

Evaluation Officer

Adam Stoll, DeWitt Wallace–Reader's Digest Fund

Documentors

For the Case Studies in Atlanta

Rebecca Jackson, Atlanta, Georgia

Valerie Lockett, Atlanta, Georgia

Andrew Plankenhorn, Decatur, Georgia

Dr. Jacquelyn Ponder, Senoia, Georgia

For the Case Studies in Berea

Marybelle Duff, Somerset, Kentucky

Malcolm Smith, Somerset, Kentucky

Olive Williamson, Somerset, Kentucky

For the Case Studies in Chattanooga

Amelia Allen, Chattanooga, Tennessee

Anne Garland, Chattanooga, Tennessee

Sammy Gooden, Hixson, Tennessee

For the Case Studies in Lincoln

Carolyn Brown, Lincoln, Nebraska

Dr. Ruth Ann Lyness, Lincoln, Nebraska

For the Case Studies in Denver

Nancy Cornwall, Boulder, Colorado

Marjorie Larner, Boulder, Colorado

Jessica Oakley, San Francisco, California

For the Case Studies in New Haven

Julie Giordano, West Haven, Connecticut

Julia Nicefaro, Hamden, Connecticut

Deborah Stewart, Hamden, Connecticut

Judith Whitcomb, Northford, Connecticut

Regional Coordinators

Pauletta Brown Bracy, Associate Professor, School of Library and Information Sciences, North Carolina Central University, Durham

Charles Bruckerhoff, Research Associate, Curriculum Research and Evaluation, Chaplin, Connecticut

David Loertscher, Professor, School of Library and Information Science, San Jose State University, San Jose, California

Marilyn Shontz, Associate Professor, Rowan University, Glassboro, New Jersey

Cecelia Steppe-Jones, Professor of Education, North Carolina Central University, Durham

Appendix B
Library Media Specialist Questionnaire—1997

Library Media Specialist Questionnaire
for Library Power Schools
Responding for the First Time
April, 1997

From: National Library Power Program Evaluation Team

To: Building-level Library Power library media specialists

Re: Final national questionnaire

The attached questionnaire is the final survey of library media specialists being conducted by the National Evaluation of Library Power. The DeWitt Wallace–Reader's Digest Fund and the evaluation team understand that Library Power projects have been asked to provide a good deal of information over the course of the evaluation, and those contributions have been very much appreciated. As this is the last opportunity to obtain comprehensive data about the library media programs in past and current Library Power schools, your response to the present survey is particularly important.

This form of the questionnaire is intended for all schools that have not filled out a previous survey. If you **did** fill out this survey last year, please ask your Library Power Director for a copy of the shorter survey form.

We'd like to emphasize that we understand that individual Library Power programs receiving this questionnaire will differ from one another in a number of ways. Some programs are just getting started and others have been active for several years. Furthermore, some programs have been designed to focus heavily on certain activities and others have been designed to focus more heavily on other activities.

Neither the Fund nor the evaluation team is expecting that individual Library Power programs will be focusing heavily on all of the areas asked about in this questionnaire. What is most important to our evaluation effort is that we be able to get an accurate picture of where individual Library Power programs are at this time.

We have made a strong attempt to design this questionnaire so that it will be useful to the national evaluation, and useful to you as well. It is our hope that in generating responses to this questionnaire you will gather information that can help you in assessing your own progress. This information may also be useful in informing your project planning and your program decisions. If you find information that you generate in response to this questionnaire useful, please keep a copy of it for yourself.

We would appreciate it if you could complete and return this final Library Media Specialist Questionnaire **by May 2** so that it will arrive at our office by May 5.

If you have questions about this questionnaire, please call Douglas Zweizig at (608) 265-6286 or (608) 263-2941. We are asking for your name and telephone number in case we need to clarify your response. No individual will be identifiable in any of the evaluation reports. A stamped, self-addressed envelope has been provided for you to return the questionnaire directly to us.

National Library Power Program Evaluation <LIBPOWER@macc.wisc.edu>
School of Library and Information Studies, University of Wisconsin–Madison

Library Media Questionnaire
National Library Power Program Evaluation

Please return by **May 2** to:
Charlie Hitt, Research Program Manager
National Library Power Program Evaluation
School of Library and Information Studies
University of Wisconsin, Madison
600 N. Park Street
Madison, WI 53706

Name of library media specialist _____

School name: _____

Address: _____

City, State, Zip: _____

Telephone: _____

Fax number: _____

E-mail: _____

DATE THIS QUESTIONNAIRE RECEIVED BY YOU _____

1. _____ Grades in this school (example: K-3)

   _____ Student enrollment

   _____ Number of classroom teachers

   _____ Number of specialists (such as reading/art/PE, counselors, etc.)

2. Circle the school year you began the Library Power project in your school:

   89/90   90/91   91/92   92/93   93/94   94/95   95/96   96/97

Staffing

3. Please provide name and position of **all paid personnel** who staff the library media center.

NAME	TYPE OF POSITION	WEEKLY HOURS
_____	❑ Certified library media specialist ❑ Teacher ❑ Support Staff	❑ Full time ❑ Part time ↘ if part time, _____ #hours/week
_____	❑ Certified library media specialist ❑ Teacher ❑ Support Staff	❑ Full time ❑ Part time ↘ if part time, _____ #hours/week
_____	❑ Certified library media specialist ❑ Teacher ❑ Support Staff	❑ Full time ❑ Part time ↘ if part time, _____ #hours/week

4. How many **adult volunteers** assist in this school library media center?

    # _____   Total hours per week for all volunteers _____

    [IN AN AVERAGE WEEK]

5. Has the staffing pattern changed since last year? In what way?

6. During the course of this school year, how many classroom teachers would you say you **regularly collaborated with** in planning or providing instruction?

    _____

    [# OF TEACHERS THIS YEAR]

7. Prior to your school's Library Power project, how many teachers did you regularly collaborate with in planning or providing instruction?

    _____

    [# OF TEACHERS PRIOR
    TO LIBRARY POWER]

Facilities and Equipment

8. Which of the following equipment or services does this LMC have? [CHECK (X) ALL THAT APPLY]
    - ❑ Telephone
    - ❑ Fax machine
    - ❑ Computer with modem
    - ❑ Automated catalog
    - ❑ Automated circulation system
    - ❑ CD-ROM for full text/images: encyclopedias, maps, photographs, etc.
    - ❑ CD-ROM for bibliographic sources: periodical index searching, etc.
    - ❑ On-line database searching, such as BRS, Dialog, etc.
    - ❑ Video laser disc
    - ❑ Connection to Internet
    - ❑ Cable television
    - ❑ Satellite dish
    - ❑ in-house television production facilities

9. In question 8, put a star [☆] by those items that were added during the Library Power period.

10. What is the total seating capacity of the LMC? _____ Before Library Power: _____

11. Which of these types of spaces are available in the LMC? [CHECK (X) ALL THAT APPLY]
    - ❑ Individual reading, viewing, and listening
    - ❑ Special comfortable quiet reading areas (pillows, hideaways, etc.)
    - ❑ Small group (5 persons or less) activity areas (viewing or listening)
    - ❑ Large group (more than 5 persons) activity areas (viewing or listening)
    - ❑ Storytime area
    - ❑ Areas for learning centers
    - ❑ Production areas for classroom teachers
    - ❑ Production areas for students
    - ❑ Conference rooms
    - ❑ Computer access area or lab
    - ❑ Workroom for LMC staff
    - ❑ Storage (equipment, etc.)
    - ❑ Space enough so that when a full class is working the LMC, other activities can be accommodated concurrently (e.g., production activities, small group work, individual browsing)

12. Put a star [☆] before your check in question 11 if the area has undergone renovation with Library Power Grant funds.

13. How many microcomputers are ***under the supervision*** of the LMC staff? _____

In-Service Training

14. Overall, since your Library Power program began, approximately how many Library Power in-service or professional development sessions have you attended?

_____ # OF SESSIONS

In all, approximately how many total hours did you spend in these sessions?

_____ TOTAL # OF HOURS

Of the sessions you attended, how many did you find valuable?

_____ # OF SESSIONS

Scheduling and Access

15. Which of the following best describes the schedule for classes/groups using the LMC:
    [PLEASE CHECK ONLY ONE]

    ❏ All classes are regularly scheduled into the LMC.

    ❏ Some classes are regularly scheduled, other classes flexibly

    ❏ The LMC is completely flexibly scheduled (classes, small groups, and individuals are scheduled for varying time periods appropriate to need.)

16. What changes in scheduling of the LMC have occurred since the Library Power grant was received? (Please explain)

17. We are interested in a count of the **total number of students visiting your LMC in a "typical week."** Please look at your calendar for the most recent typical week (5 full days not interrupted by events that kept students from the LMC). If you missed a day or a half day, just include the next full day or half day until you have 5 full days of calendar. How many individuals and groups used the LMC each day? If you need to estimate, please do so.
    [PLEASE GIVE NUMBER IN EACH CATEGORY.]

    Day 1

    | NUMBER OF GROUPS VISITING LMC | = | TOTAL # OF STUDENTS VISITING THE LMC |

    _____ # of large groups (2 or more classes together) containing......... _____ # of students
    _____ # of single class visits   containing......... _____ # of students
    _____ # of small groups (smaller than a class)   containing......... _____ # of students
                                             plus............... _____ # of individual students
                                                         (not in groups)

    added together equals _____ **Total** # of students using the LMC on Day 1

(CONTINUED)

Day 2

NUMBER OF GROUPS VISITING LMC = **TOTAL # OF STUDENTS VISITING THE LMC**

_____ # of large groups (2 or more classes together) containing......... _____ # of students
_____ # of single class visits containing......... _____ # of students
_____ # of small groups (smaller than a class) containing......... _____ # of students
plus............... _____ # of individual students (not in groups)

added together equals _____ **Total** # of students using the LMC on Day 2

Day 3

NUMBER OF GROUPS VISITING LMC = **TOTAL # OF STUDENTS VISITING THE LMC**

_____ # of large groups (2 or more classes together) containing......... _____ # of students
_____ # of single class visits containing......... _____ # of students
_____ # of small groups (smaller than a class) containing......... _____ # of students
plus............... _____ # of individual students (not in groups)

added together equals _____ **Total** # of students using the LMC on Day 3

Day 4

NUMBER OF GROUPS VISITING LMC = **TOTAL # OF STUDENTS VISITING THE LMC**

_____ # of large groups (2 or more classes together) containing......... _____ # of students
_____ # of single class visits containing......... _____ # of students
_____ # of small groups (smaller than a class) containing......... _____ # of students
plus............... _____ # of individual students (not in groups)

added together equals _____ **Total** # of students using the LMC on Day 4

Day 5

NUMBER OF GROUPS VISITING LMC = **TOTAL # OF STUDENTS VISITING THE LMC**

_____ # of large groups (2 or more classes together) containing......... _____ # of students
_____ # of single class visits containing......... _____ # of students
_____ # of small groups (smaller than a class) containing......... _____ # of students
plus............... _____ # of individual students (not in groups)

added together equals _____ **Total** # of students using the LMC on Day 5

18. During **the same week** (5 days) of school, how many books and other materials were checked out from the LMC? (estimate if you do not have an actual count) _____
[# OF ITEMS CHECKED OUT]

19. During **the same week** of school, did the library media specialist(s) help teach any lessons outside of the library (for example, in a classroom)?

❏ **NO**   ❏ **YES** ⇨ If **YES**, How many lessons during this week? _____
[NUMBER OF LESSONS]

20. During **the same week** of school, how long would you say a typical group stayed in the library?

On the average, **large group visits** lasted _____ minutes. [ESTIMATED AVERAGE]

On the average, **single class visits** lasted _____ minutes. [ESTIMATED AVERAGE]

On the average, **small group visits** lasted _____ minutes. [ESTIMATED AVERAGE]

General Collections

21. At this time, what is your perception of how well the library media center's resources support the instructional program of the school for each of the following areas?

[PLEASE **CIRCLE** YOUR ANSWERS FOR BOTH "Currentness" AND "Quantity."]

		Currentness				**Quantity**		
a.	Reference	NA	Poor	Adequate	Excellent	NA	Poor	Adequate	Excellent
b.	Science/Tech.(5-600s)	NA	Poor	Adequate	Excellent	NA	Poor	Adequate	Excellent
c.	Mathematics	NA	Poor	Adequate	Excellent	NA	Poor	Adequate	Excellent
d.	Geography	NA	Poor	Adequate	Excellent	NA	Poor	Adequate	Excellent
e.	History	NA	Poor	Adequate	Excellent	NA	Poor	Adequate	Excellent
f.	Biography	NA	Poor	Adequate	Excellent	NA	Poor	Adequate	Excellent
g.	Social sciences (300s)	NA	Poor	Adequate	Excellent	NA	Poor	Adequate	Excellent
h.	Fiction	NA	Poor	Adequate	Excellent	NA	Poor	Adequate	Excellent
i.	Picture books	NA	Poor	Adequate	Excellent	NA	Poor	Adequate	Excellent
j.	Literature (800s)	NA	Poor	Adequate	Excellent	NA	Poor	Adequate	Excellent
k.	Fine arts (700s)	NA	Poor	Adequate	Excellent	NA	Poor	Adequate	Excellent
l.	Foreign lang.(400s) ESOL, ESL	NA	Poor	Adequate	Excellent	NA	Poor	Adequate	Excellent
m.	Careers	NA	Poor	Adequate	Excellent	NA	Poor	Adequate	Excellent
n.	Health	NA	Poor	Adequate	Excellent	NA	Poor	Adequate	Excellent

22. Rate the adequacy of the entire collection to meet the needs of multi-cultural education:

NA   Poor   Adequate   Excellent

From *Lessons from Library Power.* © 1999 Libraries Unlimited. (800) 237-6124.

Library and Information Skills

23. Describe how, during your Library Power project your program of library and information skills has changed. Include points such as:
    • frequency changes (such as from once a week to upon request)
    • content changes (such as from information location to the research process)
    • attempts at integration with the classroom
    What do you feel is the impact on students, teachers, and learning of these changes?

Teacher/Library Media Specialist Collaboration

24. Has Library Power affected the amount or quality of collaboration in your school?

    ❑ yes   ❑ no   Please tell us in what ways:

25. Please give us your response to the following: [CIRCLE ONE ON 1-5 SCALE]

  a. Teachers in this school generally work together to do what . . . . . **Agree 5 4 3 2 1 Disagree**
      is best for all students.

  b. Teachers in this school do not generally agree on what all . . . . . . **Agree 5 4 3 2 1 Disagree**
      students should learn.

  c. Teachers in this school generally feel responsible that all . . . . . . **Agree 5 4 3 2 1 Disagree**
      students learn.

  d. Teachers in this school generally respect each other's ideas . . . . **Agree 5 4 3 2 1 Disagree**
      about teaching and learning.

  e. Teachers in this school do not generally trust each other . . . . **Agree 5 4 3 2 1 Disagree**
      to make decisions that are best for the staff.

  f. Teachers in this school generally feel responsible to one . . . . **Agree 5 4 3 2 1 Disagree**
      another for carrying out the goals of the school.

  g. Teachers in this school do not generally share their best . . . . **Agree 5 4 3 2 1 Disagree**
      ideas with each other.

Student Learning

26. Think back over your Library Power project to when a student or students had a meaningful learning
     experience in the library media center. How did you know something new was learned? What stands out
     in your mind that made it a good learning experience?

27. Please answer the following question based upon your experiences with the teachers with whom you work collaboratively. Typically, when you work collaboratively with teachers to create or carry out instructional units, who usually participates in the following processes?

[Who's usually involved? CIRCLE ALL THAT APPLY]

	The Classroom Teacher	Other Teachers	The Librarian	Other Specialists
a. Creating or writing a unit's goals and objectives	ME	OT	LIB	SPEC
b. Designing unit activities	ME	OT	LIB	SPEC
c. Designing how students will be evaluated	ME	OT	LIB	SPEC
d. Identifying & gathering materials and resources	ME	OT	LIB	SPEC
e. Delivering instruction	ME	OT	LIB	SPEC
f. Teaching information seeking/research skills	ME	OT	LIB	SPEC
g. Helping students create products/reports	ME	OT	LIB	SPEC
h. Evaluating student performance in units	ME	OT	LIB	SPEC
i. Calculating and providing course grades	ME	OT	LIB	SPEC

28. For each of the following activities that are typically associated with Library Power, please indicate whether you feel it **will continue** and **should continue** in the coming years by circling Yes (**Y**), No (**N**), or **NA** (Not Applicable—if it does not exist).

[CIRCLE ONE RESPONSE FOR **PROBABLY WILL CONTINUE** AND ONE FOR **SHOULD CONTINUE**.]

Probably Will Continue			Should Continue			
Y	N	NA	Y	N	NA	a. Flexible scheduling of classes in the library (vs. regular weekly visits)
Y	N	NA	Y	N	NA	b. On-demand use of the library by individual students or groups (vs. at pre-set times)
Y	N	NA	Y	N	NA	c. Addition of large quantities of new library materials
Y	N	NA	Y	N	NA	d. Collaborative planning with librarian on instructional units
Y	N	NA	Y	N	NA	e. Integration of new technologies into the school curriculum
Y	N	NA	Y	N	NA	f. Enlarged role for the library as a resource for teachers and students
Y	N	NA	Y	N	NA	g. A full-time librarian at this school
Y	N	NA	Y	N	NA	h. Collaboration between teachers and librarian on developing the library's collection

Collection Mapping

Library Power schools in Round 2 and 3 sites have used collection mapping as a collection analysis and planning tool. If you have a Collection Map that describes the current status of the collection, please check [x] **here** and append the Collection Map for your library.

➡ ☐ **a Collection map is included.**

Collaborative Unit Summary Chart

In the fall of 1996, Collaboration Log forms were distributed to Library Power schools. These forms asked you to keep logs of collaboratively planned units of instruction during the 1996-97 school year—noting planning activities, how instruction was carried out, and joint evaluation of how the instructional unit worked. [These forms were optional for Round 1 sites. If your Round 1 site elected not to use Collaboration Logs, please ignore this question; you have completed this survey.]

If you have been maintaining Collaboration Logs, please photocopy the **five** most successful collaboratively planned units and attach them to this questionnaire.

As a cover sheet for the units, please create a chart like the one below that lists all of the collaborative units taught this year. Then, place a star [☆] by those units that both the teacher and the library media specialist agree were successful. Use a single sheet of paper. Example:

Social Studies
    Our Local Elections-grade 6
    ☆ *Family Trees-grade 3 and 4*

Reading
    ☆ *Newbery novel unit-grades 5 and 6*

Science
    ☆ *Environment of the School Grounds-entire school*
    ☆ *Simple machines-grade 3*
    Nutrition-grades 5 and 6

Integrated Units
    ☆ *Local environmental hazards-ss and sci. grade 4*
    ☆ *Labor movements-ss and art grade 6*

If you are attaching Collaboration Logs, please check [x] **here.**

➡ ☐ **Collaboration Logs are included.**

(You have completed this questionnaire. **Thank you very much!**
Please remember to include your Collaboration Logs and Collection Map
and mail back as instructed on the cover sheet.)

Appendix C: Principal Questionnaire—1997

Dear Principal: As you know, your school participated in the Library Power project. As part of the National Evaluation of Library Power, we would like to ask you a few questions about your experience with the project. Your response is completely anonymous and will not be identifiable in any report. Please feel free to state your opinions. Please return the completed questionnaire, sealed in the envelope provided, to the Evaluation office within ten days. Thank you very much.

Douglas Zweizig & Dianne McAfee Hopkins
School of Library and Information Studies
University of Wisconsin–Madison
(608) 265-6286

Principal Questionnaire—1997

1. School Name: _____ City: _____ State: _____

2. Number of classroom teachers in your building: _____

3. School year your school became involved in Library Power: [PLEASE CIRCLE]

   92/93   93/94   94/95   95/96   96/97

ON THE FOLLOWING QUESTIONS, PLEASE CIRCLE THE NUMBER ON THE SCALE THAT REPRESENTS YOUR VIEWS.

4. At this school, how much influence do **teachers** have on: [CIRCLE ONE ON 1-5 SCALE]

		A Little		↔		**A Great Deal**
a.	The school day schedule	1	2	3	4	5
b.	Designing the curriculum to be taught	1	2	3	4	5
c.	Selecting textbooks to be used	1	2	3	4	5
d.	Selecting non-textbook materials for classrooms	1	2	3	4	5
e.	Selecting materials to be added to the library	1	2	3	4	5
f.	Setting standards of achievement for students	1	2	3	4	5
g.	Determining teaching techniques	1	2	3	4	5
h.	Governing the school	1	2	3	4	5
i.	Hiring and assigning of staff	1	2	3	4	5

5. Please give us your response to the following: [CIRCLE ONE ON 1-5 SCALE]

   a. Teachers in this school generally work together to do what . . . . . **Agree 5 4 3 2 1 Disagree**
   is best for all students.

   b. Teachers in this school do not generally agree on what all . . . . . . **Agree 5 4 3 2 1 Disagree**
   students should learn.

   c. Teachers in this school generally feel responsible that all . . . . . . **Agree 5 4 3 2 1 Disagree**
   students learn.

   d. Teachers in this school generally respect each other's ideas . . . . **Agree 5 4 3 2 1 Disagree**
   about teaching and learning.

   e. Teachers in this school do not generally trust each other . . . . **Agree 5 4 3 2 1 Disagree**
   to make decisions that are best for the staff.

   f. Teachers in this school generally feel responsible to one . . . . **Agree 5 4 3 2 1 Disagree**
   another for carrying out the goals of the school.

   g. Teachers in this school do not generally share their best . . . . **Agree 5 4 3 2 1 Disagree**
   ideas with each other.

From *Lessons from Library Power.* © 1999 Libraries Unlimited. (800) 237-6124.

6. Please rate the **amount of change** in your school or district that has occurred in the past year; these could include changes in personnel, initiatives, finances, facilities, or governance.

[CIRCLE ONE ON 1-5 SCALE]

VIRTUALLY NO CHANGES		MODERATE CHANGES		SIGNIFICANT AMOUNTS OF CHANGE
1	**2**	**3**	**4**	**5**

7. Please briefly identify the **major changes** that occurred in the last year:

8. How would you say these changes affected the school's Library Power program and activities?

9. Typically, in your school, as classroom instructional units are created and carried out, which people usually participate in the following processes?

[CIRCLE ALL THAT APPLY]

	The Classroom Teacher	Other Teachers	The Librarian	Other Specialists
a. Creating or writing a unit's goals and objectives	**CT**	**OT**	**LIB**	**SPEC**
b. Designing unit activities	**CT**	**OT**	**LIB**	**SPEC**
c. Designing how students will be evaluated	**CT**	**OT**	**LIB**	**SPEC**
d. Identifying & gathering materials and resources	**CT**	**OT**	**LIB**	**SPEC**
e. Delivering instruction	**CT**	**OT**	**LIB**	**SPEC**
f. Teaching information seeking/research skills	**CT**	**OT**	**LIB**	**SPEC**
g. Helping students create products/reports	**CT**	**OT**	**LIB**	**SPEC**
h. Evaluating student performance in units	**CT**	**OT**	**LIB**	**SPEC**
i. Calculating and providing course grades	**CT**	**OT**	**LIB**	**SPEC**

10. Question 9 lists those who might collaborate in creating instructional units and in providing instruction. **To what extent and in what ways** has Library Power affected the **collaborative processes** outlined in question 9?

11. At this time, what do you consider the most important contribution of Library Power to the **teaching** done in your school?

12. **Overall**, what would you say has been the single most important contribution of Library Power to your **school**?

13. The following questions ask about practices that may be associated with Library Power in your school.

   Question 13a. Asks you to indicate <u>the extent to which practices have been adopted</u> by your faculty (i.e., by the full faculty, some faculty members, or none at all.)

   Question 13b. Asks you to check **AE** if a practice <u>already existed</u> in large part in your school <u>prior to Library Power</u> in your school.

   Question 13c. Asks for your view on what is <u>most responsible for a practice being adopted</u> in your school: **LP** (Library Power), **SR** (other School Reform efforts), or a **Mix** of other school reform efforts and Library Power project activities. Please check **N** (None) if you feel none has had much influence on the practice.

	13a. Extent Adopted [PLEASE CIRCLE ONE]				13b. Already Existed	13c. Attribution [PLEASE CHECK (X) ONE]			
	None at all			Full faculty		Mostly Library Power	Mostly School Reforms	A Mix	None
a. Flexible scheduling of classes in the library (vs. regular weekly visits)	1	2	3	4	AE ☐	LP ☐	SR ☐	Mix ☐	N ☐
b. On-demand use of the library by individual students or groups (vs. at pre-set times)	1	2	3	4	AE ☐	LP ☐	SR ☐	Mix ☐	N ☐
c. Collaborative planning among teachers and librarians on instructional units	1	2	3	4	AE ☐	LP ☐	SR ☐	Mix ☐	N ☐
d. Collaboration between teachers and librarians on developing the library's collection	1	2	3	4	AE ☐	LP ☐	SR ☐	Mix ☐	N ☐
e. Collaboration among teachers to plan instruction	1	2	3	4	AE ☐	LP ☐	SR ☐	Mix ☐	N ☐

14. What has been the greatest challenge you've faced in trying to sustain the Library Power project and activities in your school? **What made this a challenge?**

15. For each of the following activities that are typically associated with Library Power, please indicate whether you feel it **will continue** and **should continue** in the coming years by circling Yes (**Y**), No (**N**), or **NA** (Not Applicable—if it does not exist).

[CIRCLE ONE RESPONSE FOR **PROBABLY WILL CONTINUE** AND ONE FOR **SHOULD CONTINUE**.]

Probably Will Continue			Should Continue				
Y	N	NA	Y	N	NA	a.	Flexible scheduling of classes in the library (vs. regular weekly visits)
Y	N	NA	Y	N	NA	b.	On-demand use of the library by individual students or groups (vs. at pre-set times)
Y	N	NA	Y	N	NA	c.	Addition of large quantities of new library materials
Y	N	NA	Y	N	NA	d.	Collaborative planning with librarian on instructional units
Y	N	NA	Y	N	NA	e.	Integration of new technologies into the school curriculum
Y	N	NA	Y	N	NA	f.	Enlarged role for the library as a resource for teachers and students
Y	N	NA	Y	N	NA	g.	A full-time librarian at this school
Y	N	NA	Y	N	NA	h.	Collaboration between teachers and librarian on developing the library's collection

16. What recommendations would you make to the DeWitt Wallace–Reader's Digest Fund about ways in which the Library Power initiative might be improved?

Please return this questionnaire in the envelope provided to:

National Library Power Program Evaluation
School of Library and Information Studies
University of Wisconsin–Madison
600 N. Park Street
Madison, WI 53706

Thank you for your cooperation!

Appendix D
Sample Design for the Teacher Survey

Although the population of Library Power schools could be surveyed for the librarian and principal surveys, to survey the population of approximately 20,000 teachers in Library Power schools required that a sample be drawn. A number of considerations determined the strategy used to identify members of the sample. There was no list of the teachers that would allow a random or systematic sampling. Teachers were very much involved in Library Power, but had not had much direct contact with the administrative aspects of the project. While the librarian and principal in the school were required to apply formally to become a Library Power school and to agree to the conditions of the grant, many of the teachers became aware of the program largely through contact with the librarian and principal and through participation in professional development programs. Appealing to individual motivations of teachers likely would not produce an acceptable response rate, but the survey required responses from the full range of classroom teachers, not just those actively involved in Library Power activities. These reasons dictated the choice of a cluster sample using the schools as the sampling unit and surveying every classroom teacher within the selected schools. Roughly 30 schools would produce a sample size of 1,000 teachers, an adequate number for analysis, but because such a sample would be strongly influenced by the particular schools selected, the clustering effect was reduced by doubling the number of schools. Sixty-three schools were included in the sample survey, resulting in a sample of 2,511 teachers.

To select a set of schools that would reflect the general experience with Library Power, the population of schools was stratified by three variables: the year the school began its Library Power program (1991 or earlier, 1992, 1993, 1994, 1995), the grades covered by the school (elementary, middle, mixed), and the number of teachers in the school (19 or fewer, 20–25, 26–33, 34–45, 46 or greater). From within these cells, the required number of schools was drawn proportionally and randomly. Because project considerations required that schools from each Library Power site be included in the sample, more schools than were needed for the design were added to the sample, again, randomly and preserving the proportions.

Table D-1 shows the number of schools in the population and the sample that were found in each cell of the stratification variables.

TABLE D-1
Population and Sample Data for Selection of Schools for the Teacher Survey
(Sample Drawn in 1996 and Used for 1996 and 1997 Surveys)

	Year Began LP			
	Population #	Population %	Sample #	Sample %
£ 1991	64	12.0%	11	17.5%
1992	107	20.0%	10	15.9%
1993	89	16.6%	8	12.7%
1994	140	26.2%	19	30.2%
1995	135	25.2%	15	23.8%
Total	535		63	

	Grades in School			
	Population #	Population %	Sample #	Sample %
Elementary	390	72.9%	44	69.8%
Middle	91	17.0%	9	14.3%
Mixed	54	10.1%	10	15.9%
Total	535		63	

	Number of Teachers			
	Population #	Population %	Sample #	Sample %
< 19	56	10.5%	6	9.5%
20-25	87	16.3%	9	14.3%
26-33	125	23.4%	14	22.2%
34-45	134	25.0%	17	27.0%
‡ 46	133	24.9%	17	27.0%
Total	535		63	

A supplement to the sample survey was created by including any case study schools not already included in the sample. These supplementary surveys were printed in a different color and were not included in the sample survey analysis. Results for a case study school were provided to the case study researcher for that school, along with comparative data from the sample survey, to support the development of the case study.

Appendix E: Teacher Questionnaire—1997

Dear Teacher: As you know, your school has participated in the Library Power project. As part of the National Evaluation of Library Power, we would like to ask you a few questions about your experience with the project. Your response is completely anonymous and will not be identifiable. Please feel free to state your opinions. Please return the completed questionnaire to your Principal <u>within a week</u>, sealed in the envelope provided. Thank you very much. The DeWitt Wallace–Reader's Digest Fund appreciates your cooperation.

Douglas Zweizig & Dianne McAfee Hopkins
School of Library and Information Studies
University of Wisconsin–Madison
(608) 265-6286

Teacher Questionnaire—1997

1. School Name: _____ City: _____ State: _____

2. School year you, as a teacher, became involved in Library Power: [PLEASE CIRCLE]

   92/93   93/94   94/95   95/96   96/97

3. Subject and grade levels you teach (many subjects = *general*)

   SUBJECT(S): _____

   GRADE(S): _____

ON THE FOLLOWING QUESTIONS, PLEASE CIRCLE THE NUMBER ON THE SCALE THAT REPRESENTS YOUR VIEWS.

4. At this school, how much influence do teachers have on: [CIRCLE ONE ON 1-5 SCALE]

	A Little		**↔**		**A Great Deal**
a. The school day schedule	1	2	3	4	5
b. Designing the curriculum to be taught	1	2	3	4	5
c. Selecting textbooks to be used	1	2	3	4	5
d. Selecting non-textbook materials for classrooms	1	2	3	4	5
e. Selecting materials to be added to the library	1	2	3	4	5
f. Setting standards of achievement for students	1	2	3	4	5
g. Determining teaching techniques	1	2	3	4	5
h. Governing the school	1	2	3	4	5
i. Hiring and assigning of staff	1	2	3	4	5

5. Typically, when you're designing your classroom instructional units and carrying out unit activities, do you work on your own or do other faculty members participate in the following activities along with you: [Who's usually involved? CIRCLE ALL THAT APPLY]

	Me, the Teacher	**Other Teachers**	**The Librarian**	**Other Specialists**
a. Creating or writing a unit's goals and objectives	ME	OT	LIB	SPEC
b. Designing unit activities	ME	OT	LIB	SPEC
c. Designing how students will be evaluated	ME	OT	LIB	SPEC
d. Identifying & gathering materials and resources	ME	OT	LIB	SPEC
e. Delivering instruction	ME	OT	LIB	SPEC
f. Teaching information seeking/research skills	ME	OT	LIB	SPEC
g. Helping students create products/reports	ME	OT	LIB	SPEC
h. Evaluating student performance in units	ME	OT	LIB	SPEC
i. Calculating and providing course grades	ME	OT	LIB	SPEC

6. How has your use of the library's collection **to support your instruction** changed since the Library Power project began?

   I'm using the collection much less than before   [CIRCLE ONE NUMBER] **1 2 3 4 5**   **I'm using the collection much more than before**

From *Lessons from Library Power*. © 1999 Libraries Unlimited. (800) 237-6124.

7. Think of a research project that your students have done this school year. How much help did the **students** receive from the library media center staff?   [CIRCLE ONE ON 1-5 SCALE]

	None		↔		A Great Deal
a. Selecting a topic to explore	1	2	3	4	5
b. Learning about the kinds of resources in the library	1	2	3	4	5
c. Finding materials	1	2	3	4	5
d. Using the materials/information gathered	1	2	3	4	5
e. Using technology (such as CD-ROM, computers)	1	2	3	4	5
f. Learning information seeking/research skills	1	2	3	4	5
g. Preparing reports/presentations	1	2	3	4	5

8. What do you consider the two most important contributions of Library Power to your **teaching**?

   a.

   b.

9. How often do you participate in the following types of collaboration:

[CIRCLE ONE ON 1-4 SCALE]

	Not at all	↔		Very Often	9. **LP**
a. Collaboration **with a librarian** for the planning and designing of instruction	1	2	3	4	LP ☐
b. Collaboration **with a librarian** in delivering instruction	1	2	3	4	LP ☐
c. Collaboration **with other teachers** for the planning and designing of instruction	1	2	3	4	LP ☐
d. Collaboration **with other teachers** in delivering instruction	1	2	3	4	LP ☐

☛ 10.   If Library Power has **increased your participation** in any type of collaboration listed above, please check **LP** in the box provided.

11.   Please indicate how your students typically visit the library: [CHECK ALL THAT APPLY]

☐ as a class   ☐ in small groups   ☐ as individuals

12.   Has your school library become more "flexibly scheduled" (vs. regular weekly visits) since Library Power began in your school?

☐ yes   ☐ no
⬇

If **yes**, please briefly describe how flexible scheduling has changed the ways you and your students use the library.

13.   How would you describe your level of participation in Library Power activities, such as flexible use of the library and joint planning of instruction with the librarian?

[CIRCLE ONE NUMBER]
Not active at all   0   1   2   3   4   5   Very active

We would appreciate additional information to help us understand your level of participation.

From *Lessons from Library Power.* © 1999 Libraries Unlimited. (800) 237-6124.

14. What changes in student use of the library have you noticed since Library Power began in your school?

    a. Students' frequency of using the library: [CIRCLE ONE ON 1-5 SCALE]

    Much less than before   1   2   3   4   5   Much more than before

    Please explain:

    b. Students' frequency of using the library **on their own initiative**: [CIRCLE ONE ON 1-5 SCALE]

    Much less often   1   2   3   4   5   Much more often

    Please explain:

    c. Students' attitude toward using the library is: [CIRCLE ONE ON 1-5 SCALE]

    Much more negative   1   2   3   4   5   Much more positive

    Please explain:

15. Please give us your response to the following: [CIRCLE ONE ON 1-5 SCALE]

    a. Teachers in this school generally work together to do what . . . . . **Agree 5 4 3 2 1 Disagree** is best for all students.

    b. Teachers in this school do not generally agree on what all . . . . . . **Agree 5 4 3 2 1 Disagree** students should learn.

    c. Teachers in this school generally feel responsible that all . . . . . . **Agree 5 4 3 2 1 Disagree** students learn.

    d. Teachers in this school generally respect each other's ideas . . . . **Agree 5 4 3 2 1 Disagree** about teaching and learning.

    e. Teachers in this school do not generally trust each other . . . . **Agree 5 4 3 2 1 Disagree** to make decisions that are best for the staff.

    f. Teachers in this school generally feel responsible to one . . . . **Agree 5 4 3 2 1 Disagree** another for carrying out the goals of the school.

    g. Teachers in this school do not generally share their best . . . . **Agree 5 4 3 2 1 Disagree** ideas with each other.

16. Do you play any role in helping to select materials for your school library's collection?

    ❑ yes   ❑ no

    Do you play any role in helping to assess the quality of your school library's collection?

    ❑ yes   ❑ no

    If your role in either of these areas has changed in the past couple of years, please briefly explain how:

17. Overall, since your Library Power program began, approximately how many Library Power in-service or professional development sessions have you attended?

_____ # OF SESSIONS

In all, approximately how many total hours did you spend in these sessions?

_____ TOTAL # OF HOURS

Of the sessions you attended, how many did you find valuable?

_____ # OF SESSIONS

18. For each of the following activities that are typically associated with Library Power, please indicate whether you feel it **will continue** and **should continue** in the coming years by circling Yes (**Y**), No (**N**), or **NA** (Not Applicable—if it does not exist).

[CIRCLE ONE RESPONSE FOR **PROBABLY WILL CONTINUE** AND ONE FOR **SHOULD CONTINUE**.]

Probably Will Continue			**Should Continue**			
Y	N	NA	Y	N	NA	a. Flexible scheduling of classes in the library (vs. regular weekly visits)
Y	N	NA	Y	N	NA	b. On-demand use of the library by individual students or groups (vs. at pre-set times)
Y	N	NA	Y	N	NA	c. Addition of large quantities of new library materials
Y	N	NA	Y	N	NA	d. Collaborative planning with librarian on instructional units
Y	N	NA	Y	N	NA	e. Integration of new technologies into the school curriculum
Y	N	NA	Y	N	NA	f. Enlarged role for the library as a resource for teachers and students
Y	N	NA	Y	N	NA	g. A full-time librarian at this school
Y	N	NA	Y	N	NA	h. Collaboration between teachers and librarian on developing the library's collection

19. Overall, how well does the school library collection support your needs as a teacher and the needs of your students?   [CIRCLE ONE NUMBER FOR **TEACHER** AND ONE FOR **STUDENTS**]

Supports needs of **teacher** → **Very Well**   5   4   3   2   1   **Not Well**

Supports needs of **students** → **Very Well**   5   4   3   2   1   **Not Well**

20. How has the adequacy of the collection changed since your Library Power project began?
[CIRCLE ONE FOR **TEACHER** AND ONE FOR **STUDENTS**]

	Much Better	Somewhat Better	About the Same	Somewhat Worse	Much Worse
Supports needs of **teacher** →	Much Better	Somewhat Better	About the Same	Somewhat Worse	Much Worse
Supports needs of **students** →	Much Better	Somewhat Better	About the Same	Somewhat Worse	Much Worse

THANK YOU FOR YOUR ASSISTANCE.

Please seal the questionnaire in the envelope and return it to your school office.

Be sure that your name is checked off as responding to the survey.

Appendix F
Collaborative Unit Planning Sheet

Collaborative Unit Planning Sheet

Teacher: _____ Grade levels included: _____ Library media specialist: _____
(Could be teachers/teams.
If so, please indicate the # of teachers involved: _____)

Subject area: _____ Unit title: _____
(could be interdisciplinary)

Student learning objectives of the unit: [Dates and time used in planning]

Date	**Amount of Time**
	(in minutes, *estimated*)
_____	_____
_____	_____

Proposed learning activities and products: [Dates and time used in planning]

Date	**Amount of Time**
	(in minutes, *estimated*)
_____	_____
_____	_____

Responsibilities:

Teacher(s):   Library media specialist: Both:

Log of instructional activities (Actually carried out by the library media specialist and/or teachers):
Examples:
13 Sep 96;   30 minutes;   mini-lesson on how to judge currency of info.(teacher and LMS taught);   Library
14 Sep 96;   45 minutes;   students compiled current info; checked by teacher/LMS;   Classroom

Date	**Time used**	**Activity**	**Location**
_____	_____	_____	_____
_____	_____	_____	_____
_____	_____	_____	_____

Use additional sheet if necessary. Please add **actual student assignment sheet(s)** if available.
Use the reverse side of this sheet to jointly evaluate the unit.

Teacher/Library Media Specialist Evaluation of a Collaboratively Taught Unit

[TO BE FILLED IN WITH TEACHER(S)]

Unit Title: _____

What worked well in the unit?

Suggestions for improvement:

What information skills were integrated into the unit?

From both the teacher's and library media specialist's point of view, was **learning enhanced** through collaboration?

      ❏ Yes   ❏ No

Why or why not?

From the **teacher's** point of view, what did the library contribute to this unit that would not have been possible in the classroom alone?

Was the unit successful enough to warrant doing it again in the future?   ❏ Yes   ❏ No

How well did the library media center collection respond to the unit objectives?

SCALE: 5 = excellent
             4 = above average
             3 = average
             2 = below average
             1 = poor

_____ diversity of formats (books, audiovisual, electronic)

_____ recency (books and other materials up to date?)

_____ relevance of collection to unit needs

_____ duplication (enough materials for the number of students taught?)

_____ reading/viewing/listening levels meet students' needs?

_____ average of above ratings (use this figure for quality stars on the collection map)

What materials/technology will we need if we are planning to repeat the unit again?

Appendix G
Fourteen Standards for Authentic Tasks, Instruction, and Student Performance [1]

Assessment Tasks: Seven Standards

1. *Organization of Information*: The task asks students to organize, synthesize, interpret, explain, or evaluate complex information in addressing a concept, problem, or issue.

2. *Consideration of Alternatives*: The task asks students to consider alternative solutions, strategies, perspectives, or points of view as they address a concept, problem, or issue.

3. *Disciplinary Content*: The task asks students to show understanding and/or use of ideas, theories, or perspectives considered central to an academic or professional discipline.

4. *Disciplinary Process*: The task asks students to use methods of inquiry, research, or communication characteristic of an academic or professional discipline.

5. *Elaborated Written Communication*: The task asks student to elaborate their understanding, explanations, or conclusions through extended writing.

6. *Problem Connected to the World*: The task asks students to address a concept, problem, or issue that is similar to one that they have encountered or are likely to encounter in life beyond the classroom.

7. *Audience Beyond the School*: The task asks students to communicate their knowledge, present a product or performance, or take some action for an audience beyond the teacher, classroom, and school building.

Classroom Instruction: Four Standards

1. *Higher Order Thinking*: Instruction involves manipulating information and ideas by synthesizing, generalizing, explaining, hypothesizing, or arriving at conclusions that produce new meanings and understandings for them.

2. *Substantive Conversation*: Students engage in extended conversational exchanges with the teacher and/or with their peers about subject matter in a way that builds an improved and shared understanding of ideas or topics.

3. *Deep Knowledge*: Instruction addresses central ideas of a topic or discipline with enough thoroughness to explore connections and relationships and to produce relatively complex understandings.

4. *Connections to the World Beyond the Classroom*: Students make connections between substantive knowledge and either public problems or personal experiences.

Student Performance: Three Standards

1. Analysis

   (a) *Mathematical Analysis*: Student performance demonstrates and explains their thinking with mathematical content by organizing, synthesizing, interpreting, hypothesizing, describing patterns, making models or simulations, constructing mathematical arguments, or inventing procedures.

   (b) *Social Studies Analysis*: Student performance demonstrates higher order thinking with social studies content by organizing, synthesizing, interpreting, evaluating, and hypothesizing to produce comparisons/contrasts, arguments, application of information to new contexts, and consideration of different ideas or points of view.

2. Disciplinary Concepts

   (a) *Mathematics*: Student performance demonstrates an understanding of important mathematical ideas that goes beyond application of algorithms by elaborating definitions, making connections to other mathematical concepts, or making connections to other disciplines.

   (b) *Social Studies*: Student performance demonstrates an understanding of ideas, concepts, theories, and principles from the social disciplines and civic life by using them to interpret and explain specific, concrete information or events.

3. Elaborated Written Communication

   (a) *Mathematics*: Student performance demonstrates a concise, logical, and well-articulated explanation or argument that justifies mathematical work.

   (b) *Social Studies*: Student performance demonstrates an elaborated account that is clear and coherent and provides richness in details, qualifications, and argument.

NOTE

1. Newmann, F. M., Secada, W. G., & Wehlage, G. G. (1995). *A guide to authentic instruction and assessment: Vision, standards and scoring.* Madison, WI: Wisconsin Center for Education Research.

Index

AASL. *See* American Association of School Librarians (AASL)
Access. *See* Flexible scheduling
Accountability
  for achievement, 122
  in collaboration, 65
Active learning, 116
Adler, Mortimer, 137
American Association of School Librarians (AASL), 2, 5, 13, 178, 179, 213
Assessed curriculum, 83
Assessment
  needs, 181–82
  professional development programs, 196
  student performance, 139
Assignments. *See* Authentic tasks, standards for; Learning activities
Association for Educational Communications and Technology, 2
Attained curriculum, 83
Attitude toward library use, 49–50
Authentic achievement, 103–4, 109, 116, 119–20, 136
  criteria, 145–46
Authentic tasks, standards for, 273
Awareness, 61, 73

Bank Street College of Education model
  instruction, 113
  reform, 138, 141, 144, 158, 159, 162
Bookshelves. *See* Facilities

Case studies, 12
  documentors, 15–16, 244
  regional coordinators, 16, 245
  researchers and reports, 14–15, 242–43
  site selection, 12–14

Center on Organization and Restructuring of Schools (CORS), 103–4, 105, 113, 136, 145
Centralized system, 85
Chaney, B., 36–37
Change, 134–35
Classroom instruction, standards for, 274
Coaching and mentoring, 174, 177–78
Collaboration, 2, 5, 53–54, 77
  activities, 61–66
  collection development, 19, 23–27, 31, 68, 70, 71
  and curriculum, 86, 90, 91, 92–93, 96, 98, 144
  difficulty of, 66–72, 145
  increases in, 55–60
  and innovation diffusion theory, 161–62
  institutionalization of, 200, 203–5, 209, 211
  instruction, 102–3, 106, 112–13, 117–18, 129
  levels of, 72–77
  libraries and instruction, 60–66
  professional community, 129, 155–56
Collaboration logs, 11
  sample, 271–72
Collection, 5, 16, 19, 33–34
  budget for, 22
  collaboration on, 70, 71
  continuation of practices, 31–33
  contributions of, 30–31
  curriculum, matching to, 23–27, 61, 84, 91, 98
  improvement, 20–23
  and instruction, 19
  practices, institutionalization of, 200, 206–9, 211
  proposed, 26
  support for improvement, 27–29
Collection mapping, 25, 81, 86, 90
  institutionalization of, 200
  for Library Power evaluation, 11
Comer, James, 85, 111, 134
Commitment, 67

Connecticut Mastery Test, 110–11
Constructivist knowledge, 112, 129, 130, 145–46, 147
Content areas, 94–95
Coordinated instructional activities. *See* Supportive/coordinated instructional activities
CORS. *See* Center on Organization and Restructuring of Schools (CORS)
Culture (school), 162–64, 167, 212
Curriculum, 79–82, 98–99, 200
   awareness of, 86–90
   content areas, 94–95
   development and change, 97–98
   forms of, 82–83
   goals and objectives, 92–97
   interpretations of, 79
   and Library Power, 98
   new packaging of, 91
   planning, 16
   and professional development, 166
   staff awareness, 81
Curriculum mapping, 81, 86, 90, 141, 166

Dewey, John, 138
DeWitt Wallace–Reader's Digest Fund, 1, 5
Disciplined inquiry, 118–22, 129, 145, 146, 147
Discretionary funds. *See* Mini-grants
Distar, 108
District-wide emphases, 182
Documentors, 15–16, 244

Edna McConnell Clark Foundation, 108, 123, 190, 217
Educational technology, 237–38
Eisenberg, Michael, 180
Erikson, Erik H., 138
Evaluation of Library Power, 6–7
   approaches, 7–8
     case studies, 12–16
     surveys, 8–12
   personnel, 241–45

Expectations
   and curriculum, 2, 84, 86, 91, 93–94
   and instruction, 111, 118

Facilities, 41–44
   and curriculum, 84, 91, 96, 97, 98
   renovation and flexible access, 41–44, 51–52
Flexible scheduling, 36–40
   and curriculum, 84, 98
   facilities renovation, 41–44, 51–52
   and innovation diffusion theory, 161
   institutionalization of, 200, 201–2, 209, 211
   professional community, 129
   and use patterns, 45–47
Forward in the Fifth (FITF) Kentucky
   institutionalization, 213–14, 215, 216, 221
   professional development, 172, 176, 186, 195, 196
4MAT, 195
Funding, 2, 218–21, 225
   professional development, 172–74
Furniture. *See* Facilities

GIILS. See *Guide to Integrated Information Literacy Skills* (GIILS)
Goals and objectives
   curriculum, 82, 83, 84, 91
   learning, 98, 99, 144
   Library Power. *See* Library Power, goals
Grants
   Library Power, 2–5
   mini-grants, 174, 177, 194
Group performance, 116–17
The Guide for Thematic Units, 180
Guide to Integrated Information Literacy Skills (GIILS), 106, 180

Haycock, Ken, 180
High stakes assessments, 83
Hopkins, Dianne McAfee, 6

Identification and gathering of materials, 29, 62, 65
Implemented curriculum, 83–84, 86, 90, 98
Improvement, reform as, 135
In-service programs, 175
Information literacy, 226
Information Power: Guidelines for School Library Media Centers, 2, 168, 223–24, 226, 237
Information-seeking skills. *See* Research skills
Innovation diffusion theory, 161, 162
Institutes and workshops, 174, 175
Institutionalization, 199–201, 221–22
    collaboration, 200, 203–5, 209
    collection development, 200, 206–9
    flexible scheduling, 200, 201–2, 209
    professional development, 187
    supports and impediments, 211–13
        external support, 213–14
        funding, 218–21
        leadership, 216–17
        policy, 214–15
        staff development, 217–18
Instruction, 101–3, 129–31
    analysis of, 114–18
    change or improvement question, 105–10
    collaboration. *See* Collaboration, instruction
    disciplined inquiry, 118–22, 129
    expectations, 110–14
    improvement in, 122–24
    intellectual quality, 103–5, 115
    professional community, 124–29
    standards, 274
Instructional entrepreneurs, 122
Instructional units, collaboration on, 61, 70, 71 98. *See also* Thematic units
Instrument development, 9
Integrated practice, 224–27, 238
    and educational technology, 237–38
    instructional unit design, 231–33
    quality, 233–35
    research on, 238
    resource support of instruction, 227–29
    resource use, 229–31
    student achievement, 235–37

Intellectual quality, 103–5, 115, 117, 121
    and reform, 136, 155, 156, 160, 162
Intended curriculum, 82, 83, 84, 86, 91, 96, 98
Interactive instructional activities, 61, 73, 74, 77
Interdisciplinary curriculum, 200
Interdisciplinary units. *See* Thematic units

Kentucky Education Reform Act. *See* KERA (Kentucky Education Reform Act)
KERA (Kentucky Education Reform Act)
    institutionalization, 214, 216, 217
    instruction, 123, 124
    integrated practice, 236
    professional development, 195, 196
    reform, 139, 143, 144, 162
Kuhlthau, Carol, 6, 14

Johnson, Debra Wilcox, 6

Leadership
    and institutionalization, 216–17
    by librarians, 183–85, 195
Learning activities, 103. *See also* Authentic tasks, standards for
Levin, Henry, 134
Librarians
    as leaders, 183–85, 195
    role institutionalization, 209
    roles of, 2
Library media center, uses of, 45–51
Library Media Specialist (LMS) Survey, 8, 247–57
    access and use, 37–38, 41–48
    collaboration, 203–4
    collection, 20–22, 29, 32, 207–8
    instruction, 126–27
Library Power, 2–6
    continuation, 209–10
    evaluation. *See* Evaluation of Library Power
    goals, 2, 189–91
        collaboration, 53, 189
        curriculum, 80
        instruction, 102
        reform, 189
    history, 6–7

Library Power Advisory Committee, 84
Literacy League, 31, 123, 124, 195, 214, 217
Local control, 85
Loertscher, David, 6, 180
    collection mapping, 25, 179
    needs assessment, 181–82

Meetings, annual national, 174, 178–79
Mentoring. *See* Coaching and mentoring
Mini-grants, 174, 177, 194
    collections, 22
    curriculum design, 157
Mitchell, Lucy Sprague, 138
Model schools, 182–83
Multicultural component of collections, 23
Multiple uses, 41

National assessments, 83
National Center for Education Statistics, 8, 9,
    20, 36, 225
Needs, professional development
    assessment, 181–82
    differing, 192
Networking, 174, 176–77, 180

Organizational capacity, 155, 162, 167
Outcomes, 83, 135

Paideia Project, 85, 140, 144, 157, 162
    instruction, 108, 109, 123, 137
    professional development 190, 217
Parallel instructional activities, 61, 73, 74, 77
PEBC. *See* Public Education Business Coalition
    (PEBC) Denver
PEN. *See* Public Education Network (PEN)
Performance standards, 274–75
Piaget, Jean, 138
Policy, 214–15
Primary research, 119. *See also* Research skills
Principal Survey, 9, 259–62
    collaboration, 56–58, 68–72
    collection, 24, 27, 29, 32

    curriculum, 92
    institutionalization, 201, 202
    instruction, 126–27
Problem solving, 107, 112, 129, 130
Professional community, 124–29, 130, 162, 225
    and reform, 136–37, 155–60
Professional development, 165–68, 172–80
    challenges, 191–93
    collaboration, 60, 64–65
    curriculum, 84–85, 86, 92, 93, 96, 97
    and institutionalization, 187, 217–18
    instruction, 118, 124
    as Library Power strategy, 170–72
    methods, 174–79
    principles, 168–70, 193–96
    stages, 180–88
    value, 188–91
Public Education Business Coalition (PEBC)
    Denver, 123
    collection, 31
    professional development, 171, 176, 178,
        186, 190
Public Education Network (PEN), 5, 13, 213,
    214

Reform, 2, 83, 85, 133–34, 160–64, 167, 168
    assessment-based, 85
    case studies, 137–40
    collection, 31
    definitions, 134–35
    institutionalization of, 200
    instruction, 102, 123–24, 129
    intellectual quality, 136, 145–55
    library use and collaboration, 140–45
    and professional community, 136–37,
        155–60
    reform programs, 135–36
    standards-based, 85
Regional coordinators, 16, 245
Research skills, 62, 65, 94, 109–10, 119
Researchers and reports, 14–15
Resource–based instruction, 102–3, 105–6,
    109, 110, 113, 114, 129
    and collection, 31

institutionalization of, 200
  professional development, 166
Resource equity, 111, 121
Restructuring, 2
  curriculum, 83
  defined, 134
  instruction, 102
  and professional community, 136–37
Role relationships, 134

SASS. *See* Schools and Staffing Survey (SASS)
School visits, 174, 175–76
Schools and Staffing Survey (SASS), 8
  collection development, 20–23
  integrated practice, 225
  library media center scheduling, 36–37
  use, 45
Seating capacity, 41
Shared instructional activities, 61, 73, 74, 77
Site selection, 12–14
Size, 134
Sizer, Theodore, 134
Staff development. *See* Professional development
Standards
  authentic tasks, 253
  instruction, 274
  intellectual quality, 103, 112
  and restructuring, 136
  student performance, 274–75
Stoll, Adam, 223–39
Storytelling, 93
Stripling, Barbara, 180
Structure, 212
Subject matter specialization, 200. *See also*
    Curriculum
Supportive/coordinated instructional activities,
    61, 73, 74, 77
Survey response rates, 9–10

Surveys, 8–12. *See also* Library Media Specialist
    (LMS) Survey; Principal Survey; Teacher
    Survey

Target ordering (books), 91
Tasks. *See* Authentic tasks, standards for;
    Learning activities
Teacher Survey, 9, 267–70
  collaboration, 58–59, 62–63, 204–5
  collection, 24, 28, 29, 32, 206, 209–10
  curriculum, 86–88, 92–93
  instruction, 126–28
  library use, 48–50, 205–6
  sample design for, 263–65
Team instruction, 96
Thematic units, 96, 102, 166. *See also* Instruc-
    tional units, collaboration on
Time considerations, 67, 134, 191–92
Trelease, Jim, 180
Trunk units, 91
Trust, 131
Turnover, 130

Use of library media center. *See* Flexible
    scheduling

Value beyond classroom, 145, 146, 147
Videos, 174, 177
Vision, 191
Voyage of the Mimi, The, 138, 158
Vygotsky, Lev S., 138

Webb, Norman Lott, 6
Wehlage, Gary, 6, 14, 85, 195, 233

Zweizig, Douglas L., 6